To: M

Spread the message.

Kevin C. Dreher

03/18/01

(404) 298-9098

SURVIVAL GUIDE FOR BLACK MEN IN AMERICA

You Don't Have to Be Extinct

XAVIER C. DICKS

FARRY BELL PRESS

Farry Bell Press, Inc. P.O. Box 361166, Decatur, GA. 30036
www.farrybellpress.com

Printed in the United States of America
First Farry Bell Press Printing: November 2000

ISBN: 0-9647003-2-8
LC: 97-60037

My Personal Testimonial

I love the Lord with all my heart, all my mind and with all of my soul. I wrote this book in direct obedience to the will of God.

I will tell you that writing this book was not easy. While writing this book, I encountered all sorts of trials and tribulations. I almost lost the roof over my family's head, I didn't make any money in my law practice, my car was taken (I later got it back), I ruined my credit and almost lost my faith.

Still, I knew that God had given me a spiritual mission. He revealed to me the knowledge to solve some, if not all, of the problems that Black men face. All I had to do was to trust him and put the knowledge down as only I could at that point in time. Then spread this knowledge across the land. I put all earthly tasks and desires aside and did as God asked me to do. I trusted God's calling even though I did not understand it or know what the outcome would be.

Now, the blessings of heaven are being showered upon me. I have and will receive the greatest blessing of all, peace of mind and being able to do God's work. I have been touched by God and will never be the same.

My advice to all who read this book is to put God first in your lives, praise him, seek his kingdom, study his word (read the Bible), be obedient (keep his commandments) and do what God calls you to do and everything else (loving spouse, family, wealth, purpose and health) will be granted unto you.

May God bless all those who read this book.

Xavier C. Dicks
God's Servant

FOR
BERTA

To the most beautiful woman in the world, the greatest wife,

mother, lover, and most of all, my best friend . . .

ACKNOWLEDGMENTS

Praises are to God for allowing his humble servant to use his talents to write this book. I also want to express my sincere thanks to all of the people who gave me a chance and read my first book, *The Time Has Come,* when I was an unknown author. Thank you for encouraging me to write yet another book which I hope will affect the lives of even more people in a positive way.

A very special thanks goes to Dr. Eduardo Montes (1954-1997). He was a man who really did not know me, owed me no duty and yet helped me, a stranger, more than he will ever know. Without him, this book would not have been possible. Thanks Eddie.

Of course I want to thank Rev. George O. McCalep, my pastor at Greenforest Community Baptist Church in Decatur, Georgia, who continues to teach me and inspire me to grow in the spirit and live as God intended me to and **Pastor Creflo A. Dollar, Jr.**, of World Changers Ministries in College Park, Georgia, who affects my spiritual life on a daily basis through his tape ministry.

TABLE OF CONTENTS

PROLOGUE

Blacks Males are on the Verge of Extinction and the Effects on American Society.

Black men are becoming extinct in America. Extinction is defined in the dictionary as being outdated, obsolete, dead, no longer present and lacking survivors.[1] Extinction, as it relates to Black men, is defined as not living productive, fulfilling lives. This means getting married to a loving mate; raising a family; earning enough money to provide the necessities of life, having a high standard of living and enjoying what life has to offer; controlling your own destiny; and evolving into something more both technologically and spiritually than the previous generation so that the next generation can cope with life's ever changing variables better than you did.

The concept of extinction is not new. The most notable example of extinction is what happened to the dinosaurs.

Dinosaurs roamed the earth up until 65 million years ago. They emerged from primitive reptilian ancestors sometime in the Triassic period of geologic time, which extended from 248 million to 213 million years ago. They became dominant during the Jurassic period, for the next 70 million years, and continued strong until the close of the Cretaceous period, some 65 million years ago.[2]

Then for reasons not entirely certain, the dinosaurs disappeared. Something happened 65 million years ago, at the end of the Cretaceous period, something so devastating that it altered the course of life on earth. With seeming abruptness, as geological time goes, almost half of the genera living throughout the world disappeared, animal and vegetable, marine and terrestrial, large and small.[3]   Gone in the great dying were all the ammonites, those flat shellfish related to the chambered nautilus and squid.   Gone were many bivalves, reef-building animals, sponges, and all but a few species of the single celled marine plankton so critical to the food chain; one-fourth of all marine families perished. Gone too were the pterosaus, most of the little marsupials, and all the large tetrapods.   No species living exclusively on land and weighing more than twenty-five kilograms seemed to have survived, and the most conspicuous of the nonsurvivors were the dinosaurs.[4]

The something that happened 65 million years ago is one of the most intriguing and perplexing mysteries of science. Scientists from many disciplines over the years have tried to solve this puzzle.   They have put forth numerous theories as to what happened to cause the extinction of the dinosaur.

Some scientists have suggested that dinosaurs disappeared because the climate deteriorated (became suddenly or slowly too hot or cold or dry or wet), or that the diet was inadequate (with too much food or not enough of such substances as fern oil; from poisons in water or plants or ingested minerals; by bankruptcy of calcium or other necessary elements).

Other scientists put the blame on disease, parasites, wars, anatomical or metabolic disorders (slipped vertebral discs, malfunction or imbalance of hormone and endocrine systems, dwindling brain and consequent stupidity, heat sterilization, effects of being warm-blooded in the Mesozoic world).

Another theory put forth was that perhaps the dinosaurs were the victims of racial senescence (racial old age). Scientists believed that a race of animals, like the life of an individual, goes through stages of growth and decline. It has its youth, its period of adaptation and maturation, its more settled middle age, and finally, its period of senility.[5]

Unable to solve the mystery of what happened to the dinosaurs, scientists proposed even more theories. These theories included blaming dinosaur extinction on evolutionary drift into senescent overspecialization, changes in the pressure or composition of the atmosphere, poison gases, volcanic dust, excessive oxygen from plants, meteorites, comets, gene pool drainage by little mammalian egg-eaters, overkill capacity by predators, fluctuation of gravitational constants, development of psychotic suicidal factors, entropy, cosmic radiation, shift of Earth's rotational poles, floods, continental drift, extraction of the moon from the Pacific Basin, drainage of swamp and lake environments, sunspots, God's will, mountain building, raids by little green hunters in flying saucers, and lack of standing room in Noah's Ark.

While there have been many different theories proposed, they all have one thing in common. None of them have been proven conclusively to be the reason that dinosaurs became extinct.

The explanation for why there is no conclusive theory for the cause of the extinction of the dinosaurs is because it happened so long ago. It occurred tens of millions of years before the existence of man. In other words, man was not there so all he can do is speculate. The only thing that appears certain is that dinosaurs ceased to exist 65 million years ago.

However, unlike the dinosaur, we are observing the extinction of the Black male first hand. In the case of the Black male, we see both the causes of extinction and the effects on American society in general and us as individuals in particular.

To begin to understand the causes of Black male extinction, it is first important to recognize the signs that it is occurring. The signs that Black males are becoming extinct are obvious. You see Black men walking down the street, dirty and smelly, with all of their belongings in a trash bag or in a grocery cart. You see Black men standing close to a building urinating in daylight with people walking and driving just a few feet away. You see long lines of Black men standing at the various feed the hungry programs throughout this nation because these Black men can't even provide the basic necessities for themselves. No one can argue that too many Black males between the ages of 17 and 35 are in jail because they committed a senseless crime. Once they are in jail, they are no longer productive members of their families, communities nor society.

Another obvious sign that Black males are becoming extinct is the increasing rate of high school and college drop-outs. This lack of education parallels a host of other signs that point to extinction such as high unemployment, lack of hope and direction, and ultimately poverty. It is a sad sight to see large numbers of homeless black men cluttering up city libraries just to get out of the cold, yet they are unable to tap into the wealth of knowledge right at their fingertips because they can't read.

A less obvious sign is the growing number of single Black men in America. Black men are not marrying Black women. He does not seem to be able to match up with her in a long term, committed relationship.

You see groups of Black men standing on street corners or sitting on park benches for hours at a time for no apparent reason than just hanging out. And when these men are not hanging out, they go inside to use drugs in order to get high to escape their reality. The next day this cycle of hanging out and drug usage is repeated. Sometimes you see the same Black men standing on the same corner, year after year.

The most important sign of Black male extinction is the lack of spirituality possessed by most Black males. Black men have gotten away from the teachings of Christ. Most are non-believers. This is only decreasing the time to complete extinction because there is no foundation upon which to evolve both from and to.

What is truly sad is the fact that these signs of extinction are manifesting themselves in younger and younger Black men and that most Black men are beginning to accept their fate because they feel powerless, blame its causes on someone else or because they believe their place in this life is part of some pre-ordained, man-made master plan.

Of course when one race is on the decline (becoming extinct), members of the declining race and every other race in that society is adversely affected. What this means is that every person in America is affected as a result of Black men becoming extinct.

Just like the signs that Black men are becoming extinct are obvious, the effects of his becoming extinct are no less obvious on American Society.

The most obvious effect is the commission of crimes any and everywhere there is a large population of Blacks. Since Blacks tend to populate the downtowns in most large cities in America, those downtowns are unsafe. Notable examples are Atlanta, New York's five boroughs, Chicago, Detroit, Los Angeles, Oakland, Newark, Baltimore, Miami, Washington D.C. and any other city that Blacks make up more than 15% of the population.

Of course there is the usual loud, obnoxious music coming from cars being driven by Black males.

It is very difficult to walk down any main street in America that has Black males as part of the population and not be subjected to panhandlers. It gets so bad that when you see any Black man approaching you not dressed in a suit and tie, you just know that he is going to ask you for money either to catch the bus or for food.

Suppose you were having a heart attack. You happen to be near a public pay telephone. You can barely reach into your pocket and find that one quarter and dime. You put the money into the slot and dial 911. Your chest feels like it is going to burst as you try to tell the operator what your problem is and where you are located. Just as you lean on the phone base for support, you get cut off because there is a short in the cord which you adjusted when you moved. Guess what? The 911 operator can't call you back because most of the pay phones in metropolitan areas can't receive incoming calls. Why? Because conventional wisdom is that Black males conduct drug deals via pay phones and if these phones can't receive incoming calls, it cuts down on the number of drug deals done over the telephone.

Another effect that Black male extinction has on society is that it has caused most downtown establishments to refuse to offer public restrooms. The reason is because the homeless, most of which are Black males will use these restrooms to bathe in, use as a shelter from the cold or simply congregate at a business establishment because it has a restroom.

Have you tried to enjoy a public park lately? Chances are that you can't because it will be filled with dirty, grungy, Black men with sleeping bags occupying the benches. This is especially true during periods of warm weather.

One of the major impacts on American Society caused by the extinction of the Black male is White flight. Here Whites and a growing number of Blacks relocate to the suburbs in order to get away from crime being committed by Black males and all the general aggravation associated with Black men being near you. When Whites relocate to the suburbs, the best stores and services relocate with them, causing most downtowns to be desolate and slummy. Most major cities in this country will only have governmental facilities and sports arenas downtown with a few private sector firms strewn in between. Now it is more costly to live in suburbia than it is to live downtown. If the current trend continues, there will no longer be any meaning in the term downtown.

Another major impact of Black male extinction is less obvious. This effect is seen in the way buildings, parks, apartment complexes, and shopping malls are designed. The central theme is that things are constructed so that Black males will not congregate on or in front of the premises. For example, buildings are designed with huge setbacks. The space between the sidewalks and the buildings are taken up with flowers and other shrubbery so that you look like an idiot hanging out there. Shopping malls are built so that you don't have consecutive stairways between floors. If you go up one flight of stairs or escalators, you have to walk quite a distance before you can then take the stairs or escalators up to the next level. Many convenient entries into the malls are eliminated altogether to discourage lingering near these entryways. Most apartment complexes have gates that surround the entire perimeter and require codes at the front gate to gain entry.

What about all those annoying security checks that you are subjected to when you want to enter most buildings. Of course international and domestic terrorism plays some role here, but the major reason for the checks is because Black males carry guns and the only way to keep them out of buildings is to have metal detectors.

And let's not forget how the delivery of services at establishments such as fast food and convenience stores has been affected. These places now have thick shatterproof and bulletproof glass covering their entire fronts with a little window or turntable just large enough to put your money through and to get an item through. When was the last time you could pull into a service station and put gas into you car without having to pay first?

The extinction of the Black male has caused this society to spend so much time focused on fighting and trying to prevent crime that this society spends little if any time focused on increasing educational standards, improving the standard of living, exploring the universe, curing disease and understanding the meaning of life. More monies are being spent on the criminal justice system (hiring police, constructing jails, building larger courthouses etc.) than is being spent on education and self improvement (schools and library construction, research institutes, grants for research, recreation centers etc.).

In a general sense, the effects of the extinction of the Black male has caused feelings of uneasiness, fear, anger and downright hatred of the Black male in this country. The negative effects of the Black male has made this country a far less desirable place to live than it would be if he were not part of this society. Unfortunately, while the Black male is becoming extinct, the effects that it is causing from the degradation of the public school system to the right to quiet enjoyment and the pursuit of happiness is becoming intolerable.

The purpose of this book is to provide a survival guide, which if followed and applied, will prevent the extinction of the Black male in America.

Unlike the dinosaur, Black men are human beings. As such, Black men are sentient beings. They have the power of their minds and the use of their hands. They can change the way they operate in this society.

Furthermore, the other races that make up this great country must decide if they will simply standby and watch the Black male become extinct and endure the negative impacts that go with it or if they will take an active role to help prevent the extinction of the Black male. While the ultimate responsibility rests upon the shoulders of the Black race to do what needs to be done, the other races must assist because the fate of the whole country is at stake. Just as the human body cannot survive if one of its major systems or appendages becomes diseased, neither can a society.

This book operates from the premise that all of the negative stereotypes regarding the Black male are in fact true. The reasoning here is that just like the alcoholic must admit that he or she has a drinking problem before they can work on being cured, Black males must admit that they have all the serious problems that Whites and yes, other Blacks say that they have before they can make the necessary changes. All stereotypes have a factual basis originating from observing countless behavior patterns in a race or group and then predicting certain future behaviors from observing past behaviors. Blacks must understand that it is not important whether or not people stereotype you, but rather if in fact the stereotypic behavior is true and detrimental to you and others.

Using this as a starting point, this book first identifies the current status of Black men in America. Then all of the causes that have led up to the current state of extinction of the Black male are discussed. These causes are grouped into three categories. Those attributable to Whites, those attributable to Blacks themselves and general causes. Then the steps are listed in a systematic fashion which will stop the current extinction of the Black male and prevent extinction in the future.

After showing how to prevent extinction, this book proposes a survival fitness test as a way to constantly monitor whether or not Black males as a group or individually are once again heading toward extinction.

Finally, this book contains a forecast of what will most likely happen to Black males in America. One thing is certain, if Black males in this country continue to do the things that they do and not follow the steps outlined in this book, they will become extinct.

Read this book with an open mind. When presented with facts that seem negative, rather than get mad, ask yourself if they are true based on your daily observations.

The purpose of this book is to promote change. It is never an easy task. There is usually criticism and anger directed toward the change agent. But all of it is worth it here because the survival of a race of men is at stake.

PUBLIC SERVICE ANNOUNCEMENTS

In every book, there are usually 6 to 10 blank pages due to the fact that by convention, new chapters are to begin on a right-hand page. So if a chapter ends on the right, the next page, which is a left-hand page, will be blank. Rather than have these pages blank, I have decided to help people by allowing them to reserve these pages to promote their businesses.

As the author of this book, I urge you to utilize these people. They are the best at what they do and I vouch for them. If you do use them as a result of seeing them in this book, let them know.

I understand that this is the first time that this has been done in a hardback book, but it will be a trend that I will continue each and every time I write a book.

Thank you.

PART I. STATUS OF BLACK MALES IN AMERICA

Everyone knows that the current state of the Black male in this country is less than encouraging. The problem is that few people can agree on what exactly is his current state. What exactly is wrong with the Black male? Why does he do the things that he does? Obviously you have to figure out what is wrong before you can figure out what will work most effectively to solve the problems.

This section identifies all of the things that are currently wrong with the Black male or at the very least are having a negative impact on his life.

Either Putative Father and/or Illegitimate Child

Putative father means that you are alleged to be the biological father of a child and not know it, and the odds are that you don't live in the same household with your child. Illegitimate child means that you were born out of wedlock, i.e., when you were born, your father and mother were not married.[6]

Most of the Black males in this country either do not have their biological father living in their household, and/or they themselves are illegitimate. These same Black males may also be the father of a child and do not reside with the child. What this means is that either you the father are not there to raise your child or you are the child and you have no father living with you to raise you.

With no father living in the house, there is no one to teach the Black male child the basics of life. Of course you will get countless arguments from mothers and Black males raised by their mothers that it does not matter and that they turned out okay. But the thing to understand is that we are not talking about the rare exceptions, rather we are talking about the general rule and what happens when there is no father in the home.

There is no one there to teach the Black male child even the simple rules of life and those are how to be a man and what your responsibilities are to yourself, your family and society.

Even worse, without the father, the Black male does not get a good Christian upbringing where the child is taught about the life and teachings of Christ by attending church on a regular basis and then having these Christian principles enforced through discipline and correction on an as needed basis.

Children need mentors of the same sex and the same race to pattern their behavior after. They need the guidance and direction that only a father can provide. Who else is going to teach the Black male child how to love himself and love others. Who is going to teach him a good work ethic, i.e. make the child do his chores and do them right. Who is going to teach him manners. How to respect and treat his fellow human beings and have respect for the property of others.

You often wonder why Black males do not love and respect Black women. One of the main reasons is because they have not had a loving father around their house and been able to observe how he treated his woman, in their case, their mother.

When these young men grow up without fathers, they take it as normal to abandon their own children and not fulfill their own responsibilities as fathers. This cycle repeats itself time and time again in the Black race.

Black male children have no one to set the standards for them. Thus they do not learn how to dress properly, how to perform to the best of their ability in school and in life.

Not having a father in the home is the root cause of 90% of all of the problems that are experienced by Black males in America. These problems stem from a lack of values. If these male children do not get these values before they are 12 years old, they can never be taught them. Society cannot serve as a surrogate father. It does not and will never work. By the time society gets involved, the formative traits of the child are already there. How the child responds to teaching and discipline is already imprinted. It cannot be changed. This is why the criminal justice system is not a deterrent to these children. They continue to commit crimes even though they may have served time in prison before.

Even if society gets involved early on, no one other than a father can be there day in and day out to make sure that whatever values are being instilled are constantly reinforced and followed. Nurturing can only be done on a one on one basis. Values can only be instilled on a one on one basis. Not through public policy.

Undisciplined, Uncontrollable and Immature

The effects of not growing up with a father to provide the discipline and values necessary to live in this society are manifested first and foremost in the behavior of Black males.

As you observe the behavior of most Black males you see a similar pattern exhibited by most of them. They take no responsibility for self or property. They will destroy anything and anybody. Black males certainly do not respect other peoples' privacy and quiet enjoyment.

Look at how Black males walk down the street. They will walk right into you. Sometimes they are walking down the sidewalk four abreast. Have you ever pulled up behind a car blocking traffic only to discover that it is a Black male stopped in the middle of the street having a conversation and yelling obscenities to the frustrated drivers he is blocking to go around or wait.

When you have Black males around, you are going to have loud music. It does not matter what time it is day or night. You hear these loud stereos sometimes when their cars are just going down the street, sometimes at three o'clock in the morning.

Black males account for almost all of the trash that is thrown from passing cars or dropped on the sidewalk. The countless millions spent each year on clean up and property damage repair is directly attributable to the Black male.

Because discipline and values are not possessed by Black males, they absolutely can't and won't follow the rules. The failure to follow even the simplest rules ultimately is the reason why these young males wind up coming into contact with the criminal justice system. This rule breaking runs the gamut of simply running a red light, to speeding, to drug usage, to ultimately committing murder.

This is not to say that all children that have their fathers present and that do in fact receive the discipline they need turn out to be model citizens. Sometimes children just turn out bad. However, the overwhelming majority of children that have their fathers present do better than those that don't have their fathers present.

Closely paralleling discipline is maturity. Young Black males are becoming less and less mature. What seems to happen is that Black men seem to stop maturing mentally at about age 16. They seem to be frozen in time. You have thirty-year old Black men acting like and doing the things that a sixteen year old does. All a Black male wants when he is in is twenties is a car, any car in which he can put shiny wheels on and drive around with his buddies all day long looking for trouble. Young Black males do nothing to plan for the future which includes looking for a mate to start a family and getting an education to learn a usable skill to make money to have a decent life.

This lack of maturity is highlighted when the Black male deals with the Black female because the average Black female in her mid to late twenties is mature and acts like an adult. So while the Black male is acting childish, the Black female is working on her future. The problem is that the only men that she can find that matches her maturity level are about twenty years older than she is and even then the Black male in his early forties may still be acting like a 16 year old, chasing women and spending most of his money on cars and clothing.

This lack of maturity of Black males is also obvious when you compare young Black men to young men of other races. Young men of other races, say Asian or White, when they are in their early twenties, are concentrating on how to make money and raise a family. They are in college and studying their brains out as hard as they can because they know what their responsibilities are. These men also get married before the age of thirty. So while the brother is out spending his last dime on an old piece of car, these Asians and Whites are getting their futures in order. So by age thirty, Asian and White men are earning $40,000 or more, the young Black male is still at home, acting like a teenager. His whole existence is spent trying to get some woman in bed or kicking it with his buddies.

The reasons for this lack of maturity may again be attributable to the lack of a father figure in the home to teach the Black male what it means to be a man and the responsibilities that go along with it such as raising a family and being financially stable. There is no one to teach the Black male about being able to not only take care of his immediate family, but to be able to leave a legacy for those future generations that will follow him so that they don't begin their lives in poverty.

Uneducated

The most important commodity in the 2000's is an education. Along with good values, it is the most important building block that one needs to make it in this society. You will never develop into the optimum you, without an education.

Black males are the least educated group in American Society. Most Black males drop out of high school at the 9th grade level.[7] Of the few that remain in school, most of them will not complete college.

As a result, 30% of Black males in America can't read nor write. A higher percentage than that are functionally illiterate.[8] This means that while they may be able to discern some or all of the words that they see, they can't process the information given in order to grasp a particular concept or take the action presented by the words. The ability to read is what separates the losers from the winners, the wealthy from the poor and the informed from the brainwashed.

Reading is a form of active learning. It is this type of information input that you retain the longest. More of your neurons are at work when you read which is why you are far more creative and alert when you are reading than merely watching and listening to something. Audio and video are passive forms of learning and must be reinforced many more times than written material. Don't be fooled into thinking that when you are using a computer that the information that you are receiving is mostly video. In actuality, you are reading from the screen, either words or symbols. Black males can't and don't use computers because they can't read.

Because of this lack of education, Black males don't meet the minimum standards for most high paying careers. This explains why too many Black males wind up with Blue collar jobs. These jobs don't require intellectual energies, but instead require repetitive, mindless, manual labor. Ninety-five percent of Black men work jobs such as UPS and Federal Express drivers, pizza and all kinds of deliverymen, policemen, security guards (watchmen), mailroom clerks, sanitation engineers, cooks, bellhops, grounds keepers, bouncers, handymen (repairmen), janitors, bus drivers, cab drivers, carpenters, hospitality workers, barbers, mailmen (postal clerks), hospital orderlies and aides, machine operators, retail and grocery store clerks, waiters, service station attendants, chauffeurs, mechanics, butlers, fast food workers, parking attendants, firemen, farm workers, apartment and building managers, temporary agency workers (day laborers), telemarketers, manufacturing and textile factory workers and the few remaining blue collar jobs you can think of (I bet you can't think of anymore).

These baseball cap wearing Black men can and do pay their bills, but they are never going to control their own destinies. Rather, they are at the whim of their bosses or companies, more or less expendable as the need arises. These men are not planners and shapers of the future, rather they are comfortable with the status quo and anything that disrupts their daily routine is met with confusion and anger.

The negative impact of uneducation does not stop there. It gets even worse. The gap between Black males and females is widening both in terms of intelligence and finances. The Black female is becoming more educated and thus more financially independent while the Black male is becoming more deficient in both of these areas.

The lack of educational parity between Black males and females is probably the single most important reason why Black men and women are not able to remain in stable relationships. Black men can stimulate the Black female body, but they cannot stimulate her mind and thus cannot communicate with her.

After a period of time, all the physical stimulation in the world is not enough for a woman without mental stimulation. When a woman can no longer get mental stimulation from her man, she then starts to not want the physical stimulation and ultimately, does not want to be with that man. In other words, if you have a woman's mind, you automatically have her body, but if you just have her body, you don't really have her.

What has happened is that Black women no longer respect the Black male. Women don't enter into long term relationships with men they don't respect. Thus the Black male has lost his ability to marry Black women.

Can the negative effects of not having an education get worse than that? Unfortunately they can.

There is an inverse relationship between the amount of education one possesses and the amount of crime one commits. In other words, the less education one has, the more crimes he is likely to commit.

The Black men that are committing most of the crimes in this country are uneducated. If you survey the jail population, you will not find many high school graduates and few if any college graduates.

An education seems to broaden one's horizon. It seems to give a person hope. At the very least, it takes the magic and uncertainty out of life and enables one to see that you are responsible for doing those things that will better you in the long run. People with an education always feel as though they have an alternative. Even if they are living at the poverty level, they feel that it is only temporary.

To get an education, requires discipline. This discipline seems to spill over into all other areas of life. Educated people tend to want to earn something rather than take or steal it from someone else.

Now why don't Black men get an education? One reason seems to be that they equate getting an education with trying to be White. They act as though getting an education is bad. Some Black men say why bother. Even if you get an education (degree), no one is going to hire you anyway.

Another reason is that their fathers and mothers are not educated. These parents themselves don't understand the value of an education. As such, they don't demand that their Black male child get an education. If parents don't demand that their children get educated, you can bet that society will be unable to create the desire in children to get an education. And in the end, why should society be responsible for you beyond making sure that you have taxpayer access to the educational system.

Unemployed

There will never be zero unemployment in this country. At any given time there will be people looking for work because they are just entering or re-entering the job market, they are changing jobs, they were laid off or their company went out of business or they were fired.

No one knows for sure exactly how many of these out of work people there are. Likewise, no one knows for sure how many people are employed because when people are not looking for work, they are not accounted for in either group. After making the best guesstimate for both groups, the number of unemployed people is divided by the number of employed people to come up with what is commonly known as the unemployment rate. That number traditionally has fallen somewhere between 4% and 8%. These numbers are for the entire country and all races.

Unfortunately, when you are calculating the unemployment rate for the Black male that number conservatively increases to approximately 35% overall. That's right, the number probably is even higher because as stated above the number of Black males not looking for work is not factored in. What this means is that at any given time, more than one-third of Black males over the age of 18 are not earning a living.[9]

Again, the reasons are obvious. Many Black males are simply lazy and will not work. After all, they have not been taught a meaningful work ethic. Without the father figure around, there is no one to teach them that a man works no matter what. Even if the job is beneath him, he still provides for his family.

As stated earlier, many Black men are not educated and thus don't meet the minimum job standards. Their skills are so bad, that even the Blue Collar employers will not hire them.

There is a cycle here that some people are not aware of. What happens is that these Black men don't have usable (employable) skills, so they can't get a job to earn a living, so they resort to either crime or other heartbreaking alternatives. The crime happens to be selling drugs or stealing. The heartbreaking alternatives are such things as standing at the gas pumps asking people to pay them to let them pump their gas. Or worse yet, running up to cars at a red light with a dirty rag asking drivers to give them some money for streaking up their windshields. There is also the old faithful alternative which is just beg (the old ask for a quarter syndrome).

There are also large numbers of Black men that are unemployed, not because they can't find a job, but because the job that they find they consider beneath them. They refuse to work at fast food places like the other brothers or if the salary paid for the job they find is not enough to support their lifestyles, they stay home. They would rather starve than take these jobs until they can do better.

While the Black male is sitting on his buttocks, the Black female is putting food on the table. She knows that both she and her lazy mate have to eat. So the Black female, has no shame working these menial jobs until she can do better. Just look at who is on the freeways each morning between the hours of seven and nine o'clock. It is hundreds of thousands of Black women in their little econo-boxes going to work while their mates are still snoring. These women not only go out to work and put food on the table, but they are expected to come home after a hard days work, have sex, cook, and take care of the kids.

Poor

If you are not earning money, and no one is giving you money and you are not left a nice inheritance, you wind up financially broke, better known as being poor. A conservative estimate is that 85% of the Black males in this country are poor.

Poor is defined as earning on a yearly basis, from no money at all up to earning less than $40,000.00 per year. Anyone earning less than that can't pay for their baseline necessities such as utilities, groceries and rent (they sure as hell can't buy a house).

It is easy to see how all these negatives fit together. Since the Black male has no work ethic, he won't work to the best of his ability to learn a usable skill or trade, then he will settle for unemployment and ultimately wind up poor. And not just poor, but to the point that he can't even eat, so he becomes a beggar. If he can still eat, meaning someone else (his mother or some little sister) is taking care of him, he may still enter into a life of crime because he still wants what everybody else has and that is expensive trinkets.

Like all the other negative things in a Black man's life, being poor also has the obvious consequences. Black men don't earn nothing so they don't own nothing and therefore they don't take care of nothing. This is why Black males destroy property such as breaking out windows, setting things on fire, scribbling graffiti all over walls, throwing trash on the ground everywhere they go and letting the rental property where they live go into a state of disrepair.

When you are poor, you pay more for goods and services which continues to keep you poor. For example, Blacks pay more for gasoline, food, clothing, and services because the service providers factor in property destruction and theft from Black males when places of businesses are located in the Black communities. Or business owners charge more to these Blacks because they know that you don't have a choice. For example, pay phones located in run down Black communities cost more to make a local call.

Of course, poor people have bad credit, so credit costs poor people more. When they apply for credit it will be twice the going rate.

There are lot of Black men out there with ideas in their heads that would change the way society does certain things. The inventions that these Black men could bring to fruition are mind boggling. But, they don't have the money (capital); so instead of being rich, they are begging.

What about the link between being poor and dying early. Poor people don't live as long as wealthy people.[10] Sure there those of you that will say, but my grandmother or grandfather or aunt lived to be a hundred and she was poor. But that is incorrect because those people were not poor. They owned their houses, and farmed their own land. Many didn't have all the material wealth that this generation craves, but they sure as hell were not poor (particularly in spirit). Our grandparents did more with what little they had to plan for our future than we are doing with what we have to plan for the future of our descendants.

Very Insecure, Especially When It Comes to His Woman

One of the most aggravating things that women hate in a man is insecurity which manifests itself as jealousy. There is perhaps no male in the world that is more jealous than the Black male. He thinks that everybody wants his woman. He is jealous of a woman even if he is not married to her and is not supporting her. He expects to have complete control of his woman. He does not want her to go places, to talk to other men, or to have male friends. In other words, he attempts (unsuccessfully) to keep his woman in a shell.

Most Black men want the supermodel looking, Rhodes Scholar type of Black woman who is moving up the career ladder. If these men are unlucky enough to get such a woman, it quickly becomes apparent that these Black men can't measure up to these women in ability nor taste. These men can't service these women.

Of course this leads to jealousy and to an all consuming inferiority complex because they know that they are less educated and make less money than these women. These men feel the pressure that they have to do more and more to keep these women. These men begin to think (rightly so) that their women are having affairs with their co-workers. They worry about how short their woman's dress is or how much make-up she has on or they try to make their woman account for every minute of her time when she is away from home.

Over a period of time (a very short period), these men become control freaks. When this does not work (it never does), these men become frustrated and angry. Often times, they abuse these women, verbally and physically. Even if they divorce or break up with these women, the anger and desire to control these women does not go away. Too often, these Black men kill the women and on a few occasions themselves so that nobody else can have their woman.

This could all be avoided if Black men looked for a spiritual connection with a potential mate rather than just a physical connection. But they never do. They want the finest woman they can find so that they can show her off to their friends and family. This makes the man feel like he is successful and desirable. They would be better off with someone who loves them and is loyal to them and who is on the same mental and emotional level.

Habitual Drug User

While the frequency of overall drug use in America is down, it appears to be on the rise in the Black male population.[11] Crack cocaine has become the quickest and cheapest way to escape from reality for Black men. It is comforting to see that rare Black man going down the street who is not high.

One reason for such high drug use in Black males is because they feel hopeless and helpless. They can never see their situation getting better. They have no job, no woman, no place to call home and no future to look forward to.

Another reason is because they are uneducated. This lack of education is what leads to the feelings of hopelessness and helplessness in the first place. They don't have usable skills or trades so there is no way to earn a living. This just adds to their low self-esteem and gives them more justification in their minds to escape reality.

It should be pointed out that not all Black men who use drugs are down and out (at least not to start with). Many of these men were professionals or well paid blue collar workers. They began to use drugs for recreation. This recreational use soon became an addiction. Ultimately, they wind up in the same boat as the escapee users.

Drugs in general and crack cocaine in particular have become the overall scapegoat for lack of effort and responsibility possessed by most Black males. It is easier to blame the effect and availability of drugs than the person using the drugs. What is important to understand is that drugs in and of themselves are not bad, rather the problems are the extent of the usage of the drugs, the unlawful behavior to obtain the drugs and the negative effects on self, family and the community.

Understand also that the mentally weak, who usually are uneducated and undisciplined, fall prey to every vice that comes along. The vice of choice right now happens to be crack cocaine. When a new vice comes along, Black males will quickly take it and experience all the negatives associated with it.

Having Sex Not Marriage nor Money is Primary Motivation

Black men seem to be driven to pursue women for the purpose of having sex more than anything else in their lives. These men place having sex above making money, raising a family, getting an education, getting married or just generally being committed to one woman.

Just listen to the differences between conversations going on in a group of White males and those going on in a group of Black males. The Whites will be talking about politics and how some new ruling will affect their ability to make money. The Blacks will be talking about how they screwed some woman or boasting how soon they will. The Whites are talking about making money, the Blacks are talking about getting laid.

No one is certain as to why this is true of the Black male. Black men are not the only sexual men in the world. For example, Italian men are well known for their sexual prowess. Yet these men are some of the most money making machines on the planet. Just think of the best foods, the best cars, the best suits and you think of Italian made.

This is one area where one can only speculate. Perhaps the Black male has more testosterone flowing through his veins which would certainly explain his superior athletic prowess.

Maybe he is in fact more well endowed, although, there have not been any studies done to show that Black men have larger penises. Nor has there been any proof that there is a relationship between sex drive and penis size.[12]

The most likely reason why Black males are sexually driven more than the males of other races is because Black males have nothing other than sex to gauge their masculinity and success. Unlike males of other races who use their position, power and wealth as barometers of their success, Black males use the number of sexual encounters as their barometer since most Black men don't have desirable positions (careers), power nor wealth. Since Black men don't have anything else, they use sex as a way to dominate (as least in their own minds) a woman. They look at is as a form of ownership. If I screw her, she is mine.

It could be that education again plays a vital role. Across the board, educated men, Black or White, seem to be able to balance the drive for sex with the desire to make money. It seems that when one is working hard, doing the things that need to be done on a daily basis, giving it their all, they don't spend near as much time chasing women. Successful, wealthy men don't chase women, poor, non-achieving ones do.

Another thing that is unique to the Black male is that he has no intention of getting married. He just wants to have sex as often as he can with his woman but does not want to make a commitment to her. That commitment would include marriage and taking care of her. You hear Black men all the time labeling a Black woman as trying to trap them or that the woman is being materialistic like a White woman. Yet at the same time they expect her to be available to them any time that they want to have sex. The moment the woman wises up and makes any type of demand that she be treated with dignity and respect, that she becomes more to the man than just a sex object, the Black male starts to call her names and belittle her. But he never proposes to or provides for her.

Primary Perpetrators of Crimes and Violence

Black men commit more crimes than any other race on the face of this earth. Not only do they commit more crimes, more often than not, these crimes tend to have violence associated with them. The Black men who are committing crimes are doing so at an increasingly younger age. The average age of incarceration is 21.[13] The frequency of crimes committed by Black males is also on the rise. A felony is committed by a Black man in this country every forty to sixty seconds.[14]

Why do Black males as a group commit so much crime? The answer you get from most Black people these days is that it is the system. Black people argue that the system is set up in order to arrest, prosecute, convict and incarcerate Black men more so than the men of other races. The one thing that Black people won't admit is that even if what they are saying is 100% true, Black men still commit the crimes. The system is not making these Black males commit the crimes. Black men themselves are making that decision.

The question becomes, why are they doing it? Again, the factors that come into play in other negative areas hold true here.

Education is a big one. The Black men committing violent crimes are uneducated. Just visit any jail and take a poll of the inmates and you will find that few if any completed high school. In other words, college graduates do not commit violent crimes as a general rule.

Crimes are being committed by Black males at an increasingly earlier age because Black males are dropping out of school earlier and have nothing to do during the day. As a consequence, committing a crime and the mental rush they feel from the danger they face and the pain of the victims, provides some stimulation to their feeble minds. A mind will always occupy itself with something. It will be either productive or non-productive. This explains why even when Black males drop out of high school, they still show up after school adjourns to harass those who are still in school because they have to have something, anything to do.

Paralleling education is discipline. The two go together. Educated people tend to be more disciplined. The more disciplined you are, the more you tend to adhere to good morals and values. You make better choices even if they are not the easiest or most popular ones. You don't follow the group as easily. You use your own mind.

Obviously, there are those who argue (they like to argue) that I know people who have good morals and values, are not educated and they still don't commit crimes. Again this is the exception. If you really look at this person or persons, you will find that they are usually over the age of 30 or they come from a family who is educated or at the very least hardworking. But you better believe that most Black males who commit crimes indeed do fall under the basic stereotype (undisciplined and uneducated).

Some Black men commit crimes out of frustration. This is their way of lashing out, getting back at the system. They blame the system for their failures and rationalize their crime as but a by-product of the system not doing more for them. It is also a way for Black men to feel that they are in some form of control. It is a way to prove their masculinity to themselves and to others (usually fellow gang members). It shows that they have loyalty to the group and that they are not afraid (just stupid).

Non-Productive and Non-Participants in Society

'The truth is the light' is an expression that has been around for hundreds of years. Another expression is 'the truth hurts'. Yet another is 'the truth is always painful'. How about 'the truth shall set you free'? The truth of the matter is that it is more important to know the truth than not because ultimately truth will prevail.

The truth is that Black men have some serious problems. Until these problems are admitted (brought to light), no matter how painful (it hurts), these problems cannot be solved (Black men set free).

Right now, this moment in 2000, Black men make life miserable for everyone including other races, the Black race, Black women, and Black children. Black men seem to just be here, in the way, causing trouble.

If you look around the world and characterize other races, you always identify them with something. For example, Germans are known for their cars (I want one), the Swiss are known for their watches (Rolex), the Italians are known for their cars (Ferraris), suits (Armani and Bertoni), and fine foods, the Japanese for their cars (Lexus and Toyota and Nissan), and electronic products (televisions and radios and computers), the American Whites for their technology and industry and space exploration, the Chinese for any product that costs less such as clothing, toys, Chinese food, etc., the Arabs for their oil, the French for their wines and it goes on and on throughout the world.

But when it comes to Blacks, specifically Black men, you can't name anything of substance except sports and entertainment which are not products. The one thing that you do associate with Black men is crime. In other words, Black men don't produce anything for resale. Black men will never be free until they produce something that the world needs and respects.

This non-productivity is manifested by non-participation in society. Black men don't produce nothing, they don't build nothing, they don't own nothing, and they have nothing (other than athletics and entertainment) to offer to society. So how can they participate in society? The answer is that they can't. So society's response is to put Black men in jail. Out of sight, out of crime and ultimately, out of mind.

Sure, there are those who will read this book and say that this sounds cruel and cold-blooded. For those who feel that way, just look around and see if Black men are important ingredients of the technological (computer) age and space exploration. Ask yourself if you can name one thing that Black men have improved? If you can, how about two things? Worse yet, ponder upon this question. Ask yourself what would society miss if Black men vanished from the face of the planet tomorrow? The answer is crime, violence and loud stereos. Sad but true.

Still There Are Some Successful Black Men

Not all Black men are criminals. Not all Black men are poor. In fact there are some extremely wealthy and successful Black men. Not only are these men successful in terms of making money, but also do an excellent job of raising their families and giving something back to their communities.

It is easy to understand how someone who has read up to this point would think that the intent of this book is just to point out all of the negatives about Black men. That is not what this book is about. Rather it is about honestly identifying all the problems that the Black male has.

Sure there are some successful Black men, but in the scheme of things, they are the exception and not the rule. For every successful Black man, there are ten thousand examples of those who are down and out. So one Black man is driving a Mercedes, living in a five bedroom house with money in the bank while the other ten thousand are living in the projects, homeless, in jail, begging on the corner or committing crimes.

If you added up all the athletes, the entertainers, corporate vice-presidents, and business owners (restaurant and night club owners), you would only total one percent of the Black males in this country.[15]

But the whole purpose of this book is to be a guide to turn this mess around. With that in mind, there is a list of some successful Black men included here so that Black men can see that this is what they want to strive to become.

These men were chosen because they meet all or most of the criteria set forth in the Survival Fitness Test outlined in Part VII of this book.

Some Examples of Hardworking, Successful, Black Men

The following list includes some examples of successful Black men. Success is not just financial, but also includes men who have overcome less than desirable circumstances. There is biographical information contained on each man, although not all information is exactly the same.

Example # 1: Vance L. Harper. He is 38 years old, married for ten years and has two children, ages eight and five. He holds a Bachelor's Degree in Criminal Justice from Fort Valley State College. He spent several years in the field of criminal justice.

Vance is the owner of Nick's Barber Shop, 4830-B, Redan Road, Stone Mountain, Georgia 30088. He specializes in hair care for Black men including grooming and recommending hair care products. He has been operating for seven years and has seen phenomenal growth, the kind of growth that fortune five-hundred companies would kill for. His annual gross income is in the multiple six figures and is steadily improving.

What is it that makes Vance and his business so successful? He is successful because, as he says, he understands what it takes to make a good impression on people and he is sincere about providing good service. As he puts it in his own words, "I take the time to make my clients feel good, comfortable, and relaxed in a calm and pleasant atmosphere. We make them feel as though they are important. We listen to them and we cater to them. We make them feel as though they matter, and they do. We treat the women customers as queens and the men customers as kings. Not only do we treat our men and women like royalty, but we work with the children as well. We work with them not only in our business, but also in the community. We teach the children to love and respect one another. We also employ several "fatherless boys in our establishment and we show them what it is to be a hard working Black man in society. The bottom line is that in my business we show all of our clients, men, women, and children the true meaning of love and respect."

What advice does Vance offer to other Black men who want to become successful? "It is very simple. It does not matter what you do in life, you have to do it to the best of your ability. It does not matter if you are a sanitation worker or barber. If you want to be successful and make the money, you have to work more than eight hours a day. The time that you will actually have to put in will be closer to 14 hours per day. There is no way to get around not putting in this much time, especially when you are starting out. Always be punctual, and show people love and respect. We need to take the time to listen to the needs of our clients, and not be afraid to help people. It is important to be there for each other and put in the necessary time to make things work. Teach your children to do their best in whatever they do. Make sure that instead of just telling your children what they need to do, also show them by example. Be God fearing and teach your children to know God and know that he loves us and that he is able. All of these things are vital and important to the future of Black men."

Example #2: Marvin Allen. He graduated from the U.S. Naval Academy in 1979. He served six years as a commissioned officer on active duty. Today he is a reservist with the rank of Commander. After being on active duty in the Navy, Marvin worked in manufacturing for Proctor and Gamble. He has been married to Wanda Evans (a successful entrepreneur in her own right) for 11 years and has three sons.

Marvin owns Philjon's Neighborhood Grille restaurant located at 2841 Greenbriar Parkway, Atlanta, Georgia. This is a sports bar that is patronized by the community seeking a place to socialize, relax and eat good food. He has been in business for four years.

Marvin will quickly tell you that all of his successes are blessings and the result of continued efforts backed by determination. In his own words, "I am a 'wizard' and I do not allow others to impose limits on me. When I set my goals, I get focused to develop action plans which serve as my road map. When others say I can't, I become even more determined. 'No's' don't stop me and I will continue my efforts until I find my 'yes'. I would have never found my 'yes' without the power of knowledge. It is true, knowledge is power! Know yourself, know your business, know your customer, and know the Lord."

Marvin shares this advice with other Black males who would like to be successful. "Commit yourself to your goals and do not allow anyone or anything to get in your way. You must not only want to achieve your goals, you must be willing to work to achieve your goals. Identify helpful resources and learn how to best utilize your resources to attain your goals. Remember, always do your best and don't be afraid to fail."

Example #3: Mark A. Lomax. He has been married to Trimona Brandon for seven years. They have three sons. Mark graduated from Heidelberg College with a B.A. He received a Master of Divinity from Trinity Lutheran Seminary and a Doctor of Divinity from United Theological Seminary.

Pastor Lomax has 18 years experience in the ministry and currently pastors First African Presbyterian Church in Lithonia, Georgia. Unlike many pastors who have become so important and too busy to spend time with the congregation, Pastor Lomax spends 20 yours per week at the Church. He makes himself available for counseling of members and teaching and training on a one on one basis. Pastor Lomax places his flock (his members) above all other interest including television interviews and appearances, popularity and outside business interests. His commitment to teaching the word and his effectiveness in doing so is shown by the numbers of people who attend bible study at his church, but are members of other churches in the surrounding community. Pastor Lomax is never too busy to talk to you and offer you spiritual guidance. He is indeed a servant of the people.

What makes him such a giant among other pastors? He will quickly tell you that, "It is my tenacity, perseverance, faithfulness to God, dedicated service to others, hard work and diligent study."

What advice would he like to share with other Black men to make them more successful? "Identify life's purpose as quickly as possible. Pursue life's purpose with determination. Set reasonable, achievable goals. Plan your career carefully. Manage your career wisely. Don't burn your bridges. Respect the dignity and worth of every human being. Take time for the 'Little Guy'. Give attention to detail. Walk with integrity. Treat others as you would like to be treated."

Example #4: Matthew Ware. He is the owner and operator of Padgett Business Services of Atlanta. His business is located at 3636 Panola Rd., Lithonia, Georgia. This is an accounting firm. He has been in business for seven years.

Matthew has been married for eight years to Noreen Banks and has two children. He graduated from Fisk University.

Matthew could have moved his business to any location that he so chose, but decided to remain in his own community to provide services to his neighbors. He has been very successful, earning well into the six figures. He lives the dream that most of us have and that is to not only have your own successful business, but to also own the building in which your business is located in.

As Matthew puts it, "To be a success, you must have a willingness to work long hours and stay educated on tax laws and accounting changes. You must have the ability to explain accounting information and treat clients right. Most of all you must have God's blessings."

His advice to other Black men is, "Be willing to fight for your dream and work hard to achieve them. Always be honest to those people who are willing to pay you and make sure you always advertise. Remember, anything worth having is worth the hard times, tears, joys and prayers."

Example # 5: Adebowale Adedeji. Bo, as he is referred to by his friends, has been married for 15 years. He had three children, two daughters and one son, Adetokunbo, who is deceased. Bo never attended school formally, but has been trained to a level that would be equivalent to a baccalaureate degree. He is quick to point out that he will forever be a student and hopes to never graduate from learning the lessons that life has to offer.

Bo is the owner operator of Africa By Design. This business is located at 6118-C Covington Highway, Lithonia, Georgia. He has been in business for five years. As the name implies, his business sells any and everything that is remotely related to Africa. Bo also hosts regular events featuring guest speakers dealing with topics that affect the lives of Black people.

What about being successful? Bo says, "I would not say that I am successful just yet, but I am beginning to succeed. I am learning my business everyday. Part of my progress can be attributed to the art of listening to the God in me and the ancestors. They tell me what to do and I do just that. However, I am still learning to listen. Everyday I adjust to my business environment and needs. I, like all Black men must go back to school to learn the art of business and the art of self-activation. These are very important to business progress. When I really look at it, my success begins when I can help other people into business and maintain them in business. I look forward to each day of my life."

Bo's advice to other Black men is very simple. "To me the greatest atrocity you can ever commit is the act of not listening and believing in your dreams and ultimately not pursuing them. So listening, believing, and acting on your dreams equals success."

PUBLIC SERVICE ANNOUNCEMENT NO. I

If you need legal services, use the following law firm:

DWIGHT L THOMAS, P.C.

ATTORNEY AT LAW

TRIAL LITIGATION

(MAIN OFFICE)

142 MITCHELL STREET

SUITE 401

ATLANTA, GA. 30303

OFC: (404) 522-1400

FAX: (404) 522-9004

194 PEACHTREE STREET

SUITE C

ATLANTA, GA. 30303

OFC: (404) 523-2325

FAX: (404) 523-5020

CRIMINAL TRIAL PRACTICE

STATEWIDE ONLY (800) 968-7748

PAGER (404) 415-2954

PART II. HOW AND WHY WHITES CONTRIBUTE TO BLACK MALE EXTINCTION

Anyone who thinks that Whites don't play a role in the extinction of Black males is simply naive. The truth is that in the 2000's, the methods that Whites use are much more subtle than those used prior to the 1960's.

It is important for the reader to understand that these baseline methods are not likely to be changed. Instead they are going to have to be dealt with. The only way that they can be dealt with is by Blacks becoming better, spiritually, mentally and financially.

It is equally important to note that not all Whites are bad (hum?). There are good and bad people in every race. But what is being discussed here are some innate (natural and yes, racial) tendencies.

White Male Fears Black Male

In most of the world, the White male is larger than other males. For instance, compare the White male to Asian men, or Italian men, or Indian men or even Arabian men. Time and time again you will observe that the American White male is larger in stature.[16]

This is not true when it comes to American Black men. They are the only men on earth that are physically superior in every way to White men. Black men are taller, more muscular, have broader shoulders, better butts, (larger where it counts?); they are just more manly.

As a result, women (all women) find Black men more sexually attractive. If you don't believe this, just let a buffed Black man stand in a crowd of puny White males and see who the women are getting sexually aroused for. Even if White men are large in stature, they have no sex appeal except for maybe their eyes, or hair, or some other wimpy feature.

This sexual inferiority complex is the main reason why White males have displayed a consistent hatred of Black males. He does not hate Black women as shown by the fact that he has had sex with them since the plantation days. During that period, White males created the Jezebel syndrome. The reasoning for this was that to link female honor to purity would have proven sexually inconvenient for southern White men had they not bifurcated the sexuality of White and Black women. The creation of Jezebel provided the rationale for allowing sexual relations between White men and Black women by White men.

By regarding Black women as a class of women who set little value on chastity, he argued that slavery protected Black women by saving them from the alternative of being cast out of society in the manner "justly and necessarily" applied to promiscuous White women.[17]

Sexual access to enslaved women discouraged White men from debauching "pure" White women and provided White men with easy gratification for their hot passions without violating southern codes of honor. Nor did he have to account to anyone if pregnancy ensued.

As a result, this sexual inferiority complex that White men feel toward Black men has led to a fear and hatred of Black males much deeper than other men which White males have come in contact with.

A White male's worst nightmare is that a Black man will take his White woman. Not only might he take her, but he might treat her just like he, the White male has treated Black women, just objects for sexual pleasure. These fears that White men have are not unfounded. When a White woman gets the chance to be with a Black man, she jumps at the chance. Look at how White women behave when they go to the Caribbean, a place where it is acceptable to be with Black men. And of course, once White women go Black, they never go back is the way the expression goes.

The fear that the White male has regarding the Black male is not just sexual. It is also mental. The White male knows that if a Black male is as educated as he is and is given the chance to compete, the Black male will win. This is proven time and time again. If one Black male is given a chance to climb the corporate ladder, he will become a vice-president even though he is one Black in a company that has 2,000 (often hostile) managers.

Black men are very creative. In fact, most of the twentieth century inventions were created by Black men. Where do you think the ideas for cellular phone technology, the mailbox, the refrigerator, the traffic light, and on and on came from? They came from Black men working and trying to fit into Corporate America.[18]

So how do White men respond to being sexually and mentally inferior to the Black male? They do everything in their power to keep Black men from making money and just having a fair chance.

The laws are skewed against the Black male. The penalties for crimes that he commits are harsher (see discussion on page 86). The most obvious thing that White males do is not hire Black men in positions of power. If you look at all of the television stations around this nation you will see one thing, a Black woman co-anchoring the television news with two White men.

The reasons why White men hire Black women in managerial positions and not Black men are because the White men accomplish two things at once. First, he does not have a talented, well dressed, broad shouldered, tight butt Black man to compete against. Second, if he hires only Black women, he can have dominion over both White women and Black women, i.e., have sex with both of them.

Look at any company in America and you will see this pattern over and over again. White males can get away with this under the guise of minority hiring. Proudly having you believe that not only did they hire a Black, but that they hired a Black woman, covering both race and gender concerns.

Finally, as more and more Black women are hired and paid high salaries, the White male knows that she will look up to financially wealthy White men and look down on unemployed, poor Black men. This also decreases the number of Corporate Black male role models.

King and Queen Syndrome

Whites have displayed a consistent pattern of behavior over the last one-thousand years. One trait in particular that they have shown is that they believe that they are better than other people simply because they are born with Blue blood. This belief goes all the way back to the times of the old English kings and queens. Now, just as then, Whites believe that the only purpose of other races is to service them. In other words, Whites don't value any other people who are not White.

Every time Whites have come into contact with non-White people, they have enslaved them. Not only did they enslave them, they took their land and riches without any remorse because they did not value these other non-White people as being equal. Just look at the colonization periods of the 14th and 15th centuries. When Whites went to a country for the first time, they said that it was now discovered. They claimed it for England even though there were people living there. Not only did they claim it, they killed if necessary to gain control of the land as though the people were just a nuisance that needed to be eradicated. Of course if it was profitable, the people were enslaved.

It is important to understand that this has nothing to do with White bashing. This is just the way that Whites are. This is not to say that they are the only people that are that way. The behavior that Whites have consistently displayed when it comes to other non-White races is the same behavior that is always displayed by dominant cultures.

The Han Dynasty was in power in China during the period of about 200 B.C. The rulers of this dynasty sincerely believed that their power to rule came directly from heaven.[19]

Blessed by the divine message that authorized these rulers to rule over all peoples, the "Sons of Heaven" would go off to war. Tribute or slavery--these were the choices available to the inferior races destined to be their subjects. The noble joy of mastery over lesser peoples and the pleasures afforded by easy access to domestic slaves and fine gems, furs and perfumes was surely deserved by the agents of Heaven who brought virtue and civilization to all nations.

If you look at all conquering races, you will find that they too believe this. This is especially true of Whites.

What Blacks don't understand is that it is not a question of racism, but a question of valuation. Whites simply value themselves more than they do Blacks and other races (see discussion on technology, page 82).

The poorest, uneducated redneck values himself more than he values the wealthiest most educated Black. When the redneck can't logically explain how a Black can do more and have more than him, the redneck will then form militia and White Supremacist groups so that he can then attempt to perpetuate his beliefs by force and fear.

Most times, Whites don't even feel that they are doing anything outside of that which is preordained when they hire Blacks in positions of servitude because they sincerely believe that the role of Blacks is to service Whites from cleaning up after them to raising their brats to doing all the menial labor that is beneath Whites.

This valuation in America is never going to change. No culture (race) has ever changed the way that it values another race.

But wait, Whites are not the only ones that devalue other races in America. Even Black devalue other races. Look at how Blacks behave regarding Mexicans. Blacks don't believe that the Mexicans have value. This is because, Mexicans don't have technology, they are not wealthy, they don't really produce any desirable products, nor are they very educated for the most part. In fact, Blacks view Mexicans like Whites view Blacks. They are people that you need to do menial tasks that you don't want to do.

Blacks do not try to be like the Mexicans. Blacks don't want Mexicans living near them. Blacks don't want to interact with Mexicans. In fact Blacks treat Mexicans like Whites treat Blacks. So this valuation phenomenon is universal.

Another thing that Whites and other dominant (conquering) races do a good job of is convincing the conquered and/or enslaved race that they have no value. These enslaved races incorporate this belief deep down in their psyche. The result is that these conquered races then try everything that they can to imitate the conquerors. They try and dress like them, act like them and look like them. They try everything that they can to associate with the conquerors. These enslaved races even treat each other like the conquerors treat them, i.e. substandard. These enslaved races even become ashamed of their culture and heritage. Just look at how American Blacks view Africa both as a continent and as a collection of individual nations.

Black must begin to understand that they are not the only race that this has happened to, nor will they be the last.

Cheating Husband Syndrome

The cheating husband goes around and dates and has sex with other women. If he is caught and asked why he did it, he usually tries to explain to his spouse. He will say something like, "Oh, she was looking so good that I could not help myself" or "See I was at a party and I was drinking and having a good time and she came on to me and I could not resist". How about, "Her legs were so pretty and her ass was looking so good and I am a man, you know." What about the very famous, "Baby, it just happened, I didn't mean for it to, but it just happened."

No matter what the reason given, there is one thing that cheating husbands universally expect from their spouses. When they are caught red-handed, they expect their spouses to forgive them. The reasons that these cheating husbands give as to why they should be forgiven usually fall into the category of "It was just sex, there were no feelings and it won't happen again."

Ah, but what if the wife is caught cheating? What happens when she says, "Oh honey, I was out with my girlfriends and I saw this guy and I got turned on and we had sex?" How about, "Honey I was drinking and I saw this guy with broad shoulders, sexy eyes and such a tight butt that I couldn't help myself." Again, what about the very famous, "See honey, it just happened, I wasn't looking for anything, I don't know how it happened, please forgive me?"

Now what is likely to happen? Universally, the cheating husband, even though he may have been forgiven on a prior occasion, is not going to forgive his wife. The idea of another man making love to his woman is something that he will not accept; not just today, not just tomorrow, but never. This cheating husband is likely to get so pissed off that he may abuse his wife or divorce her. One thing is certain, he is not going to forgive her.

What is the analogy here as it relates to White people? Like the cheating husband, Whites discriminate in their hiring and promotion practices, they treat Blacks unfairly, and so on.

When called on the carpet about something regarding unfair treatment of Blacks, just like the cheating husband, they try and explain it away. They will say something like, "Oh, it just seems like it is discrimination, but maybe anytime something does not go the way Blacks want it to go, they yell discrimination." How about the very famous, "Even though it looks like discrimination, there does not seem to be any harm done?" Many times you will hear, "I didn't know that I was discriminating and if I was I didn't mean to."

Just like the cheating husband, Whites expect to be forgiven and if not forgiven, forgotten. Either way, they will pretend that it is not so bad. Ultimately, they will tell you that they are not perfect and discrimination is just a part of life.

But oh my gosh, let a Black, just like the cheating wife, appear to have discriminated. Just let a Black person get hired or promoted ahead of a White and the only reason that you can find on the surface is that the person may have been promoted based on skin color (or heaven forbid, quota). Just like the cheating husband, Whites can't accept it. Never mind that they have obviously discriminated for centuries, they go crazy.

Whites don't scream discrimination, they yell, reverse discrimination. They want you to think that this is much worse than the discrimination that they do. Like the cheating husband, they want you to know that here it is a White person being discriminated against by a Black person. It is much, much worse.

When Blacks begin to understand the psyche of Whites this way, they can then begin to understand why Whites are so up and arms about affirmative action. The propositions in California are not just happening for no reason. The very thought that a Black person can get a position and make more money or be treated better than a White person just because of the color of their skin is outrageous. This is unfair they say. Whites even have the nerve to quote the civil rights legislation regarding equal treatment regardless of race, creed, or color (all the same thing actually). Again, never mind that just like the cheating husband, they have discriminated for centuries. The point is that just like the cheating husband, it is now happening to Whites and it seems worse somehow.

If you really think about this cheating husband syndrome and how it truly explains White behavior when they feel that they are wronged, it will help Blacks to understand White behavior regarding the O.J. Simpson trials.

Jury nullification is a term that Black males should be very familiar with. It is a term that refers to what happens when evidence is presented to a jury and the jury obviously rules differently than what a rational, reasonable person would rule.[20] In other words, the verdict is not substantiated by the facts.

What many people believe in America, (some Blacks and all Whites) is that O.J. Simpson killed Nicole Brown Simpson and Ronald Goldman. They believe that the verdict returned in the criminal trial was incorrect and racially based. Specifically, that you had a majority Black jury that found a Black man innocent of a crime. But here not just any crime, rather you had a Black man that got away with killing two Whites. You also had a wealthy Black man who used his money and power to get the best lawyers (Black ones ultimately) to get away with murder according to Whites.

Look at how the cheating husband syndrome applies here. Whites have gotten away with killing Blacks over the last century in overwhelming numbers. Even in the Rodney King State Court trials, where you had video taped evidence showing conclusively that the officers involved were wrong, an all White jury acquitted the officers. After all, Rodney King was Black, the officers were White.

But like the cheating husband, Whites cannot accept the acquittal of Mr. Simpson. Especially by a majority Black jury. This is wrong. It is unfair. You even have Whites to go so far as to say that their own system of justice is now flawed.

Like the cheating husband, Whites will never accept the outcome of either the criminal nor civil trial. The civil trial is just as important as the criminal trial. The difference in the civil trial is that you also had the king and queen syndrome at work.

In the above section, it was stated that Whites value themselves more than any other race, especially Blacks. Think about it for a second, O.J. Simpson is accused of killing not one, but two Whites. From a value standpoint, both Nicole Brown Simpson and Ron Goldman are at the lower end of White society. Neither were educated, money making Whites, but they are still valued more than O.J. Simpson by Whites because he is Black and there just cannot be the perception that a Black man (a commoner) could kill two Whites (a king and queen) and get away with it especially because the Black man had money and power and used their own system against them.

The civil verdict and awards was a message to Black people. It had nothing to do with justice in the purest sense. The message to Blacks was that we, Whites are going to punish you for killing Whites and for having the audacity to find one of your own innocent for killing us. Never mind that we have done this to you countless times, it is worse when it happens to us. Never mind that neither Ron Goldman nor Nicole Brown would have earned more than $500,000 in their lifetimes. To us Whites, we are going to say that they are worth 8.5 million dollars plus 25 million to teach you a lesson.

The psyche of Whites will never let them get over the deaths of Nicole Brown and Ron Goldman. Whites will never be satisfied even after O.J. Simpson is dead and buried. Whites will moan and groan about this from now on because deep down in their psyche, they feel that Blacks don't value these two deaths.

Like the cheating husband, the anger and the hatred will continue to build. No White person can say with 100 percent certainty that Mr. Simpson did it. In fact if it ever came out that someone else did the killing and it was certain that they did it, say a White person, the Whites in this country would self-destruct.

No Desire to Share Economic Pie

Ultimately the one thing in our society that is the great equalizer is wealth. It is not power nor achievements. Both of these two without wealth are meaningless.

People value how much money a person has over what that person does. For example, a neuro-surgeon is probably one of the smartest people in our society, but he is not the most respected nor sought after (unless you need brain surgery) person. Athletes and entertainers are far more revered because they have money.

You take two people, exactly the same in terms of education, position and power, except one is a millionaire and the other is not, it is certain that the one that has the money will get the most clout.

People that truthfully say that they don't care about being rich or not are either all ready rich or they are insane. You cannot live in this society with any kind of quality of life without money.

The one thing that Whites have in this country in abundance that Blacks do not have is money.   Money gives Whites control. This money (and technology) is the main reason that Blacks look up to Whites because this money allows Whites to build and operate the things that they have.

Whites have no intention of sharing their wealth with Black people, especially Black males. If Black males have money, they will not look up to Whites. Whites can't innately feel superior to Black men with money. In fact when a Black male accumulates a certain amount of money (and it doesn't have to be that much), he doesn't even want to be associated with the Whites male (not true of the White female, the brother will get him one).

This is another reason why White males don't hire Black males in positions that make money. The moment these Black men make money, they become role models for other Black males and all other women.

Whites will never change regarding how they love money and Blacks must stop trying to change them .

Actually, Blacks must understand that Whites don't owe Blacks any duty to share their economic wealth with Blacks. True economic wealth must be earned because wealth is more than just having the money, it is a mind set. This mind set drives you to earn more and more.

Whites Will Do Anything to Maintain Racial Purity

Genetically speaking, there are dominant and recessive genetic markers for human traits.[21] For example (a very simple example), if x is a dominant gene (say for being Black), and y is a recessive trait (say for being White), then anytime you have a dominant gene present, you would have a Black person. Under this scheme with these two markers, the formula that potential offspring from the mating of a Black and White would be either (xx), (xy), (yx). You could never have (yy) (unless two Whites mated). So anytime you had Blacks and Whites mating, you would have Black offspring 100% of the time. It would not matter if you had a Black male and White female or a White male and a Black female. The result would be the same, a Black child.

When viewed in the strictest scientific observation, the first generation of offspring would be a mixture of Black and White, i.e. varying degrees of both. But in the next generation, if this offspring from the first generation mated with a Black, then their offspring would be far closer to being totally Black. If you have this second generation offspring mating with a Black, then the third generation would be completely Black. You could never stop the process to complete Blackness. All you could do is slow it down by having the offspring from a Black and White union to mate with a White. But again, the Black gene being dominant would still manifest itself in the bloodline and the moment anyone in this bloodline mated with a Black, you are just one generation away from total Blackness.

Whites have always known this. This is why they will do anything to prevent large scale mating between Blacks and Whites. They know that if this happened, in three generations, there would be no pure Whites left.

Sex is always the worry, it is the heart of the matter. Why do you think that Whites will let their children play with Black children until they get to the age of about seven. At this point a concerted, conscious effort is made to discourage any further contact so that by the age of ten or eleven, the White child would have had two to three years of no constant contact with Black children. This continues until puberty or the sexually active years.

This worry about having sex with Blacks is so ingrained into the collective consciousness of Whites, that the White male will do anything to prevent Blacks males from mating with White women. Here it is 2000 and Whites continue to condition Blacks that they have broken some kind of universal (divine) law when they date and mate with Whites. They continue to ingrain this in Blacks by hanging them, murdering them and just generally discouraging interracial couples.

This sexual worry only applies to Black people. Whites will tolerate Asian matings and Hispanic matings because the genetic markers for these groups are no more or less dominant than Whites.

As mentioned in an earlier section, the White male fears the Black male. Most of that fear has to do with sex. Not only can't the White male measure up to the Black male in terms of sexually attractiveness, nor sexual performance, but most importantly, he can't measure up in terms of sexual perpetuation of the race.

The world is dark. With the exception of Europe, the United States and Australia, the world is dark. Whites know that they make up a small part. They will do anything to maintain their heritage.

Primary Distributors of Drugs and Guns to Black Community

Ask any Black person around this nation what does he or she think is the single most important thing that is causing the demise of the Black community and you will most likely get that it is crime related to drug usage.

It appears that no Black community is immune to the drug problem. Many Black people believe that if you got rid of crack cocaine, you would get rid of crime. This is obviously not true. It is the inherent mental weakness in the mind of the drug user, not the drug that is the problem.

Still whether it be crack cocaine, heroine or some other hardcore drug, Black people don't have the ability nor resources to manufacture, package and distribute the drug to their own communities.

Most of the raw materials needed to produce crack cocaine for instance are grown in South America, specifically Colombia. The raw material, the coca plant must be harvested and flown to the United States in order to then be chemically processed into crack cocaine.

Blacks don't have the airplanes and boats nor do they have the connections in South America to transport coca plants to the U.S. Blacks also don't have the chemical facilities and know how to then process the coca plants into crack cocaine. Finally, Blacks particularly don't have the ability to work together to distribute crack cocaine nationwide and ultimately into the Black community.

The evidence is mounting that even the CIA may have been instrumental in the wide spread distribution of crack cocaine in Black neighborhoods in the Los Angeles area (and probably other major metropolitan areas) in order to finance the Contras and no telling who else.[22]

When it comes to the distribution of guns in the Black community, the same facts ring true.   Blacks are not capable of the manufacture, sale and distribution of guns to the Black community. Yet there is massive distribution of guns in the Black community. Even in junior high schools where Blacks make up a significant part of the student population, guns are a problem.

Where do Blacks get guns? They get them from Whites. The easiest place to get the guns are from the umpteen pawn shops located in the Black community. Who owns the pawn shops, Whites do.

Why is it that local, state and federal law enforcement officials don't do more to prevent the manufacture, distribution and sale of crack cocaine and guns to the Black community? Why is it that most of the emphasis is on prosecution of the end level user, Blacks, and not on prevention, i.e., stopping the manufacture and distribution?

The answers to these questions are very simple, money and genocide. By taking the path that law enforcement officials take, they (and they are White) accomplish several things at one time, they first make money off Blacks, then they indirectly kill them because drugs and guns kill, and if the Blacks don't die, Whites put them in jail and out of society. Even while in jail, Blacks are still making money for Whites (see discussion under Criminal Justice System in Part IV).   Also, if you really went after the people who really manufactured and distributed drugs and guns, you would have to go after White people and in this case wealthy, well respected, ivory tower Whites.

What happens is that Whites promote tougher crime bills which usually contain longer and longer jail sentences for the end user, but not for the front end provider.

Let's focus on guns for a moment. Whites don't really want tougher gun control laws because if you had the background checks that are needed and very easy to implement, the White pawn shop owners (most of whom belong to and support the efforts of the National Rifle Association) would lose money. They would lose money because most of the felons who buy guns would no longer buy them from pawn shops nor gun shops because they would get arrested. Who are most of these felons, they are Blacks. If the Blacks did not buy the guns, the pawn shop owners would lose money.

Just imagine for a moment what would happen to the sale of hand guns, both legal and illegal if every time a gun was sold in a shop, the person who purchased the gun had to be photographed and fingerprinted. But for the above reasons, it is not happening.

It is also very unlikely that the true distributors of drugs to the Black community will ever be prosecuted because, who, especially what White, is going to arrest and prosecute factory owners, car dealership owners, upscale restaurant owners, corporate presidents, mayors and ultimately, top level government cronies? It won't happen because their place in society is protected from governmental prosecution through years of bribery. That bribery is justified because the ultimate victims here are Black and are not valued as human beings.

PUBLIC SERVICE ANNOUNCEMENT NO. 2

If you need excellent food and would like to open your own franchise:

daVIDO's

$3.75 PIZZA

6118 Covington Highway
(Covington Square Shopping Center)
Lithonia, Georgia 30058
(770) 808-5855

daVIDO's $3.75 PIZZA is a new pizza concept started in Atlanta, Georgia, featuring authentic Italian pizza, delicious hot wings and real philly cheese steak sandwiches.

daVIDO's $3.75 PIZZA is known for its great food, excellent customer service and value pricing. We are committed to developing our business while making a positive impact on our community.

Partners involved with daVIDO's $3.75 PIZZA will have unlimited opportunities to earn above average income and make a significant contribution to their neighborhood. We are looking for entrepreneurs committed to doing well by doing good. We are looking for partners who want to make a difference.

daVIDO's $3.75 PIZZA can make your dream of owning your own business come true. **For further information, call David L. Holt, owner,** at (770) 523-8969.

PART III. THE ROLE THAT BLACKS PLAY IN CAUSING BLACK MALE EXTINCTION

One of the hardest and most painful things for Blacks to talk about is the role that they play in causing their own problems. They have spent such a long time blaming Whites and God for their situation and as a result, they resist any viewpoints that point to other reasons for their problems.

The reality is that Blacks themselves share much of the blame. This section looks at the factors that are playing a role in the extinction of the Black male that are a direct result of the actions and behavior of Blacks.

Too Busy Trying to Integrate With Whites

Blacks have been exposed to decades of programming in this country by Whites that Blacks are inferior. This programming, whether openly done or subtlely done, is so ingrained into the psyche of Blacks that Blacks will do anything to try and be like Whites. This includes trying to lighten their skin color, changing their hair texture, trying to live in White neighborhoods, associating only with Whites if possible, trying to dress, talk like and just generally trying to be White.

Blacks have tried so hard to integrate with Whites that they have turned their backs on their own culture and ultimately on other Blacks. Blacks for the most part are more loyal to Whites than they are to each other.

Here it is in the year 2000 and you have Blacks that are so proud to be the only Black working for a company. They never stop to think that they are not the only Black that is qualified to work there, rather they just feel good that they are the only Black there. Not only are Blacks glad to be the only Black working in a company, but these Blacks will do things to insure that other Blacks are not hired. They want to continue to be the only Black working there as if it is some accomplishment or honor (actually it is stupid). What is worse, these Blacks act as though they have been betrayed or disgraced by another Black if that second Black gets hired in the same company or department.

Blacks have spent so much time trying to integrate with Whites that they have spent little or no time mixing with each other. Blacks have not really worked together on any large scale. Most of their efforts have gone into trying to prove their self worth to Whites even to the detriment and exclusion of other Blacks.

Watch Blacks during lunch time and see what is happening. You will see a group of Whites accompanied by one Black. The Black person will be talking so much and trying to fit in that the Whites can't get a word in edgeways. And while you're at it, try and speak to the Black person if you are Black and see if they speak back or even acknowledge that you spoke to them.

This drive for Blacks to integrate and be like Whites is so bad that Blacks just can't seem to do anything by themselves. Blacks must associate with Whites or they seem like they will go crazy.

Blacks Don't Want to Admit to Seriousness of Their Problems

When you try to discuss with a Black person or persons the issues that affect Black people, you will usually get the following responses. After about two or three sentences, you will begin to hear a discussion about God and how God is punishing this person or race and how God will fix this or that and how Blacks don't know God and on and on. Rarely will you meet a Black person who is able to discuss any kind of issues without quickly turning from that issue to a discussion about God this and God that.

Another thing that Blacks do when you try and discuss Black issues is to point fingers at other races. For example, when you say that there is a lot of crime in our communities, Blacks will quickly say, well Whites commit crimes, or Asians commit crimes. If you attempt to discuss the drug crisis in Black communities, again you get the finger pointing of well Whites use drugs or some other race. This finger pointing goes on and on. This finger pointing makes no sense. The act of pointing out that other races have the same or similar problems that Blacks have does nothing to begin to solve our own problems. This is like a patient going to the doctor and being told that he has been diagnosed with lung cancer and the patient telling the doctor that well other people have lung cancer or other people smoke. You see how stupid that is. It does nothing to stop this patient's cancer or change his habits so that he will not develop additional cancer.

Another thing that Blacks do is give you the exceptions. They will point out that one exception in a thousand and think that the problem is overstated by you or that it does not exist. Talk to Blacks about the high unemployment rate and lack of education among Black males. They will respond by saying well I know this guy who works in a company or I know this guy who graduated from medical school. How about the other nine hundred and ninety-nine who are unemployed and uneducated? Life is not about exceptions, it is about the general rules. You certainly would not apply this logic to getting your pay check. You would not say well I get my check at least one pay period out of the year. No you would realize very quickly that you are not being paid and would not tolerate your employer's explanation that well I know you got one pay check.

When you do get a Black to talk about the issues for a moment without jumping to a discussion about God, or pointing at other races or pointing out an exception, you get the old emotional washout. Blacks wear their emotions on their sleeves. When they hear something that they can't argue against just for the sake of argument, they get their feelings hurt. They get angry. Sometimes they get so mad or hurt that they start to cry or want to fight. Often times they will get off of the issue and begin to attack you personally (like so many of the readers will do to me who read this book).

Why is it that Blacks seem to want to do anything except admit the truth? It may be because they would become very depressed if they faced reality. The reality is that things are far worse than they want to admit. Black males are killing each other. Blacks are worse off than they have ever been. Blacks do commit crimes. As a race, we are the least productive, the least educated. We have a serious teenage pregnancy problem. Black males are falling behind the Black female in every way. Blacks don't have purpose and direction. Our Black boys do populate the jails more than they populate the school system. Where you have Blacks you do have loud stereos. As a group, we are afraid of each other and don't trust each other. We don't like each other.

Maybe Blacks feel that by not admitting these problems, that they will go away. Or maybe they don't have to face them. Maybe we are ashamed of the problems and as long as we can pretend, we don't have to face the shame.

One thing is certain, just like the alcoholic, the first step to solving a problem is to admit that you have it. And until Blacks admit that they have all of the problems outlined here, they will never do anything to fix them until ultimately, they become extinct.

Blacks must learn to talk about their problems, both as individuals and as a group. They must get beyond the finger pointing, blaming God stages and really explore in-depth the root causes of these problems and then look for viable solutions.

Blacks Are Their Own Worst Enemies

Look at how Blacks treat each other in this country. They treat each other worse than anybody else treats them. Isn't it ironic that Blacks keep trying to get other races, especially Whites to treat them as equals and with dignity and respect, and yet Blacks don't treat each other with dignity and respect. In other words, Blacks expect Whites to treat them better than Blacks treat each other.

It is true that there are a lot of Whites that dislike and down right hate

Blacks. But the hatred that Whites have for Blacks pales in comparison to the hatred that Blacks have for each other. This hatred that Blacks have for each other is so deeply rooted that it may never get better.

Blacks have a history of treating each other badly. In fact, during the periods of slavery, most of the Blacks that were captured in the jungles of Africa were not captured by Whites, but rather by Blacks themselves and brought to the Whites.

During the early days of slavery, Whites needed people to grow and harvest rice off the coast of South Carolina and Georgia. There were few peoples in the world who could successfully grow rice. There were the Asians (the Chinese, the Thais, etc.), but they were not the kind of people that you could enslave. Then there were the Africans who populated an area in Senegal and Gambia and were called Wolofs. These people were expert at growing rice. When the White slavers went to this area, they quickly discovered that they could not get their ships past certain points, so they built forts at these points.[23] Nor could they find the Africans when they went into the jungle. But guess who ran the Africans down and chained them and brought them back? Us.

The slave trade would not have been as successful as it was had it not been for Blacks selling each other out. In fact, every time Blacks have caught the short end of the stick, it was Blacks helping to cut the stick off.

Even in America, you had Blacks selling each other out. When a slave ran off from the plantation, who was it that helped track him down and bring him back. Who helped the master keep up with the gossip about the escape plans of the slaves? Us.

Is this self defeatist attitude still pervasive in Blacks in America today? You better believe that it is. Blacks will get mad with each other and align themselves with Whites to help bring down other Blacks. Even if they don't align with Whites, they feel that they are doing something by telling Whites, usually in the form of notifying the newspapers or radio. These Blacks will bad mouth each other all over the White media. Blacks are proud to air their dirty laundry out in the White public.

When Whites want to find out what Blacks are up to, the first thing that Whites will do is to interview other Blacks. Of course, Blacks will spill the beans and be so proud of it.

Blacks are more loyal to Whites than they are to other Blacks. They will work for the common good of America which means the betterment of Whites and the detriment of Blacks.

The finger pointing Blacks will argue that other races have in-fighting. And they are right, other races do. But the difference is that other races keep the in-fighting amongst themselves, they don't let other races know the specifics of what is going on. These other races have the ability to put the in-fighting aside for the good of the group, particularly when other races threaten whatever it is that they are trying to accomplish.

It has been said that Blacks are like crabs in a crab bucket. When one tries to climb out of the bucket, the others reach up and pull him or her back down. Which means that you don't have to put a lid on the bucket to keep them in. If you apply this analogy to Blacks, it means that Whites don't have to do things anymore in a deliberate way to keep Blacks down because Blacks (just like the crabs) will pull each other down. And they will pull each other down for no reason other than one Black is trying to do better and they don't want to see that happen. They will do that even though the actions of the Black that is trying to do better doesn't affect the other Black at all.

Perhaps the most telling example of Blacks being their own worst enemies is in the area of law enforcement. Blacks are the only race that will go under cover in their own neighborhoods to entrap and arrest their own people. You will never see other people such as the Japanese, the Chinese, the Colombians, Whites or Jews help the legal system in this country to prosecute each other. Black police officers will go into Black communities and solicit crime by posing as drug buyers for cocaine knowing that Blacks don't make cocaine nor do they distribute it.

What is the justification for the actions of Black police officers? The same as it always is for Blacks. It is a job. I will sell out anybody in my race, even my own blood relatives in the name of doing my job. Pay Blacks five dollars or more per hour and they will do anything that is detrimental to their race. Of course it must be mentioned that there are a lot of foolish Blacks that still think that it is our country and our justice system. To those idiots, just go to any courthouse and jail and see who is there.

The other races and peoples mentioned above have a code of honor and loyalty. Nothing and no one comes before their race. But not Blacks. It seems as though everyone and everything comes before being Black.

What about the way Blacks apply laws and rules to each other? Here again, unlike other races, Blacks apply rules and laws to each other harder and harsher than they do to anybody else. Look at how Black judges apply the law to Blacks and how they apply them to other races. How many times have you as a Black person let out a sigh of relief when there was a White person to apply the rules instead of a Black person. Why do you do this? The reason is because the Black person is going to apply the law to the letter and beyond against you and act as though they have done something.

Blacks Don't Value Each Other

Earlier there was a discussion about how dominant and conquering races were able to make the conquered race feel inferior. This inferiority manifests itself in terms of valuation. Whites knowingly and unknowingly have done an excellent job of making Blacks feel inferior.

Blacks don't value themselves as individuals and thus don't value themselves as a group. The sad part about all of this is that the only way that Blacks can change the way that they value each other as a group or race is to change the way that each Black feels about him or herself individually. This is next to impossible when your own reference point is measured by how another race values you.

What's worse is that Blacks value themselves less in the 2000's than they did in the 80's, than they did in the 70's, than they did in the 60's and so forth.

Look at how Blacks treat each other when there are only Blacks interacting with other Blacks. A prime example is the service that Blacks get from other Blacks in restaurants or just businesses in general. The Black providing the meal or service acts as though it pains him to serve another Black. He or she acts as though it lessens them to provide the service or that he or she is doing a favor to serve another Black. Basically, they do the bare minimum and never with a smile on their face. Yet they will bend over backwards to provide service to a White or another race. In fact, they will go out of their way to make sure that the White customer is happy, grinning ear to ear while they're at it.

Then there is Black on Black crime. Young Black boys and men don't value each other's lives. They will kill another Black simply because of the way that someone looked at them. Yet these same Black killers don't kill Whites because they value the lives of Whites more either because they know that they will be hunted down and prosecuted or inside they just feel that Whites have more value.

What about when it comes to valuing accomplishments or information? Here Blacks don't value other Blacks unless these Blacks have been legitimated by the White media. You as a Black person could tell another Black person the secret of immortality. You could lay out step by step what they needed to do and the Black person would not do it. Even though you could show them that you were 200 years old, they wouldn't follow up because the information came from a Black person. But let the Black person with the information or accomplishment appear on television or in the newspaper and the other Blacks will scramble to just get near that person because Whites have legitimated this Black person.

This devaluation of Blacks by other Blacks is so bad that Blacks want to treat the accomplishments of all Blacks the same. The janitor wants to treat the P.h.D. as his equal in terms of accomplishments. Blacks don't want to give the doctors and lawyers and scientists their due. Again, they want to pretend that everybody is equal.

This is not saying that the people with degrees are innocent either. The first thing that a Black person does who gets an education or makes some money is to disassociate him or herself from other Blacks. They walk around and act as though they are better. They do their best to convince their White friends that not only are they not like those other Blacks, but in reality, they are merely Whites trapped in Black bodies.

The supreme devaluation of Blacks by other Blacks is that when Black men in particular become half-way successful, the first thing that they do is run out and marry a White woman. They will do this even if they have to get a divorce from a Black woman whose back they have climbed upon to get where they are. Black men do this because they feel that by having a White wife, they have therefore arrived and are thus legitimated by this trophy wife.

To add insult to injury, there are those so called civil rights and Black activists running all around the country talking about the plight of Blacks and how Whites are to blame and yet every night they go home to a White wife. You talk about being disingenuous (lying about how they feel about Whites). If ever you see a Black activist married to a White woman, don't trust them, because they are not sincere. How can they be?

Blacks Will Not Help Each Other

The worse Redneck will offer assistance to a Black person if it is not going to hurt the Redneck. Yet Blacks will not help each other. If any group of people in the world needs to work together and help each other, it is Black people. In light of all the things that non-Black people have done to Blacks, you would think that Blacks would bend over backwards to help one another. But they don't.

Why this is so is not completely understood. Maybe when Blacks are dealing with each other and they have a choice to help they don't because it is at least one time that they can feel in control of someone else and determine the outcome of that person's life.   All of the rest of the time, Blacks are being controlled by other races.

Blacks seem to let petty jealousies get in the way.   Blacks seem to feel that before I will help some other Black get ahead, I'll let us both suffer instead. Why help someone else when they may do more and become more than I am. With my help, that other Black person might make some money.   Blacks will not let this happen.

If Blacks were honest with themselves, most successful Blacks would have to admit that most of their personal success was the result of a White mentor helping and showing them the way.   This is especially true if money was involved.   You are more likely to get financial help from a White person than a Black person, even if the Black person is wealthy beyond his own personal needs. Before that Black person will lend another Black person a financial helping hand (a capital loan), the Black with money will make a multimillion dollar contribution to a college, very often a White college.   These Blacks will take you to lunch and spend two hundred dollars to impress you, but wouldn't lend you fifty dollars on a venture.

Again, it is so bad that if you are referred to someone in a particular area by a friend or business associate to assist you in terms of information or money, the wind is usually knocked out of your sails when you learn that the person is Black because most of the time they are not going to help you.

Unfortunately, the bottom line here is that if a Black person has the opportunity to either help another Black or not help another Black, the usual response is that the Black person is not going to help.

Black Men Don't Communicate With Each Other

Blacks in general don't speak to each other.   For the most part, they won't even acknowledge one another with a simple greeting.   Not even a 'hello'. If you don't believe this try the following test for two days.   On day number one, speak to one hundred White people and see how many speak and greet you back.

Then on day number two, speak to and greet one hundred Black people and see how many speak back to you. You will find that at least 90 of the Whites speak back and only about 50 or less of the Blacks speak back.

If you are a Black male and were to narrow your test to just Black men, you would find that only about 25 of the 100 will acknowledge you.

The significance of this is that in order to have communication, you must first greet a person. After the initial greeting, you then may enter into a dialog of some kind and ultimately exchange feelings and ideas.

Black men don't speak to one another and ultimately they don't communicate with one another. What causes this?

One factor may be just plain and simple distrust of one another. Black men may feel that if they let another Black man get to know them, then some how he is going to be betrayed or taken advantage of.

A factor could be that Black men don't value each other and thus feel that the Black man speaking to them has no value.

Of course some brothers are so busy trying to be important that they feel it is beneath them to acknowledge another Black man. You've seen them. They drive BMW's, wear alligator shoes and expensive suits. They seem to get mad when spoken to by a brother that is not as well dressed. They feel as though you have done something wrong. They look at you like, don't you know who I am? Don't you know how important I am?

Now what happens when Black men do get together and begin to talk? The first thing to bare in mind is that you never see more than two or three Black men together in a conversation. Again, just look around during the lunch hour and see for yourself. You will see lots of tables with gossiping sisters in groups of five or more, but not the brothers.

When the brothers do talk with one another they usually try to pretend that they have so much and are doing so well. They have this big deal or that big deal. They are so booked and pressed for time. Ultimately their conversations turn to women or sports.

And it is just out of the question for Black men to discuss their problems with each other.   Unlike the sisters who tell each other about their money problems, their children, their love lives, and just generally more than you would ever want to know, Black men don't share anything with each other.

It seems as though Black men think that discussing and sharing their problems with other Black men is a sign of weakness. Black men then are never really honest with one another about their families or financial situations. Black men never vent their problems with other Black men. Instead, they let their problems boil up inside them until they literally explode and sometimes hurt someone.   Many of the Black men who abuse their spouses or girlfriends probably would not do it or do it far less often if they would talk about their situations with another Black man.

Of course while the brothers are acting stuck up, trying to impress each other and not speaking and greeting each other, they miss out on opportunities. The person they pass by and not speak to while they have their noses in the air is usually the person who has the resources and knowledge that the stuck up brother needs in order to do even better.

The result of all of this is that Black men don't network with each other. It is impossible for Black men to plan and build and control their own destiny as a group because you must work together to accomplish this. The more other people work together, the less Black men seem to do so. We must start speaking to each other if we ever hope to work together.

Without working together, how are Black men going to solve the problems with their children? How are they going to work together on the crime and poverty in their neighborhoods?

Unfortunately, Black Women are Part of the Problem
Many Black women will take offense to this section.   This is understandable in light of the fact that Black women have carried the Black race in this country for the last one-hundred years. She has raised the children, most

times by herself. She has put food on the table, clothing on the backs of herself, the children and some times on the adult Black male. The Black male has not been there for her, neither financially nor emotionally. In some instances, when the Black female broke her back to support an up and coming Black male, she found herself betrayed and deserted once he became successful. So many times she had to endure the sight of a White women enjoying the fruits of her labor while she and her children suffered. Without the strength of the Black female, the Black race would not have survived to the degree that it has today.

Still, Black women are part of the problems leading to Black male extinction. How can that be you ask in light of the above paragraph? Please read on to find the answers.

Many Black women still have the 1980's and 1990's mentality that is promoted by Ebony and other magazines that you should not limit your search for a mate to white collar Black men. Instead, give the hard working blue collar men a chance.[24] The message that Black women got from this was that you lower your standards in order to find a mate. But this did not and will not work. The reason is that while blue collar men will work very hard, put food on the table, and pay the bills, they tend to be content. They don't tend to work at improving their station in life by getting more education or getting a better job. Meanwhile, Black women are constantly striving to better themselves educationally and financially. They want more and to do more. Ultimately this causes pressure on the blue collar Black male. He begins to feel that he is not good enough. This then leads to friction in the relationship. When the blue collar brother develops an inferiority complex, he then begins to fight back through either verbal or physical abuse. He begins to resent not only his woman but all Black women. He then proceeds to dog out every Black woman that he meets from that point on. All of this happened because he entered into a relationship with a woman in which he did not measure up to from the start.

Some Black women have given up on Black men and no longer give them encouragement and support. They do this because they have had one bad relationship in which a brother abused them. These women have tried to look to White men as the answer instead of working with Black men to solve a problem that they both perpetuate. When Black women do this, they lose both ways. She will never be accepted by the White male's family because they are concerned about the heirs that such a relationship will produce. These relationships only last about three years on average. At the same time, because these Black females have closed their minds to even the possibility of dating Black men, they miss out on meeting the man that God has chosen for them.

Then you have those Black women that have been hired by the White corporate world, usually as a receptionist, but some times in a good high paying position. After a few days on the job, they begin to take on the persona of the White corporate culture. They begin to judge their Black male spouse or mate by the White corporate male standard. They see financially successful White males all day long. They go to meetings with them, to lunch with them and some times to bed with them. Then they come home to their Black males who might be unemployed or who make less than a tenth of what the White male is making. These Black females never stop and think that this is by design, to hire her and not the Black male. Instead she starts strutting around, looking down on her man, saying that he does not measure up. It never occurs to her that what she should be doing is to learn as much about the company and the business in general where she is and to bring that information back home so that she and her man can learn how to potentially start a business of their own. Instead of bringing home an attitude, she should be bringing home the pertinent business forms and practice manuals. She should think of herself as being the eyes and ears for her man, not as the replacement for him.

Some Black women are so busy competing with Black males that they can't work with them to improve the overall Black experience. These women try so hard to make more money than Black males, to drive a bigger Benz or Bimmer, live in a bigger house and to have better job. In doing so they sacrifice not only their children or potential children, but they sacrifice their own well being. They think that money will provide happiness, but it won't. What these women do is try to go through life without a man. But ultimately the lack of companionship catches up to them. Then they usually fall for the first fool that smiles at them and become victims of abuse.

The thing that Black women have done more than anything else that causes Black male extinction is to provide easy access to non-married, non-committed sex. Black women have lowered their spiritual and moral standards. They have lost respect for themselves and don't demand respect from Black males. The justification for this is that there are not enough good Black men to go around and that if I don't do it some other sister will. There are Black women who will get into their cars and drive thirty miles to see a man, have sex with him and spend the night. There are Black women who will allow a man to come and see them on a Friday night at midnight (booty call), spend the night, but this same man won't come by during a Sunday afternoon. This women's liber attitude does nothing to cause men to be men. There is no demand by that Black female that a Black man be responsible and respectable.

This sexual permissiveness that is so pervasive in Black females speeds up the cycle of Black male extinction in that not only do they have sex, but they have unprotected sex. As a result, there are too many illegitimate children in the Black race. There are too many Black women trying to raise Black children by themselves. If Black women are going to provide sex so easily, at least they should use birth control. Hopefully, there are not a lot of Black women out there who still think that having a child for a man is the way to keep him.

Not all Black women want to raise children by themselves. But there are some who do. They don't want the child's father around because they don't like him anymore or they are spiteful or whatever. But the fact is that Black women can't raise the Black male child by herself. They have double standards when it comes to children. They will place high demands on Black female children. Just let a mother come home from work and the dishes are not done and the house is not cleaned and there is a female child there who is twelve years old and up. The mother goes crazy. Mothers will not let a daughter go out of the house looking like a bum. Rather, they comb her hair, do her nails, make sure she has matching clothing, in other words, she must look like a lady.

These same mothers make little if any demands on Black male children. They will let them lay around the house in a filthy room. There is no expectation of doing house work. Mothers feel guilty about not having the father there. They will let the boys leave the house looking like they are homeless. Mothers don't demand that the boys make as good of grades as they do the girls. The reasons that mothers can't raise the boys is because mothers are nurturers by nature and not disciplinarians like men are by nature. So the boys suffer while the girls flourish.

Again, you will get those people who quote the exceptions, but again, go to the jails and see how many of the boys and men that are there had fathers in the home.

When you add all of these things together, the way the Black male has abused and used the Black female, all the hard work and financial struggling that Black women have had to endure to make sure that the family could eat, the competition she has faced in a White male dominated corporate world, these things have taken their toll on the Black woman. Many Black women have become bitter from having to be provider and protector. They have become Black male haters. Black women have been forced to act like a man, and yet she can never be a man. This has led to an attitude of I will get all I can from a Black brother, even sex, but I will no longer commit myself to him nor will I encourage him, nor attempt to build a future with him.

Low Expectations and Standards

Blacks all over the country have been in an uproar about Ebonics. They feel that is a way for Whites to set Black students up for failure in the real world when they graduate from high school.

What is Ebonics and whose idea was it? The term comes from the words "ebony" which means black and "phonics" which means language.[25] "Ebonics", first coined in 1973, refers to a grammatically consistent and rich African-American speech pattern with roots in West Africa. Key components include not conjugating the verb "to be" ("I be joking") and dropping final consonants from words ("hand" becomes "han"). Linguists have long debated whether Ebonics constitutes a distinct language or a dialect, often dividing along ideological lines. Some people even argue that any language is merely a dialect spoken by large numbers of people.[26]

Approximately three years ago, teachers from the Oakland school system enrolled in a state Standard English Proficiency (SEP) training program to sensitize teachers to students who spoke black English. SEP techniques were then applied to the classroom. For instance, in "Flossie and the Fox", Flossie is an African-American girl who speaks in a vernacular that has been called Ebonics and the fox speaks standard English. Teachers might pull words from the text, pointing out differences in syntax. "I be Flossie Finley," Flossie says. Or "How do a fox look?" The teacher then asks, "Is this written in Ebonics or standard English?" The technique is called "contrast analysis".[27]

On December 18, 1996, the Oakland school board passed a muddled resolution to treat Ebonics as a second language. By unanimous decision, the board voted to recognize Ebonics as the "primary language" of many of its students, and to teach students in their primary language in order to both maintain the "legitimacy and richness" of the language and to help students master standard English. Describing Ebonics as "genetically based," the resolution suggested that schools might seek federal funds earmarked for bilingual programs. This is what set off the furor over Ebonics.[28]

The intentions of the Oakland school board were honorable. They were trying something, anything to raise the achievement of Black students. The Oakland school system was not the first system to try such things, even Ebonics.

It is not the school systems that are at fault here, rather it is the Black race that shoulders the blame. What we are seeing in our elementary and high school students are the manifestations of our own low standards and expectations.

As a group, Blacks have the lowest standards and expectations of any other group on the planet. We are at the bottom in every measurable category. We simply do not and cannot compete in anything except sports.

Standards and expectations start at home. It starts with demanding that our children keep their rooms clean and orderly. That their clothing be worn properly. That they have good manners, especially when dealing with their elders. We don't demand that our children do the very best that they can from the start. This means at the kindergarten level. Whatever you do for a child at this level is like a form of imprinting. It can't be altered later.

Every day you see the effects of low standards and expectation in the Black community. If you have a residential community of predominantly Blacks, you will find that the yards are dirty, i.e. the grass needs cutting and the leaves need to be raked. The houses are in a state of disrepair. There are old cars in the driveways. When a commercial area is predominantly Black you usually find that the buildings have windows broken out, there is graffiti all over the place, litter is everywhere. If a business is Black, the first thing that you notice is that the place is not clean, not to mention that the customer service is poor.

These low standards and expectations carry over into education. Blacks as a group accept poor performance from their students. Somehow we have come to accept a "C average" as okay. Somehow Blacks themselves perpetuate the belief that being Black automatically means that you can't make good grades. Ebonics is not a language, it is laziness in learning the English language. This failure to put in the time and effort to learn the language is then glorified and justified by calling the broken English, slang or that it is cool. Yet, when other races come to America, they can learn the language. They may have an accent, but their English sure as hell is not broken.

It is not just English that Black students have trouble with, but it is all areas of formalized education. The reason for this is again, it takes hard work, (time and effort) to master any subject. The lower the standards and expectation, the harder it is for a student to put in the time.

Even on the extremely rare occasions when Blacks work together as a group, the standards within that group are low. People show up late, pay their dues late and perform substandard. The only time that Blacks perform up to par is if there is White intervention or participation because the Whites set the standard.

It is very sad when you can't name one business, one product, one area of endeavor other than sports (there Whites still set the standards through coaching and ownership) where Blacks out perform other races. The simple fact is that Whites and Asians demand the best from themselves as individuals and as a group all the time, while Blacks just want to get by.

The standards for the Black male have become so low that most parents are proud to inform you that their son is not on drugs and is not in jail as if that is something to strive for. Since this is the standard, it goes a long way to understanding why young Black men are not expected to achieve in the classroom, to earn a profitable living by becoming doctors, lawyers, business owners and scientists and to raise their families and serve their communities.

These low standards and expectations that Blacks have is the reason that Blacks, particularly Black men do so poorly in life. It is the reason that they accept poverty and unemployment. Laziness is the measuring stick of your standards and expectations. Until Blacks raise their standards in every area, they will continue to suffer at the hands of Whites and every other race that gains a foothold in America.

Negative Impact of the Civil Rights Movement

The Civil Rights movement was the greatest and the worse thing that happened to Blacks in America.

It was the greatest thing for Blacks because it resulted in Blacks being granted human rights. Blacks got the right to vote, attend taxpayer supported educational institutions, eat at restaurants, work in major industry jobs at the management level, and just basically enter through the front door.

The Civil Rights movement also had residual, positive effects. It raised the conscious level of a nation, sensitizing its people to the wrongs that had been done to Black people. Because of this movement, people of all colors were able to interact for the first time in ways they never had before. Blacks had hope and dignity and Whites had friends and neighbors. Other races enjoyed rights in this country that they would not have gotten had it not been for the struggle of Blacks.

No other movement could have liberated Blacks from the discrimination that they experienced in America prior to the 1970's.

Unfortunately, the movement lasted too long. It lasted so long that Black people became fixated with it. Blacks failed to take the next step. That step is two fold. Part one is working to improve the individual. As individuals, Blacks need to become more educated both philosophically and practically. We need to work on our individual morality and spirituality. We need to raise our individual standards and work ethics. Part two is working together as Blacks for the betterment of Blacks. Once we got our basic freedoms, it was time to stop concentrating on Whites and concentrate on ourselves.

For whatever reason (ignorance, glory, greed), Black leaders (so called anyway) have continued to perpetuate not only a dead movement, but a movement whose basic premise is now wrong.

The premise of the movement now is one of integration. Actually, it is not even integration, it is assimilation. A large number of Blacks still want to be assimilated, i.e. give up everything that is associated with being Black, and be absorbed by Whites. They rather do this than become independent and self-determinative.

The results of promoting this dead and erroneous movement have been absolutely catastrophic to Blacks.

For one thing, Blacks have not built anything of substance since before King died. They have not built any more colleges and universities. Take a look at Auburn Avenue in Atlanta, Watts in Los Angeles and Harlem in New York. Those areas had doctors, lawyers, shop owners and other thriving businesses prior to the civil rights movement. Once the movement and the misguided premise of assimilation took hold, Blacks turned their backs on their own stuff and tried to fit in with Whites. As a result, they lost or gave up the legacy that their grandfathers and grandmothers built for them. Most of the best Black areas of the 60's are now slums in the 2000's.

Blacks have and continue to use old methods in a new world. The most often used method being marches to appeal to the inner consciousness of Whites. This does not work because most Whites under the age of 50 (most White Americans) were not active participants in racial discrimination. What this means is that all of the Whites still alive and were active participants in promoting policies of racial segregation and discrimination at the time of King's death will be dead in twenty years. So Whites under the age of 50 don't feel guilty about what has happened to blacks because they did not cause it directly. Instead, they feel disgusted for being blamed for something that they did not do.

Blacks have spent and continue to spend too much time trying to change the way Whites feel and respond to Blacks. It has already been discussed that the 'King and Queen' syndrome prevails.

Worse yet, Blacks have confused Civil Rights with economic rights. There is no such thing as economic rights. We live in a capitalistic society. The American way is Darwinism. He who is the most economically fit, wins. There is no constitutional right to jobs and promotions. Yet, Civil Rights leaders and proponents of the Civil Rights movement continue to teach weak minded Blacks that they have some God given right to the same percentage of jobs on all levels of management in direct proportion to the percentage of Blacks that make up the community where a company or factory is located. The recent perceived success in the Texaco Case and boycott perpetuates this erroneous thinking and strategy.[29]

Blacks have to get rid of anyone who calls himself a Civil Rights leader. The reason is because these leaders are not representative of Black people in the

21st century. Although they like the limelight of television, they are adding to the destruction of Blacks. These Civil Rights leaders and the Civil Rights movement continues to brainwash generation after generation of Blacks that they are the victims of the evil White man. So what you have now in America are generations of lazy, weak, pathetic, poor, crabs in a crab bucket, dumb, uneducated, crime and violence perpetrating, dope smoking, single, renting instead of owning, non-product producing, ashamed to be Black, non-business owning, non-competitive Black people.

Now lets put this movement into a 21st century perspective. When Martin Luther King, Jr. was alive, he wrote one of the best inspirational speeches in modern times called, '*I Have A Dream*'. Before he died, he adopted a song entitled, '*We Shall Overcome*'. After King's death, Ralph Abernathy said, "We Shall Overcome". Joseph Lowery said, "We shall overcome". Jesse Jackson said, "We Shall Overcome". (Okay, he also said, "Keep Hope Alive"). Hosea Williams said, "We Shall Overcome". Dick Gregory said, "We Shall Overcome". Even today, after every King celebration, you see Blacks across this nation linking hands and singing that same old, tired song.

Again, why do Blacks do this? The reason is because Blacks haven't had anyone to tell them the whole formula for achieving their destiny in America.

The formula is: "We have a dream, that we shall overcome, by working together lovingly as one, to accomplish all the things in the Black race that need to be done, so that we can achieve the highest level of technology and spirituality possible, until Jesus returns."

Easier to Blame Whites Than Take Personal Responsibility

Blacks have placed their fate into the hands of Whites. Ask any Black person why they are in the predicament that they are and they will blame a White individual, a White group or the nation of Whites as a whole. What is really sad is that Blacks feel that Whites control their destiny more than God does.

We live in the best place in the entire world as far as being able to control your own life on a day to day basis. Only in America can you go from rags to riches in one generation unlike in many countries where you have a caste system or dictatorship or worse yet the opportunities simply don't exist.

It's really funny how when Blacks get ready to commit a crime, or make love or party, how they don't need Whites. But when it is time to get an education, earn a living, raise their children and clean up their community, they become helpless and dependent upon Whites.

Speaking of crime, let a Black man get caught because he committed a crime. He will cry that it is the White media that is after him or that he is singled out because he is Black. Never mind that he may have embezzled thousands of dollars or had a mistress on the side or misappropriated funds to buy cars and houses. No, he screams that Whites are after me. He refuses to take personal responsibility.

Ultimately, you control your own destiny. Whatever you become in life is the result of what you did or didn't do. As for Whites, sure they may or may not be an obstacle, but there are many obstacles in life, you are responsible for overcoming them. Whites don't control you on a day to day basis. You decide when you are going to get up, when you are going to sleep, how hard you are going to work and how you are going to prepare for your future.

It's time for Black men to stop making excuses. It is time to stop blaming White men. It is us. Ultimately, everything that is right with the Black race and everything that is wrong is because of us. If you have failed in life, the person responsible is the one that stares back at you in the mirror.

It is nobody elses fault other than Black men that our youth are committing all of these crimes, our women have lost respect for themselves and the rest of the world runs over us. It is time to stop blaming Whites and stand up and be men.

Failure of the Black Churches

Blacks as a group go to Church as much or more than any other race in

America. Go to any Black Church around this nation and it is filled to capacity. Visit any Church and you will see singing and shouting and praising God as only Black people can. Black folk for the most part are Church folk. They are spiritual people.

So in light of all this Church going and worshiping, how has the Black Church contributed to the extinction of the Black male?

Black Churches, especially those located near metropolitan areas, have grown large and are now showplaces for the rich and well to do. The members get caught up in the structure, i.e., how big the building is and how many people the sanctuary seats. In other words, my Church is larger than your Church.

Black Churches don't serve the communities in which they are located because most of the members that belong to a particular Church drive an average of 15 miles to get to Church. Most Blacks rarely belong to the Church that is closest to them. What is really sad (as well as stupid) is when a person who belongs to a Church is boasting about all of the programs that particular Church has only to hear someone in the community where the Church is located not having a clue as to what those programs are and in most cases not even knowing that they exist.

The focus in most Black Churches is the minister and the music. If the minister is not young and dynamic and on television, the people don't want to attend that Church. Speaking of music, some Church choirs rival rock bands in terms of the sounds they make (lots of drums) and the way they perform. The end result of ministers delivering their messages by jumping up and down and the performance of the band (sorry, choir) is that you have a circus like atmosphere in which the members come to be entertained and not get spiritually enriched. If the entertainment is good enough and word of how good the performance is gets out, people will drive thirty miles to see the show. Meanwhile, with all the hoopla, the Black men of the Church are not getting the values that they need.

Black Churches have become involved in too many non-biblical ministries such as the singles ministry, the credit union, senior centers, family life centers, and political ministries. On average, there are now as many as 45 ministries at most Black Churches. As a result, Black Churches attempt projects and programs better suited to the community.

It is easy to see how Blacks make the mistake of trying to use the Church for politics and social programs because this approach worked to a limited extent pre-1970 when there was basically only one Church to a community and people did not drive out of their community to go to a different Church. Also, during that era, the Church was the only forum in which Blacks had to do anything. Oftentimes, the Church was the only building that Blacks had in common. In the 2000's this approach will not work because again, the people that attend Churches don't live in the community where the Church is located. The members that make up the Church body now don't work side by side all week and then attend services on Sunday, rather most Church memberships now are a collection of strangers who happen to worship together on Sunday and never see each other during the week.

In attempting projects and programs better suited to the community, the Black Churches have drained community resources both in terms of manpower and money. To run these monstrosities, people, particularly the men have to spend so much time at the Church that they don't spend time in their own communities mentoring and acting as role models to young Black men. To build and maintain these monstrosities requires money. Blacks as a group spend most of their disposable income outside the home building Churches instead of building businesses. So what you have is a group of people building bigger and bigger structures but not having financial ownership and profit in these structures. Meanwhile these same people own no laundries, gas stations, grocery stores, department stores, video stores, car repair shops or anything else that these people need and use on a day to day basis. Obviously, if you burn down the Black Church, you destroy the only things that Blacks own in the community.

The Black Church does not develop Black males as it once did. You take any great orator and leader in this country that is over 40 and chances are that many of the skills that they possess that made them successful can be attributed to the teachings they received in Church.   Before the Church got so big and uppity, young Black males could say speeches in front of the congregation, they could sing, participate in plays, read Bible verses during the service and so forth. Now, the Black Church has separated the young people (Black males) from the main service which means that there is no longer any nurturing and shaping of those youth by adults.   Young Black males don't get to do things that build their confidence by being under the scrutiny of a large crowd.   Further, Black ministers protect the pulpit and the service to the point that other Black men never get a chance to share their views.   Instead, you get only the view point of the minister, i.e., his political and social slant only.

There is entirely too much time spent on emphasizing tithing.   Of course this is understandable considering how much it cost to continue to build and maintain these monstrosities.   Imagine how wonderful it would be if Black Churches spent as much time cultivating and shaping the value systems of Black males as they do on soliciting tithes.

Perhaps one of the greatest sins that Blacks commit is that Blacks have reduced God and his Church as a means to get material things.   The message is that you go to Church, pay your tithes and things will fall from the sky and you will be rich.   You have Blacks who live their whole lives believing this and go to the grave in poverty.

Finally, there are too many Black Churches.   Go to any metropolitan area and you will find as many as 25 Black Churches for every five mile radius.   In essence, there is a Black Church on every corner in the Black community.   Yet these Churches don't communicate, neither the pastors nor the members.   As a result you have duplication of effort, i.e., three Churches located within 1000 feet of each other all trying to build a senior center.   In other words, in a given community, even if the people in that community did attend the Churches located there, the Churches still could not serve the community because the people are getting mixed messages.   You have this one Church saying do this, the other

Church is saying do that, yet another Church saying do something else. You might have as many as ten Churches all trying to accomplish a different agenda with the net effect of them canceling each other out. What a waste of resources.

Unless Churches are going to be complete communities like the Egyptian pyramids and have everything under one roof like the sanctuary, living quarters, school, stores, places to work, then they can't possibly serve as the center of the Black communities of the 2000's. Instead Black Churches will be nothing more than cash cows for White lending institutions and construction companies. These large monstrosities will merely be monuments to the legacies of the egos of the minister at the time.

PUBLIC SERVICE ANNOUNCEMENT NO. 3

If you need any type of insurance, please use:

ALL CITY INSURANCE AGENCY

2964 Ember Drive, Suite 136

Decatur, Georgia 30032

Auto   **Homeowners**   **Life**   **Health**

Ron Parker

Agent

(404) 212-1820

PART IV.   GENERAL FACTORS THAT HAVE CONTRIBUTED TO THE EXTINCTION OF THE BLACK MALE.

There are a number of factors that are contributing to the extinction of the Black male that are subtle in nature. The blame for these factors can't be attributed to a certain person or group, but they are nevertheless as real and devastating as any of the factors discussed up to this point.

These general factors may have more of an impact on the Black male in the coming years than any other factors. The reason for this is that the individual and racial factors are not going to change, but these general factors are going to play a more and more important role in the lives of Black men than ever before.

The dangerous thing about these general factors is that they are so subject to interpretation and it is difficult sometimes to see the negative impact that they have and most importantly, who is to blame.

It is suggested to the reader that they read this portion of this book with an open mind. There is not a lot of research that his been done regarding the effects of these areas and some of the conclusions drawn in this book may run completely contrary to conventional wisdom.

The Role of Television, Movies and Talk Radio

If you had to pick one thing that has changed the lives of people in the world in the twentieth century more than anything else, probably television would be it. Obviously, a very strong argument could be made that computers have made the most impact.

One thing is certain, there are very few people that don't watch television. We watch television for entertainment, to get the latest news and in many instances, just to keep us company.

The effect of seeing something on television is mind boggling. So much so that advertisers spend hundreds of millions of dollars per year to promote their products on TV. Many of us can remember television jingles from our childhood. The reason for this is because the subconscious stimulation from television is long lasting. If you watch it on television over and over again, the mind begins to accept it as being true. What is really scary is that many people believe that what they see on television is in fact true or it would not be on television.

When it comes to Black men, television portrays them as being funny, as being a criminal, as being uneducated and as being poor.

The negative and criminal portrayal of Black men is endless. This type of programming goes on hour after hour, day after day.

One of the newer fads is the so called real life cop shows. The cop shows show a steady diet of White cops chasing uneducated Black men. Once caught, they are slammed to the ground, placed in hand cuffs and stuffed in the back of a police car.

Another similar fad on television is the judge shows. Here you have countless Black men paraded through the courtroom, (without a lawyer I might add), and sentenced unmercifully day in and day out.

The subliminal message here is that Black men are criminals and Whites are the good guys trying to make the streets safe for Whites. So if you see a Black man in real life, he too is probably a criminal just like on television.

This negative portrayal of Black men is just as prevalent on the big screen. When Black men are in a movie, once again, they are always the criminal or the flunkie. Black movie characters are never smart and wealthy, but always funny, street smart and dumb.

When a movie is all Black, i.e., made primarily for a Black audience, the writers and producers feel that the Black audience always has to laugh. That a

Black movie can never be serious such as a mystery or sci-fi. Most often when a movie is Black it is about bank robbers and thieves. Once again, the subliminal message is that Black males are murderers and bankrobbers and dope dealers.

The negative programming is even promoted by Black film makers such as Spike Lee and Eddie Murphy. Just think about their movies for a second and you will again see the trend that the Black male character must be funny and stupid.[30] What do you do when even the Black film makers believe that Blacks will not go see a serious, educational message type of movie? The funny thing here is that any White drama, mystery or adventure movie that makes it to the top only does so because of the Black viewers that go see it too.

It should also be mentioned that Black men are not the only ones put down in the movies. The Black woman is also portrayed negatively such as being a whore or a criminal with no respect for herself or her man.

There is another major media tool that is used to negatively portray the Black male and that is radio. There are two types of negative influences from the radio in the 2000's. The first is White radio shows and the second is Black radio shows.

The White radio shows are usually talk radio. Their messages are straight forward. They simply say that Blacks are inferior and criminals. Whites are superior. They broadcast this message all over the nation during the daylight hours. The host is usually a 'Rush Limbaugh' clone who picks the negative topic for the day and then gives a basic premise. He then fields callers for three hours. White talk shows are able to legitimize racial hatred of Blacks and promote White supremacy under the guise of entertainment. Nevertheless, the message is clear and is repeated often.

The Black radio shows are about being funny, playing music and never being serious about issues that affect Black people. The number one Black radio stations in any city have basically the same format. The announcers are juvenile, always laughing and joking, and the focus is on playing music. The times that these Black hosts do interact with callers it is to have the 14th caller identify some song after hearing a three second sound bite of the song. Here it is the 2000's and the only mental stimulation that Blacks get off the radio is to identify some song!

What is even sadder is that the Black radio shows are promoted by White owned radio stations who make millions of dollars from advertising while the Black listener is fed a steady diet of mental garbage.

The Impact of Technology

Of all the words that are currently used in the English language, the word technology is probably in the top five. The other words being money, crime, sex, and bills. What is technology anyway? In the simplest sense, technology is finding a way to do something better and being able to do this something better on a mass scale, i.e. anyone that can possess and understand the technology can use it to get the desired result. The key is that when the way to do something better is implemented, it usually requires less human intervention.

Technology is like sex and money, the more you get the more you want. And like sex, you want the best technology that you can get, i.e. if there is better sex or technology available, you want the best even though what you have is adequate.

Why is technology so important anyway? The reason is that the person or race that has superior technology controls their own destiny. Look at any culture that has superior technology and you will see a race that has fewer incidences of disease and hunger. Those who possess technology are not going to be victims to the environment (weather).

The race that has superior technology is always going to be the dominant race. They are also going to be the conquering race. So if you look at any race that was conquered you will see that they had inferior technology first and a lack of will second. Search through history and you will see that the Romans had superior technology such as chariots and swords. Study the colonization of Africa to the American Indians to the nuclear bombing of Japan and you will see that all of these races and peoples were conquered because they had inferior technology.

What all this means is that the race or country that has the best technology is going to dominate the world. That technology in today's world is the best computers which allow you to control the best communications, to design and build the best aircraft and submarines, to deliver the best nuclear weapons. That same technology allows you to build the best products and to deliver the best services.

When dealing with technology, there are some universal constants. First, people that invent and possess technology don't value people that don't have technology. The corollary here is that those who have the best technology are valued the most and those who have the least technology are valued the least. In real world terms, the order of valuation in todays world is Whites (American Whites, Germans, Britons, Swedes) are valued the most, followed by Asians (Japanese, then Chinese, then Koreans). The people valued the least are Blacks and Mexicans, both of whom possess no technology. The important thing to note here is that human valuation in today's world is based more on technology than sheer material wealth. For instance, the Arabs are very wealthy due to oil, yet they are not valued as highly as those who possess technology. Another point that drives this home is that even if a Black or third world person is wealthy, they still are not valued as highly as a person from a technological race with far less financial means. Black people themselves value other races more than they do themselves because Blacks have no technology. This is why Blacks will patronize White and Japanese products faster than they will buy from each other because Blacks value Japanese (who can't stand Blacks) and of course we know that Blacks value Whites even to the point of wanting to be White. Again it should be mentioned that Blacks don't value people from third world countries (which by definition means that they have no technology) such as Mexicans. Notice how Blacks who have nothing in common with people from Scotland will celebrate St. Patrick's day by wearing green and join in various parades. Yet these same Blacks can't be paid to participate in Cinco de Mayo celebrations. The reason of course is Scotland is White and valued and Mexico is not valued.

The second universal constant that is present when dealing with technology is the principle of assimilation. People with technology usually will assimilate those people that they conquered. The thing is though that the conquered people have no technology. The assimilation includes everything from changing the clothing that the people wear to changing the acceptable religions.

The technological conqueror feels no guilt in wiping out the non-technological culture because people with technology view non-technological people as being less than human. Of course, the politically correct term here is that the non-technological people are uncivilized. All that non-technological people can do for those that possess technology is to service them. Most often this servicing includes cheap or slave labor. The realization here is that Blacks who possess no technology will never have any value to Whites except as cheap or slave labor. Sure there are those that will argue that the athletes and entertainers are not slaves, but you are wrong because all they do is service Whites because the more technological a race becomes, the more periods of mindless entertainment they need to break up the technological monotony. Athletics and entertainment are not technology and a race of entertainers and athletes will never control their own destiny. They will merely perform for the particular technological race that is in power at the time.

The important point for Blacks to grasp here is that the only reason we were enslaved is because we did not possess the technology and strength of will to prevent it from happening. Most Blacks erroneously believe that God is punishing them or Whites are some evil devils placed here to torment them when in reality it is only a question of survival of the technologically fittest.

This then brings up the point that most Blacks erroneously believe that we were enslaved and continue to be discriminated against because we are in the minority (more Whites than Blacks) in America. The reality of it is that the numbers have nothing to do with it. Let's reflect for a moment. When England colonized India, the population of Great Britain was roughly 25 million. The population of India was roughly 400 million. The number of English people actually occupying India was less than one million. In South Africa, Whites were outnumbered a hundred to one. So you see, it has nothing to do with the numbers, but the will of the People and the technology they possess. Can you image Japan being enslaved by America. It can't happen even though Japan is only the size both in terms of land area and people of one of our large states.

The third constant that is applicable when dealing with technology is the principle of cost. Technology cost the least to the producer and the most to the end user. Because Blacks don't possess any technology, they pay the most for it. The cost of technology will continue to rise for the end user because the end user becomes more and more dependent on the technology. The producer of the technology sets the price as high as the end user can afford. The price has nothing to do with the cost of production. Once you have been exposed to the use of technology, you can never go back to a non-technological state (sort of like sex, once you have had it you can't do without it).

Now that we understand the role of technology and how it fits into human interactions, we can see how it is adding to the extinction of the Black male. Let's look at the effects of technology on the Black male.

Technology allows you to increase productivity with fewer and fewer man-hours which means a reduction in the labor force which means fewer jobs for Black males. The jobs that require the least decision making abilities are the first to be affected and since Black males tend to work in jobs that are repetitive and require very little thought, they are fired first.

As stated earlier, computers rule the world and unfortunately, most Black men don't own one and don't know how to use one. Along with computers there is the Internet (see discussion on page 118). As a result of the Internet, communications are becoming invisible. The Internet has resulted in a vast information superhighway and Black men don't speak, nor understand, nor have access to this wealth of knowledge.

Another real world negative effect of technology on the Black male is credit checks. Almost everything you do in America today requires a credit check and most Black men can't accomplish much because they can't pass the credit check. The reason for this is again they ruined their credit trying to afford more and more technology in the form of cars, televisions and cellular telephones which they charged with a credit card and then could not pay for.

When it is all said and done, technology speeds things up which means that Black men are becoming extinct faster because their role in this world is becoming less and less valuable. In fact the only value that Black men have right now is Athletics and Entertainment and you only need a very small percentage of the available Black men to accomplish this (roughly one in 50,000). See discussion of sports and entertainment on page 96.

The Criminal Justice System

One of the saddest sights you see in America today is a young Black woman in her late teens to early twenties with one baby in a stroller and another baby in her arms going into a jail lobby to stand in line for visitation to see the babies' father who is in jail.

No one knows for sure just how many Black men are in jail. What is for sure is that there are more young Black men in jail than are currently enrolled in college. What is also true is that there are more Black men in jails than White men, not just percentage wise, but in sheer numbers.

If you go to any Jerkwater town, Any state, USA, and drive around the town, you might not see any Black people on the street. Yet if you go to the nearest jail, you will find that it is full of Black men, even though they make up a very small percentage of the town population. You observe the same thing when you visit any courthouse in the land. Once again, it is full of Black people. The inmates are Black as well as most of the people sitting out in the courtroom. There are far more Black parents going to the courthouse on a weekly basis than going to the classroom to check on their children. In fact, the jail and the courthouse have become such a social part of Black peoples' lives that they look upon them as being normal.

Can you image how much of an increase in the Black male population you would see if Black men were released from jail? It would literally double. There would be brothers everywhere. God help us! The brothers would outnumber the sisters. The unemployment rate would skyrocket. You could not cross any street corner. The parks would be filled to capacity. And on and on.

Okay, enough said. Now the obvious question is, why are there so many Black men in jail? The answers to this question falls into two categories. The first category is obvious, the second category is very subtle.

Let's deal with the obvious category first. Black men commit the crimes. As discussed earlier, they lack the moral values necessary to lead crime-free, productive lives. Most Black men are uneducated and as such do not possess the job skills needed to get hired and make money legally. They, like everyone else need money to live in today's society. They want to have the material toys such as cars, cellular phones, expensive sport clothes, etc. The only way that they can keep up with the Joneses is to commit a crime to get the money. It has gotten so bad that most Black men feel that the only way for them to get any money is to commit a crime and they feel that going to jail is an occupational hazard that goes along with being Black and living in America.

Another reason that Black men commit the crimes is because members of their families also benefit from the financial return that comes from committing the crime. There are a lot of Black mothers who enjoy the fruits of crime in the way of furniture, clothing and the like from their sons who commit the crimes. The number of girlfriends who wear the clothing and jewelry and drive the expensive cars of their crime committing boyfriends is far more than you would think. These benefactors of crime are not really discouraging the criminal in their family to quit.

We have established that Black men commit the crimes and the reasons that they do. Now let's look at why they get arrested in such large numbers as opposed to White males. This answer here also falls under the obvious category.

The Black community is the only community where you have the solicitation of crime by police. What is sadder still is that this solicitation of crime is by Black police officers. Here you have undercover Black police and detectives going into the Black community and initiating the crime. They will approach young Black males and try to purchase drugs off of them. They will pose as buyers for stolen jewelry and electronic components such as stereos and cellular phones. There are Black detectives who will proudly tell you that they go out and arrest at least ten Black males per day.

The reasons why you have solicitation in the Black community as opposed to other communities is because the other communities, White, Asian, Jewish, etc., will not tolerate this practice. Perhaps the most important reason also is because Blacks are the only race that will go out and arrest their own people. Other races will not do this because they value each other. A White or Asian has got to do something pretty bad in order for the other Whites or Asians to go out and work under cover to arrest them. Now this concept of valuation has been mentioned several times. It has been said that Whites value Whites, but Blacks don't value Blacks. Just how much do Whites value each other? Well there has been countless instances in which a White person has been shot down in an airplane, hijacked at sea or strayed into unfriendly territory. White people will risk hundreds of lives to go and get one person thousands of miles away, even if it means that it will mean certain death to some of them. That is how strong they value each other. Blacks on the other hand, value other races more than they do themselves. This is why it is so easy for Blacks to say, 'Well, I'm just doing my job, even if it means that I have to hurt other Black people to do it.' This lack of valuation of Blacks by other Blacks also helps explain how Blacks kill each other so quickly, even when there is nothing at stake except a starter jacket or a false attempt at proving manhood.

Another reason for this solicitation of crime in the Black community is because most Black communities are not represented politically or legally. Most people that live in Black communities do not own their dwellings, in fact most live in public housing, thus they have no voice and are easy targets for law enforcement to abuse them.

Now that we have talked about the obvious category, let's spend some time discussing the subtle category. The subtle category is the driving force for the way Black men are treated by the criminal justice system. So what are these subtle reasons why Black men are arrested and jailed in such large numbers?

The first and main subtle reason is money, money, money. The criminal justice system in the 2000's is not about justice, it is about making money. This system is a money making machine. Have you ever wondered why most counties in America have a jail that is either brand new or no older than five years old, while the schools in those same counties are run down and in some cases not fit for human inhabitation? The answer is because it is much easier and far more profitable to finance the construction of a new jail than it is to build a new school house. Jails are built using short term, high yield bonds. There are large companies and wealthy private investors lining up to buy these bonds. There are also profitable stock offerings by companies that specialize in building jails.[31]

This is only the tip of the financial iceberg. Once the jails are built, they must be filled. If they are not filled to capacity, people lose money. So who do you put in jails, you put young Black males. Why not? They are not valued, they commit crimes and they expect to go to jail. Now once you have the jails filled to capacity with these young Black males, just who is making the money?

The first thing to understand is that everybody gets paid. The first entity to get paid is the City government. The way that many young Black males come into contact with the criminal justice system is by way of a traffic stop. So the cities will get their money through traffic fines (no driver's license and no insurance) and monies confiscated off of the defendant. Police officers also get their share from monies confiscated and not reported. The second entity to get paid is the criminal lawyers, most of whom are White. The lawyers get paid handsomely because in most cases they have to secure a bond for the Black criminal defendant. The average bond for a Black criminal defendant is roughly $20,000. Tacked on top of the bond is a surcharge of ten to twenty percent. Most of these defendants go to a White bonding company and pay ten percent to get out. This ten percent is not refundable because the bonding company is taking the risk that the defendant will not show up in court. Once the bond is secured, the defendant is arraigned, i.e., given the opportunity to plead guilty or not guilty. Ninety percent of the time, Black criminal defendants are pled out by their lawyers, mostly White lawyers because Black defendants are uneducated and mistakenly believe that they will fare better with a White lawyer. For entering this guilty plea, the lawyer will get roughly $2,500 to $5,000 and the Black defendant will get five years in jail. Not all Black defendants will go to jail. Many of them get probation and a fine. These fines average $500 plus the surcharges for the sheriff's fund, the benevolent fund, the jail fund and any other fund you can justify. However, once on probation, there is a monthly probation fee of $20.00 to $25.00. The sad thing is that only about 30% of Black defendants successfully complete probation. The other 70% violate the conditions of their probation (commit other crimes while on probation or test positive for drug use or fail to report once a month) and end up serving time anyway.

Ultimately the Black male ends up in jail. Once in jail, the big money really begins to flow. There are those things that every inmate needs. These necessities include the contracts for shoes, toothbrushes, jail barbershops and uniforms. In many states, inmates can no longer be brought clothing and magazines from the outside. What this means is that the jail commissaries make millions of dollars from people that are not making any money. In other words, the families of the inmates must bring money to the inmates to buy items that they need.

Does the money making machine stop here? Unfortunately the answer is no. It even picks up steam. There is a new player on the scene with its hand stuck even further out. This new player is siphoning money off of the Black inmates at a faster and faster rate. Who is this new player? It is none other than your friendly, neighborhood phone company.

When an inmate gets arrested, the first thing that he does is to get on the jail phone and make a collect call home to family and friends. He does this so that he can make arrangements to get a lawyer to make bond. If no bond is made, then the inmate has a waiting period of at least six months before he is arraigned. During this time he makes hundreds of calls, sometimes out of loneliness or just plain frustration. What the inmates does not know is that the call he is making from jail is being billed to his family at a much higher rate than a normal collect call is. Not only is the call billed higher, but there is a surcharge of as much as three dollars charged just to make the call. What this means is that phone companies are making billions of dollars from the phones they have at the jails. It does not stop there. It gets even uglier. States and local municipalities have required phone companies, as part of granting them the jail contract, to pay back to the states and municipalities up to 40% of their monies collected. This 40% is then used by some states to build more jails or hire more police. But there are a growing number of states that are beginning to use the money for the general fund.[32]

Another subtle reason for the arrest and jailing of so many Black males is the way that the laws are written and applied. Many of the laws on the books are skewed in such a way that they are designed to net Blacks. Many states have party to a crime statutes which essentially mean that if you are merely present on the scene of a crime you are just as guilty as the person that did commit the crime even though you may not have known that a crime was being committed. What this means is that at least half of the Black men that are in jail are there by association only, not for committing a crime.

Perhaps the most hideous example of the laws being skewed unfavorably against the Black males is the way that crack cocaine is used in this society to eradicate the Black male. Crack cocaine arrests account for approximately 70% of the Black males arrested and convicted. Why such a high percentage? The reason is because the laws regarding crack cocaine carry a much higher penalty than other drugs, even more than powdered cocaine (White man's cocaine). Get arrested for crack cocaine, go to jail, get arrested with pure cocaine, go home. The federal sentencing guidelines are that 5 grams of crack cocaine carries the same sentence as 500 grams of powdered cocaine.[33] The Black defendants are likely to be sentenced to much harsher sentences at a rate of more than 30 times than White defendants. The theory (justification) for this was that where crack cocaine is present, there is also violence associated with it because of drug deals gone bad or attempted theft of the monies. There was also the argument made that crack cocaine is more addictive than other drugs. Use it one time and you are hooked for life. Of course, everyone is aware of the crack babies that are born though out this nation to mothers that are on crack.

There is some validity to these arguments, but not enough to justify the genocide of the Black male. The reality is that there has not been one major car, plane or train wreck that is attributable to crack cocaine. Studies in the Journal of the American Medical Association show crack cocaine is no more addictive than other forms of cocaine.[34] Saying violence increases with crack cocaine usage is also a falsity. The simple fact is that the areas where crack is used are violent anyway. The projects and street corners in poor neighborhoods don't have any more violence since the advent of crack cocaine than before it came on the scene.

Also, if you increase the distribution of any drugs in a community, the amount and frequency of crime in that community is going to increase. The reason for the increase is because the people that use drugs in that community need more money to support their drug habits and they get this money by committing more crimes.

By perpetuating the lies about crack cocaine and its effects, Whites and a large number of brainwashed Blacks have allowed the system (Whites) to systematically remove young Black males out of the productive rim of society and make horrendous amounts of money while doing it. In recent years there have been literally no arrests in the Black community for such drugs as heroine, amphetamines, or LSD, just crack cocaine. The reason for this is because, crack cocaine is the only drug that is being distributed in the Black community. It is the only one that poor, down and out people can afford ($5.00 a hit).

Along with the distribution of crack cocaine into the Black community, you simultaneously have had a violation of the constitutional protections that people have worked so hard to get. For example, the constitution protects against unlawful searches and seizures.[35] But by using crack cocaine as the justification, it is now okay for the police to arbitrarily stop a car load of young Black males and search them and ask for identification. If a young Black male is driving an expensive foreign car, he is going to get stopped because the assumption made is that he cannot afford it, so he must be dealing drugs. What is even worse is that if a Black male is merely walking through the projects and he most likely lives there anyway, cops stop and harass him using the justification that it is a high drug area. There is another protection in the law known as entrapment where if the government initiates the crime and the person that is coerced into committing the crime would not have done so without governmental intervention, then that person is not guilty.[36] Yet across this nation everyday there are thousands of young Black males approached by undercover agents (who are now Black) and solicited for crime.

An important reason why the criminal justice system is so unfavorable to young Black males is the standards for hiring personnel in the criminal justice system are too low. To be a police officer, all that is required is a high school diploma. Often times, the police officer is just a thug with a badge. He himself would be in jail if not for being a police officer. These officers are out to show the would be defendants that they are macho and in charge. Police officers spend hours and hours at the gym and buff up their bodies only to go out and whip up on defendants. So the police officers are physically able to deal with defendants, but not mentally. The same thing holds true in the hiring of probation and parole officers. The people that get hired usually can't find any other job, especially the one that they are looking for and end up working closely with an element of society that they never intended to. It does not take long for them to become bitter and take it out on the probationer or parolee. The greatest atrocities of abuse to Black men occur at the parolee level because they have no constitutional protections because the parole system is outside the judicial system and is solely an administrative body, essentially with no one overseeing it except the governor of a state. Worse yet, the same thing holds true for the prosecutors and judiciary. Again the standards have been lowered. Almost anyone can be a prosecutor or judge. And the people that are going into these areas are now just substandard wanna-bees, seeking importance with no real feel for justice and service. Rather, they seek personal political gain and base all of their decisions on the potential political fallout that may occur. Black judges are the worse. They are out to show that they are not pro-Black and usually will sentence Blacks to far worse sentences than Whites will.

Another subtle reason for the arrest and jailing of so many Black males is that America is growing older. There are a lot of people over the age of fifty today. As the population becomes older, it is also becoming more conservative, less tolerant and more hateful. Almost everything that a young person does today, especially a young Black male is considered a crime. Adding to this is that every politician uses the fear of crime as part of his or her platform, constantly telling you that they will make the area they represent safer (i.e. put more Blacks in jail). In fact, when you mention crime, most Americans, Black and White, think of Black males.

The irony (hypocrisy) of all of this is that while politicians and people in general are so hellbent on cleaning up crime, there is little emphasis placed on educating young Blacks, making the schools safer, and building better learning facilities. Nor is there any emphasis on building recreation centers or funding summer camps. What about rehabilitation? Everyone claims that the crack cocaine user has a drug problem, yet there is little or no drug treatment programs available to the inmates once they are in jail. There is also no skills training offered so that when the inmate comes out of confinement, he can enter into a productive life. Even if the inmates were to get some skills, very few people are going to hire parolees. No, just put people in jail. Don't worry about prevention (giving our youths something to do when they are not in school), just put them in jail. And as long as it is only young Black males going to jail, there is no motivation to stop this trend. The reason is that society wants and expects these young Black men to return to jail time and time again.

Blacks have to stop letting the criminal justice system eradicate their young male population. The way to do this is to completely disassociate ourselves from this system. We have to stop working as police officers, detectives, prosecutors, bounty hunters, judges on the benches helping to sentence Blacks, sheriffs, jailers and most of all young Blacks have to stop coming into contact with the law. Black males have to stay off of street corners, especially after dark. Blacks must stop going into their own neighborhoods and posing as undercover criminals to arrest other Blacks. No other race will do this except the stupid Black race.

Blacks must stop exposing young children to the criminal justice system. Young mothers should not take their young children under the age of 16 to the jail with them when they go to visit their friends and spouses. Otherwise, these young children get conditioned that being in and at the jail is just a normal part of life and they don't fear jails. After all, children do imitate their parents. We must teach our youths that it is abnormal and wrong to go to any jail. We must instill in them that you should never go to a jail in your entire lifetime.

Blacks have to concentrate their efforts on changing the criminal justice system as it relates to them. They must exert the political pressure to make the criminal justice system focus on rehabilitation rather than punishment and imprisonment. Black should no longer accept having to pay bonds for crimes that are non-violent in nature. We must force the system to seek alternatives to incarceration instead of putting a Black man in jail for any offense. This especially holds true when drug usage is the underlying offense. We can no longer accept Black men being sentenced to ten to fifteen years for less than $100 worth of drugs. We must demand that once our young men serve their sentences, that they be restored to full citizenship which means that their records are cleared except when reviewed by law enforcement and that they be allowed to vote. What does voting have to do with committing a crime anyway? It is just a way to dilute Black voting power and remove Black men from having a say in decisions that affect their community and society in general. These demands are not outrageous since other races are already treated this way by the criminal justice system.

If Blacks don't stop participating in the criminal justice system, in five years the entire system is going to be Black. The perpetrators will be Black, the policemen, the detectives, the prosecutors, the defense attorneys, the sheriffs, the jailers, and of course the judges will be Black because they will not be paid as much as regular civil court judges who will be White. What you will have is a perpetual machine driven by Blacks to help eradicate Blacks and everyone else benefitting from it monetarily.

Negative Impact of Sports/Entertainment Created Role Models

Turn on the television and watch it for ten minutes and you are guaranteed to see some well known Black athlete in a commercial promoting some tennis, running shoe or sneaker. The theme of the commercial is that if you buy these shoes, you will be like me.

The commercialization of the Black athlete has had devastating consequences on the young Black male population. It has created the false hope that any young Black male can come from the projects and play in the big leagues without an education, become an instant millionaire, have national notoriety, commercials, women, and have all of this before the age of 21.

It is easy to understand how young Black males can fall into this trap. Even when you look at the hard numbers regarding professional sports it seems plausible to make it in the big leagues.

African-Americans make up 13 percent of the U.S. population, yet, in the three major professional sports - basketball, football, and baseball - Blacks are a dominant presence. In 1997, 80 percent of the National Basketball Association's 361 players are Black, a 5 percent increase over the 1991-92 season. Of the National Football Leagues, 1,815 players, 67 percent are Black. That too, is a 5 percent increase over the 1991-92 season. In Major League Baseball, 17 percent of the league's 1,100 player's are Black.[37]

No one can argue that professional athletes are not paid well and the best of them extravagantly for their performances in arenas, stadiums, and ballparks. The average annual salary in the NBA, not including commercial endorsements, is $2 million. The minimum starting salary is $247,500. In the NFL, average yearly pay is $767,000; the minimum starting salary is $131,000. In Major League Baseball, the average player makes $1.1 million. The minimum starting salary is $150,000.[38]

If you make it as a professional athlete, the rewards are obviously there. But what are the odds that any high school athlete will play a sport on the professional level? If you add up all of the available active positions in basketball (361), football (1,815) and baseball (1,100), you come up with a total of 3,276 positions, of which there are only about 200 that are vacant on a yearly basis. This means that the best odds of a young Black making it on the professional level are 10,000 to 1 for all the sports combined or 50,000 to 1 to play a specific professional sport.

Stated very simply, not everyone is going to be a Michael Jordan. These dreams of making it in professional sports are leading to the extinction of Black males. They look at sports as a quick and easy way to wealth and fame and as such, do not build an educational foundation. If the Black high school or college athlete does not make it into the pros, he has nothing to fall back on. He does not understand that no one cares whether or not he is successful. While in college, his winning ways on the field brings in hundreds of thousands of dollars to the university he is playing for. That same university is no where to be found if the player gets hurt before the draft or if he does not get drafted. He is simply discarded and another young Black male is put in his place and exploited.

What young Black males also don't understand is that the commercials with athletes in them are shown with only one goal in mind. That goal is to make money off of the product that is being promoted. It has nothing to do with showing them a role model. It is just a way for large sports manufacturers such as Nike, Adidas, Reebok and Converse to sell high priced goods such as sneakers and jackets. Wholesale revenues for athletic footwear companies hit $7.5 billion in 1996, and African-Americans make up a large portion of the market.[39] A few Black sports stars are getting personally rich while helping to feed the sports fantasy that is so detrimental to young Black kids.

With so many sports messages bombarding young Blacks, it's hard for parents to keep their kids focused on anything but athletics.

And if it is not athletics, its entertainment. Record companies are the flip-side to shoe companies. These record companies finance and promote many new Black acts, a lot of which sing rap music. More specifically, gangster rap. The images and messages presented to Black youths are that you can be a thug, a murderer and completely uneducated and still sing and be rich. The result is a glorification of ignorance and violence. Many young Black males look upon Tu Pac and Snoop Doggie Dog as heroes. Young Black males actually try and imitate these criminals with a microphone.

This is not to say that all rappers turn out bad. Some of them actually get legitimated. Some obvious examples are Queen Latifa and Will Smith. But the overwhelming majority of gangster rappers don't amount to more than jail birds.

With all of this promotion of sports and entertainment figures, most young Blacks are electing to try and follow in their glamorous footsteps rather than getting a solid educational foundation. The results on the Black male population are disastrous. There has been a sharp decline in college graduates as more and more Blacks go into the pros early or simply do not go to college because they are too busy chasing some record deal. This continues to deplete an already small resource base of Blacks in medicine, law, architecture, computer science, accounting, dentistry, business, commercial development, science and research, and other professions of substance that Blacks need in order to improve their society.

Even when Black males make it big in sports and entertainment, they are not a threat to Whites or Asians because these Blacks are not educated and don't know how to manage their money for themselves, their families, their communities, their race nor future generations. Rather they get caught up in the hype and their own popularity, showing off their wealth (buying expensive trinkets) to the point that they are broke at the end of their professional careers. What happened to the money? It went to Mercedes dealerships, helped to support their entourages, to White accountants who robbed them blind, into stupid business ventures, to White ex-wives and child support, and just basically back to Whites. So all that the Black athlete and entertainer becomes is a vessel to channel money through. They are too stupid to pool their money and buy businesses and do other things that perpetuate wealth to the Black community.

There is another aspect to all of this. It will probably be no longer than five or so more years and the athletic and entertainment dollar is going to dry up for Blacks. As more and more young White males become bitter at the sight of all these uneducated brothers flaunting millions in their faces, messing with White women, and breaking the law time and time again and getting away with it, the rules are going to change so that you can't play professional sports unless you graduate from college with at least a "B" average and have never been convicted of a felony. The brothers are stupid, they are given an opportunity to make more money in their twenties than most people make in a lifetime and yet they think that they are above the law. Again, this is because they lack culture and discipline and education. They are simply thugs playing a professional sport. Just look at the behavior of Mike Tyson in the second fight with Evander Holyfield or Michael Erving of the Dallas Cowboys. Also, the sports fan is not going to continually finance these high salaries by paying higher and higher ticket prices. Don't look for the television networks to continue to foot the bill either when the television ratings for sports are steadily declining.

Increased Competition from Immigrants

Up until the 1970's the hardest working person in this society and the most trustworthy was a Black man. They took care of their families the best that they could. There have been countless stories of older Black men working as janitors and sending their children to college. While these men themselves did not have the opportunities to get an education and work in good jobs, they nevertheless endured. They were unskilled laborers. They worked long hours for low wages.

The jobs that Black men held were janitors, handymen, waiters, porters, housekeepers, farm hands, yardmen and grounds keepers, drivers, minor repairmen, construction crewpersons, security guards, night cleaning crewmen, bellhops, skycaps, taxidrivers, watchmen, stock and receiving clerks, couriers, elevator operators, chauffeurs, day laborers, and a host of other unskilled jobs.

Unskilled or not, people expected these jobs to be performed to the best level that they could get for the least amount of money.

Enter the immigrants. In the 90's, a number of individuals as well as companies seized the opportunity to lower their payrolls by hiring illegal as well as legal immigrants. With the brothers having so much trouble with crime and not being able to work an eight hour day, five days a week, people started looking to other sources of labor.

So what you have in the 2000's is the situation where immigrants work in all of the traditional jobs that Black men used to work. Just go to any department store at night and look inside and notice the make up of the cleaning crews. You can bet that they are no longer Black. Take a look at the elevator operators. Go to any construction site and ask for directions. You can't get them because no one speaks English. Who are the night watchmen now? While in the malls, see who is cleaning the tables in the food courts. When ordering that hamburger at your favorite fast food place, see who is behind the counter serving you.

Why are so many immigrants now working in the jobs that were traditionally held by Black men? The reasons are numerous.

The first reason is that there are a lot of Black men, particularly young Black men, who feel that these unskilled jobs are beneath them. How could they possibly work in these jobs for $7.50 an hour and their idols such as Michael Jordan and Shaquil O'Neil are making millions. These Black men refuse to bring home three hundred dollars a week for 40 hours of hard, continuous, non-glamorous work. Instead they rather hustle and steal to get some money. Or worse yet, not work at all.

Another reason why immigrants are hired is because they work very hard. They are glad to have a job. While the pay may seem low to the spoiled Black American, to the immigrant, he is living well as compared to his native countrymen. The conditions in which they are working in America seem easy as compared to where they came from.

A big reason why immigrants get hired is because immigrants don't steal. When they clean that department store, they don't walk out with merchandize. Not only do they not steal, they don't have to be supervised. They will work hard until the job is done. They don't have to be watched and checked up on constantly. Not only that, the quality of work is top notch.

Immigrants don't complain to their employer every five minutes about discrimination, or that they are overworked. In fact, most of them keep quiet and even avoid anything remotely resembling authority. The reason for this is that many immigrants are here in the U.S. illegally. They don't won't to get deported. So they just work and keep their mouths shut. Of course, many employers take advantage of the plight of the immigrant. The employer knows that they may be illegal so he pays them as little as possible and gets the most out of them. It is a symbiotic relationship that works well for both employer and the immigrant.

Immigrants are also a part of the reason that Whites are so hell bent on destroying affirmative action. Many immigrants, just like gays and women, have benefitted from the efforts and struggles of Blacks to gain equality in this country. These groups have piggybacked on the Black movement, i.e. affirmative action. Immigrants learned how to use the system of minority set asides very effectively. Many of these immigrants were not poor, and used the system to their advantage to the chagrin of Whites. So Whites, recognizing this, began to close this loophole, eliminating opportunities not just for Blacks, but also immigrants.

When you take into account all of these factors, you can see that Blacks, particularly, Black males are being phased out of the unskilled and skilled labor market. This trend is only going to increase because the number of illegal immigrants is growing and the number of employers taking advantage of this excellent, low cost labor pool is also on the rise.

Homosexuality, AIDS and Other Diseases

Homosexuality is an area that a lot of Blacks don't like to talk about. They don't like to talk about it because when you do talk about it, it means that eventually you have to take a stand. That stand is that you either support homosexuality or you denounce it. Many Blacks have tried to skirt around the issue by adopting a "live and let live attitude" or the position that if they don't bother me, they can do whatever they like.

This book is biblically based. As such, the position taken here is that homosexuality is wrong. It cannot be justified on any grounds. In the book of Leviticus 18:22, it explicitly tells you that homosexuality is wrong. Also look to Romans 1:24-27 and 1Timothy 1:10-11.[40] To put it as plainly as possible, homosexually is a sin and it is wrong.

How then does homosexuality lead to the extinction of Black males? When Black males turn from being natural, Godly men, they turn to other men, either other Black men, White men or men of other races. These homosexual Black men then are no longer available as mates to Black women. In other words, they decrease the pool of eligible marriageable Black men. This means that the chance of a stable, nurturing Black family being formed with the possibility of future stable generations (grandchildren) are non-existent. Not only does this particular homosexual decrease the available pool of men, but each time that he hooks up with another Black man, this decreases the pool by two, not just one.

We are not just talking about the sexual implications here. There are other things that being homosexual affect. Homosexual men are unlikely to be role models because once their sexual preference is uncovered and it eventually will be, people shun them (as they should). How can a homosexual male teach a boy how to be a man when the homosexual himself is not a man? Man here being described as raising a spiritual family as God intended and living in the ways of God.

And what about AIDS (Auto-Immune Deficiency Syndrome)? Where there is homosexuality, there is going to be AIDS. Now this is not to infer that heterosexuals don't also contract AIDS. It is just that on a percentage basis, more homosexuals contract the disease, at least in the U.S. and at the present time.

Where did AIDS come from anyway? There are numerous theories about what causes AIDS. Some people believe that AIDS started out in Africa (what disease doesn't?). Many Western scientists are convinced that AIDS started in Central Africa, that it has been there longer than anywhere else, and that eventually the disease will spread into the entire population of men, women and children, heterosexual and homosexual alike. The reasoning for this is that the AIDS epidemic was discovered in 1983 raging in Central Africa, and that the main mode of transmission was heterosexual intercourse. While in the U.S. and Europe, the disease, at least initially, was confined to small, identifiable risk groups such as male homosexuals, IV drug users, and hemophiliacs.

Many Africans on the other hand are equally convinced that AIDS was introduced to them by Europeans or Americans. Some people from Zaire say it was brought in by rich American sports fans who came to Kinshasa for the Ali-

Foreman fight in 1974. Others say it was introduced in canned food donated by the developed countries.[41]

Other Africans and many westerners believe that AIDS came about artificially: that it arose from a lab mutation of the yellow-fever vaccine or from an accident in a recombinant DNA experiment; or the Soviet theory that the virus was developed in a germ-warfare lab in Maryland and deliberately unleashed by the Pentagon into African villages.

Putting finger-pointing and Black bashing aside for a moment, there are several compelling circumstantial reasons for thinking that HIV-1 (one of two strains of AIDS, the other being HIV-2) originated in Central Africa. For one thing, the African strains are genetically more diverse and they seem to have been evolving longer, i.e. older than the ones found in Europe and America. By far the highest rates of HIV-1 infection in the world are found in Central Africa, also suggesting that the virus has been there longer. The first cases in Europe were in the late seventies and occurred among Africans or Europeans who had been to Africa.[42]

Then there are the clinical features of people with AIDS. In the early cases, one of the main reasons why people died with AIDS was due to Kaposi's Sarcoma, primarily an African cancer, rare in the West.

It is much harder to establish a link between Africa and America in terms of causation of AIDS. Of course one could argue that Americans got it from their travels to Europe. One theory being that Patient Zero, one of the first known cases in America, was an Airline steward and may have contracted the disease from Europe or Canada.[43] But the actual first case reported in America dates from 1969 and comes from St. Louis, Missouri. The blood was from a dead fifteen-year-old Black youth named Robert R. His doctors, perplexed at his death, saved his blood and tissues for two decades. His autopsy revealed small, purplish lesions of Kaposi's sarcoma, a rare cancer at that point found only in text books, elderly Austrian Jews and Italians, and in Central Africa. Robert R. by all accounts had never been to Africa, nor had contact with anyone who had. The virus that killed Robert R. seems to have been closely related to strains now epidemic in the U.S.[44] Could it be that AIDS developed simultaneously in Africa and the U.S. or even that it occurred in the U.S. first?

Still others believe that AIDS is God's way of punishing those people who engage in this unclean homosexual behavior forbidden by God.

It might just be that the point of geographical origin of AIDS will never be found. The same geographical buck passing took place five centuries ago, when the then sexual disease epidemic, syphilis, broke out in the West among the soldiers of the French king, Charles VIII, who had been laying siege to the city of Naples in 1494. Four years later, Vasco da Gama's sailors took the disease to India. By the time syphilis reached China and Japan, in 1509, millions had died along the way. As the pandemic raged, the French blamed the Italians for unleashing the plague. The Italians blamed the Turks. The Old World blamed the New, and the New World blamed the Old. No one wanted to be the source of syphilis. And the source was never determined.[45]

There is yet one other possibility. It could be that AIDS is nature's (God's) way of dealing with over crowding and over population. We live in a time when the population of earth is to such a degree that the contacts between people are more than they ever have been. When large numbers of people live in close proximity to each other, such as in large cities, you usually have a relaxation of moral standards and this is accompanied by an increase in sexual contacts. With more and more people being intimate with each other, maybe they are exposed to a greater potential of getting a virus like AIDS. It is also possible that with all of the various growth hormones and pesticides in our foods, once in our systems, we may be more vulnerable to the virus.

One thing now appears to be certain, it does not matter where AIDS came from or how AIDS is contracted, whether by homosexual acts, by sharing needles, by congenital transfer, or by unsafe heterosexual behavior, Black men are now dying at a faster rate from AIDS than any other group of people.[46] What this means is that if a Black male is not killed in a drive-by shooting, or killed in a DUI, or placed in jail for criminal activity, he still may be removed from life and society by AIDS.

This is not to say that AIDS is the only disease that kills Black men in large numbers. There are others. Another disease that is a result of having unprotected sex is syphilis. There are large numbers of Black men walking around with this disease that have not been treated. They have not been treated either because they did not seek treatment or if they did, they were not given treatment. Everyone knows of the "Tuskegee Experiment". Here you had large numbers of Black men who sought treatment for syphilis and were given placebos by White governmental doctors. These Black men were followed for years to see what the effects of the disease would be on humans if not treated.[47]

There are other diseases that Black men get and die from in larger numbers than men of other races. How about prostate cancer. How about hypertension, heart disease, diabetes, kidney disease?

Why do Black men seem to get these diseases at a higher rate? It is not because Black men are predisposed to get them more than other men. It is because Black men do not get detection and treatment. The reason for this is that Black men don't go to the doctor on a regular basis because they can't afford it or they don't understand the value of regular medical checkups. When they seek medical care it is usually because the disease is in the last stages and death is soon to follow.

Blacks Don't Know and Will Never Know Their History

Why is knowing one's history so important? After all, the events that have happened in the past are just that, in the past. You can't go back and change the past. Doesn't it make more sense to look to the future and only worry about the present which directly affects the future? The answer is a resounding no.

Knowing your history is extremely important. For one thing, learning from past mistakes helps to avoid the same mistakes in the future. You can also build upon the knowledge of the past. You can look at how something was done already and build upon it instead of having to reinvent the wheel each time you want to do something. History also allows you to forecast. You can look at numerous past events and predict future events based on similar inputs producing similar outputs. Understand and know history and you may be able to determine how and why certain races and civilizations disappeared. By looking at what happened to them, we may be able to prevent it from happening to us. History is also a source of tradition. Doing something over and over again in a ceremonial fashion as it has been done through the ages helps to maintain certain things in our culture that we deem important as a society.

The obvious question then becomes, why don't most American Blacks know their history? The answer is two fold. You must again look at the role that Whites have played and the role that Blacks have played in terms of the ignorance of Blacks when it comes to knowing and understanding Black history.

Whites have made a conscious effort in America to hide the history of Blacks. They have done this by simply not teaching it. They did not teach Black history because they did not value it or they were ashamed of how it would reflect on their own inhumanity. What little Black history that was recorded was skewed toward White interpretation and assimilation. The positives were left out such as the inventions and explorations and the negatives put in such as uprisings and violence. This is not to suggest that Whites were any different than any other dominant, conquering race when it came to recording history in their own history books. When there were events that took place that didn't reflect well on future generations or were an embarrassment, you simply left those events out. After all, it is your history book for your own descendants.

The role that Blacks have played in the failure of learning their history is attributable to one main reason. Blacks are too lazy to study and learn their own history. Most, if not all of the history, whether it is true or not, that Blacks know has come from Whites. It is White people that are over in Africa digging up fossils trying to learn the origins of mankind. Whites study history religiously.

Blacks on the other hand spend little if any time learning about their own history. Aside from being lazy, perhaps Black don't won't to learn their true history. It may just be a history of slavery, dating back a thousand years. It just may be a history of being uncivilized and swinging in trees.

Blacks can no longer use the excuse that they don't have any money and resources to do the kind of research necessary to learn their history. There are quite a few Blacks with wealth in the millions. It is just that Blacks don't place any value on learning their history.

Will Blacks ever really know their history? Will they spend the time, the money and the effort to find out who they are? Probably not. Even if Blacks do make a legitimate effort to discover their true history, they couldn't do it. Most of our true history is not recorded. The way it was kept was in the minds of our elders such as grandmother and grandfather. They would then tell stories to their children and grandchildren. As time has gone by, the grandchildren have not continued to pass the history along and most of it has gotten lost. Now, most of the great grandmothers and great grandfathers have died and much of our history has died with them, never to be recovered.

What Blacks have done in the 2000's is to make a lot of self-serving, ego building assumptions about their history. Blacks assume that they built the great pyramids of Egypt. Now these pyramids were perfect geometrical structures that mankind can't build today even with supercomputers. These pyramids towered in height from nine stories high to 42 stories tall and were built before the birth of Christ with individual stones weighing thousands of pounds.[48] (See discussion on page 205). Yet, even illiterate Blacks today are running around claiming their ancestors built them! Blacks assume that they were the people referred to in the Bible in Exodus. They assume that they are God's chosen people merely because they feel that the events that are recorded in the Bible happened in a part of the world that was very hot and arid, so anyone living there had to have had dark skin, thus Black. There are a growing number of Blacks who have the audacity to believe that Jesus was Black. This is based on the passage in Revelations which describes God as "His eyes were like two burning worlds and his hair was like lamb's wool".[49] Blacks believe that the descriptions of the people of the region in both the Bible and secular documents are always of dark-skinned people. Most Blacks are always quick to point out that the artifacts of the people of that time also seem to be in the likeness of Black people.

We fail to realize that there are many other people around the world who could also make these claims. What about the people from India? What about the Arabs who populate the Holy Land? Actually, when you study the Bible and pay attention to the places that are referenced therein, you will see that most of the significant events took place in what is now known as the Middle East. The places we are talking about are Jordan, Iran (Persia), Iraq, Israel (containing Jerusalem), Syria and of course, Egypt. But Egypt does not appear to be the place where our (American Blacks) ancestors lived, rather it is the home of the ancestor to the present day Arabs. I guess it is important to mention that the Arabs did not inhabit Egypt until around 600 A.D. What about many of the Hispanics? What about the Peruvians and other people from South and Central America? These are just a few of the dark skinned, red-eyed people around the world that fit the descriptions of the people in the Bible.

The saddest commentary on Blacks as it relates to history is that Blacks don't know the history of Africa. Blacks will agree that our ancestors came from Africa. Yet our basic knowledge of Black history only goes back to slavery. In fact, many Blacks only know their history back to about 1950.

Why is knowing the history of Africa so important to American Blacks? As stated above, knowing from whence you came gives you insight into who you are and where you're likely to head in the future. It can prevent you from making past mistakes, or at least put you on notice that the potential of your making them is there. It also helps you to understand your basic, innate tendencies. A group of people are not likely to alter their basic behavior towards themselves or other races no matter what. If you know the history of someone, you can plan and strategize on how to deal with this person (s) in the future.

If Blacks knew their history of Africa, it might give them a lot of insight into why they behave the way they do now in America.

For one thing, let's start by pointing out that Africa is a continent comprised of many countries, approximately 53 to be exact. What this means is that we Blacks walking around in America are the descendants of not just a continent but many different countries. Even people from the same country have different behavior traits based on where they live in that particular country. For example, people who live in the southern states of the United States have different beliefs and behavior patterns from people who live in the Northern states. So you can imagine just how many differences there are going to be among American Black people whose ancestors come not only from the various countries of Africa, but from the numerous tribes within a particular country or region. In some African countries there are as many as 200 different ethnic groups. Compounding these differences in behavior and cultures is that most, if not all American Blacks, have no clue of where their ancestors came from other than we know that they came from somewhere on the African continent. Most of us can't trace our ancestors back past the 1870's.

Another thing that has affected our behavior in America is that we have not had any kind of racial or genetic purity and continuity. Slaves in this country were bought and sold constantly. There was mating between all kinds of Black people from all of the various tribes. There was mating between family members who did not know that they were related. And of course there were countless matings between White men and Black female slaves. Slavery itself played a significant role in Black people's behavior because the Blacks that were here in America had to adapt their natural behavior (whatever it was) to survive under the conditions of slavery.

So now in America, while Blacks have skin color in common (even skin tone ranges from high yellow to dark charcoal), they have little else. Yet Blacks are classified as one group, expected to act the same and be treated the same. Imagine lumping all White-skinned people together whose ancestry can be traced back to the continent of Europe. What you would be saying is that the Britons, the Spaniards, the Russians, the Irish, the Germans, the Jews, the Swedes, the Italians, the Czechs, and any other people from the European continent act the same. This is simply not true. Many of these White people with different origins and ancestries are natural enemies toward other Whites and some are natural friends. The same holds true for Blacks. This may explain why some Blacks just look at each other and hate each other for no apparent reason and other Blacks when they meet for the first time treat each other as lifetime friends.

It is important to understand that it is not just Whites or Asians that lump all Blacks together in one group, but Blacks themselves do it. When a Black person in America does something outstanding and is granted both the notoriety and the award for the accomplishment, all Blacks expect and demand that this person thank and pay tribute to other Blacks that went before him. Even though the previous Blacks in the field may only number one or two, every Black group and Black interest with an ax to grind wants the credit; from the NAACP to the local Black Church and all Blacks in between. The Black person that accomplished something may have never had any contact or even heard of many of these Black groups or interests. The case in point is Tiger Woods winning the 'Master's Golf Tournament'. When he acknowledged being both Black and Asian and that he was a small part Caucasian, Blacks in America became angry. They said that he turned his back on his race or he was ashamed of being Black.

Yet when a Black person commits a hideous crime or does something that is not popular, these same Black people, groups and interests cry that it is not fair for all Black people to be held accountable for that particular person's deeds. They will quickly point out that this lawbreaking Black person does not represent them and it is racist and stereotypical for other races to suggest that he does.

As always, what does all of this have to do with causing or adding to the extinction of the Black male?

For starters, if Black males knew who they were and from whence they came, they might begin to appreciate who they are and stop trying to be someone else. Right now, Black men are trying so hard to be somebody, anybody but Black. Black men try to look, act and be White. If Black men are not trying to be White, then they are trying to be Muslim, changing their name to something that originated from the Arab world such as Abdula or Mohammed. These Arabic names and culture have about as much to do with being Black as English names and culture.

Oh, but if Black men just knew their history and heritage, then Black men might begin to feel a bond between each other rather than acting as strangers and enemies even when they really don't know each other. Knowing who they are might stop the feelings of hatred and distrust of one another.

The second thing is that if Black men knew their history, especially African history, they could begin to explore their behavior (why we do the things that we do) in terms of themselves instead of through the White man and just slavery and its effects. Right now, whatever negative behavior that American Black men possess, they blame it on slavery. However, the reality of it all seems to be that the freer Black men become in America, the more they seem to behave like their African counterparts.

Look at how American Black men treat their women and you will see that they treat them just like their African counterparts. Just like in Africa, Black men here don't respect their women nor are they faithful to them. Have you ever seen a Black woman just walking by herself, just minding her own business. If you have then you know that the brothers take the fact that she is by herself to mean that she is available and just wanting to be pounced upon. In fact, Black men can't stand to see a Black woman by herself, they must go up to her and pester her. Even if a Black woman is at a club or restaurant with her spouse or significant other and the spouse or significant other gets up to go to the bathroom, it won't be but a few seconds before the Black man that was observing the couple is going to run over and make a play for the woman while she is waiting for her date to return. She is simply shown no respect. Does this have anything to do with the fact that in many African countries, Black men have multiple wives? In places like Nigeria, Black men marry many wives, but it is only the first wife that is given a wedding and considered legitimate. The others are just married and treated any kind of way.

All Black men want is sex and more sex. In Africa, AIDS is transmitted the most by heterosexual sex which is directly attributable to the sexual behavior of the African male. The pattern seems to be repeating itself in America with the transmission of AIDS in the Black community following the same pattern; more and more heterosexual transmissions of AIDS.[50] How about the way brothers here in America try and dominate and control their women, even to the point of beating them or out and out killing them? Just look at any of the African countries, Rwanda, case in point, and observe how when the men have their insignificant tribal wars, they not only kill the men, but they rape as many women as they can, impregnating them with children so that they can wipe out the enemy race. In fact the worse atrocities of rape and mutilation of women in history have been in Africa.[51]

Why is it that Blacks love loud music so much. The louder the music and the more drumbeats it has, the better Blacks love it. Everything that Blacks do in terms of transferring and receiving information is done so in some relation to the beat of drums. The television commercials that Blacks like the best always have singing and dancing in them. Blacks are the happiest when they are singing, dancing and beating the drums. Isn't it funny how Blacks in America used to get mad or ashamed when they looked at an old *"Tarzan"* movie and the way it depicted the natives in the way they dressed, danced and sung. Yet, today if you went to any Black Church, the behavior that you would see during service is exactly the same, both in terms of the drumbeats, the singing, dancing and even the dress somewhat.

Is it possible that the way Black men in America display so much gold jewelry on their bodies and their love for shiny things also have something to do with their African heritage. Why do Black men put so much gold in their mouths. Black men in America do like shiny things. If they buy a car, any car, even a Mercedes, they are apt to put shiny rims and wheels on it? Are they just doing it or are they doing what is innate to them?

For years, Black men have blamed the violence that they commit in their neighborhoods on crowded conditions and other reasons which they attribute to being designed by the White man to wipe them out. But when you look back to African countries and communities, you will see that Black men have always been violent. They have always killed each other just because they didn't like each other.

Black men in this country, America, have never worked well together or related well toward each other. In fact most of the Black on Black crime in this country (especially drive-by shootings) are perpetrated on Black men by Black men. Again, this is not unique to the American Black male, rather when you look at how Black men behave in Africa, the behavior is the same. There, Black men don't work together either. They have been warring between tribes for the heck of it for centuries. I know that there will be those readers that will argue that the Arabs are the same way, always killing each other on principle and religion. But here we are concerned with saving ourselves, not finger pointing. To have something, anything of substance, you must work together. You have to pool your resources and work together for the common good. Blacks in America can't seem to get it together and do this. But again, this is not unique to American Blacks. Africans don't work together and pool their resources either. They too are dependent on Western intervention to build anything of substance.

Let's talk about the way Black men in America dress. We wear the weirdest hairstyles and clothing. We don't want to dress uniformly like other races. We will wear the loudest colors in both our clothing and shoes. Most of our clothing has to be almost ceremonial, unique, stand out from the crowd. We have to be seen and noticed. Black men will do anything to accomplish this, even if it means dyed hair and body piercing.

We have already discussed how American Blacks have spent most of their recent history trying to assimilate with Whites. All of this time we have thought that it was because we were here in America and were taught to mistrust and misuse one another. In other words, we were treating each other like our captors treated us. But when you look at the way Africans who come to America behave, the behavior is the same. Immediately upon arriving on the shores of America, Africans try to hang around with Whites, they want to become part of the group. They disassociate themselves from American Blacks as if they don't won't to be grouped with them or that they are better than American Blacks. The behavior of Africans is identical to American Blacks. These two groups spend little if any time trying to reunite with each other (see discussion on page 202) and most of their time trying to be with and like somebody else.

The simple fact of the matter is that in the 2000's, American Blacks are more like Africans than anybody else. We have spent all this time in America for the last 400 plus years and it has not made any difference. We have not become more American, we have become more African. The reason for this is that we are African, not American and simply living here is not going to change our basic, cultural tendencies.. All we have done with all of the Affirmative Action struggles and freedom marches is to focus on things that are not going to help improve us. We must now focus on ourselves, not on what Whites think about us and how Whites treat us.

Blacks May Just Be Inferior

Throughout the world Blacks are in last place. This is true in terms of overall accomplishments, production of goods, delivery of services, wealth, power, and standards of living. Blacks are not driven on their own and in and of themselves to be the best that they can be. When Blacks are the best at something, be it sports, entertainment or modeling, it is under the direction and supervision of some other race, usually, the White race.

Blacks are not driven to explore and conquer the earth and the known universe. Blacks just might not be builders and producers. It's conceivable that we may just be a race of entertainers and partiers and to ask anything else of us is to ask for something that is not in us.

Could it be that Blacks can't change with the times in order to work and cope with an ever changing environment. Could it be that if we were left all to ourselves, we would reek havoc on ourselves and others. Without Whites (American and European), would we have any order at all in our lives?

The question, simply stated, is, "Are Blacks inferior"? Inferior is defined in terms of how we stack up relative to other races and whether or not we put our abilities and talents into constructive (profitable) action. I admit that this is finger pointing somewhat, but we need to have a gauge or measuring stick to see where we are.

A premise of this book is that Black males around the world are 500 years behind on the human social evolutionary scale. The following discussion is the justification for making this premise.

Technology is a manifestation of your social evolution. You can determine how far a group or race of people have evolved by looking at the technology that they produce.

Man has been evolving step by step since he left the cave. He discovered fire and how to start, maintain and control it. He made stone knives, weapons and other tools in order to make other things that helped make his life better. This early man then began to run in clans or packs so that he could do things quicker and on a larger scale than by himself. This progression has continued from the invention of the wheel, to the electric light bulb, the telephone, the automobile and airplane, the computer, modern medical techniques and on and on.

The reason that technology is the best indicator of social evolution is because in order to have technology you will have had to evolve from working and thinking as an individual to working and thinking as a collective group. Without collective intelligence and collective effort, you can't have technology.

When you look at races and groups of people around the world, you will quickly see that those who are technologically superior such as the Germans, the White Americans, the Japanese, and the British, all work together as a cohesive unit. The races that are on the bottom, those with no technology, don't work together. Instead they are always bickering and backbiting and can never work together as a group. Take a look at Blacks and Hispanics, they are a mass of conflicting impulses, everybody doing his or her own thing.

This notion of having the ability to work and think collectively together as a group is not new. If you go back to Biblical times you can find an excellent example showing how the power of working together and having political unity, which means nothing more than having a collective goal, can accomplish great things. Here we are talking about the building of the tower of Babel. During this time all of mankind spoke a single language. As the population grew and spread westward, a plain was discovered in the land of Babylon. It was quickly populated and the people who lived there began to talk about building a great city, with a temple-tower reaching to the skies (technology at work). This was to weld them together and keep them from scattering all over the world. So they made great piles of hard burned brick, and collected bitumen to use as mortar. But when God came down to look at the city and the tower they were making, he said, "Look! If they are able to accomplish all of this when they have just begun to exploit their linguistic and political unity (see, working together), just think of what they will do later! Nothing will be unattainable for them! Come and let us go down and give them different languages, so that they won't understand each other's words! In that way God scattered them all over the earth and ended the building of the city.[52] God himself knew that if people could not work together, speaking the same language and having the same vision (working as a collective), then you would have confusion and these people could not build anything of substance, i.e. have technology because it takes group effort.

If you are looking for an obvious present day example of just how important it is to have collective thinking and effort as a race (in this case, the American White race) and what you can accomplish technologically when you do, then look at the Internet.

What is the Internet and how did it begin? Near the end of the 1970's, many companies began to install computer networks.   Several computer manufacturers introduced small minicomputers with sufficient computational power to handle many users. To interconnect minicomputers and to permit the rapid transfer of information among them, many organizations began to install Local Area Networks (LAN). Because LAN technology was both inexpensive and easy to install, many individual departments within companies purchased, installed and operated their own LANs.

Companies soon discovered that when groups or departments within organizations began to build and operate computer networks there were advantages and disadvantages. The advantages were when granted independence, a group could choose a network technology appropriate for their needs. They could budget funds to pay for the LAN installation and operation. They could decide who had access, and could devise policies regarding network use. Other advantages of LANs were that engineers devised many LAN technologies with a group being able to have a particular LAN designed to have a particular speed, ease of use and availability of interfaces for specific computers.   The disadvantage of LAN technology was that various LAN technologies were completely incompatible. What that meant was that multiple LANs couldn't be plugged together. The reasons for this were as follows: first, a given LAN technology was engineered to operate over a limited distance with each LAN specifying a maximum cable length. Adding more distance to a LAN would result in a malfunction. Second, each LAN technology had its own specification for electrical signals like voltage and frequency; different LAN technologies may be electrically incompatible. Third, each technology had a way of encoding information (e.g., a form of modulation); the encoding used by one LAN system did not make sense to another.

In addition to LAN technologies, another form of computer networking emerged in the 1960s and 1970s. Scientists devised ways to build networks that connected multiple computers across large geographic distances. These networks were called Wide Area Networks (WANs). The technology used in WANs were basically the same as that used in long distance telephone systems, with WANs using modems to send the signals. However, WANs did more than connect two computers across a single transmission channel; a WAN used computers to unify a set of transmission lines into a coordinated system. To do so, a WAN included a small, dedicated computer at each site that attached to the transmission line and kept the network operating independently from the computers that used it. The dedicated computer received an incoming message that arrived from another site and delivered it to one of the local computers. It accepted a message from any of the local computers and sent the message across the transmission line toward the destination.

The disadvantages of WANs were many. They cost far more than LANs and they required more planning and significantly more hardware. Different WAN technologies were electrically incompatible with one another so one couldn't create a larger network merely by plugging wires from one type of WAN into another. The biggest disadvantage of WANs was that they were completely incompatible with LANs.

Anyone who uses multiple computers that connect to two or more separate network systems understands how inconvenient the scheme was. For example, if one computer was attached to a LAN and another was attached to a WAN, neither had access to all resources in the organization. A computer attached to a WAN could access resources and information on remote machines, but couldn't access information on local machines and vice-versa.

Fortunately, by the late 1960's, the U.S. Department of Defense became interested in using computer networks. The military set up and funded what was first known as the Advanced Research Projects Agency (ARPA); later known as the Defense Advanced Research Projects Agency (DARPA). ARPA was given the task of researching networks using a variety of technologies. By the late 1970's, ARPA had several operational computer networks and had begun to pass technology on to the military. ARPA projects included a wide area network called the ARPANET as well as networks that used satellites and radio transmission for communication.

ARPA began to deal with the problems networks faced such as each network connecting a set of computers, but no path existing between computers on separate networks. ARPA started with a few basic ideas, awarded grants to researchers in both the industry and academia, and arranged for the researchers to cooperate in solving the problems together.[53]

The key idea in the ARPA research was a new approach to interconnecting LAN's and WANs that became known as the *internetwork*. The experimental prototype of what is in place now is known as the Internet. It uses a variety of computer software that makes it possible to interconnect networks. This software makes all of the interconnecting networks operate as a seamless system. Exactly how the software makes the Internet operate is beyond the technical scope of this book.

What is so important about the Internet to our discussion is that no longer are just people in this technological society working collectively, but now their computers are hooked together so that their knowledge can be assessed collectively which has increased collective knowledge a thousand fold. So now, both man and machine work collectively and not as individual units. You now have the ability for hundreds of thousands of people to work on a problem, all at the same time. Without Whites working together to achieve a common goal, the Internet would not have been possible.

Other things that you must have in order to have technology are high standards and order. Again, when you look at technological races, you will find that they are driven by competition leading to high standards and a desire for order where as primitive races are driven by emotion which is manifested by blame, excuses and a need for sympathy (pity).

People in a technological race or society compete for everything. They reward those who are the best at what they do and punish those who are the worst at what they do. Competition is the great equalizer. It does not matter who you are, what you have or who you know. If you are the best at what you do and you apply your abilities, you will get rewarded.

Without competition, you are not going to have high standards. The reason for this is because competition continues to raise the standards. As people try to beat out other people, they work harder, smarter and achieve today what was not possible yesterday. Highly technological races will always have the highest standards possible for every area of human endeavor. Competing for everything ensures that the standards are the highest possible at any given time.

There are those people out there (Black people mostly) who will argue that anyone who thinks that you have to compete, have technology and be wealthy is nothing more than having bought into (been brainwashed) by Western European doctrine. But lest ye not forget that the beginnings of wealth, of technology and competition is supposed to have originated in Africa and Blacks are supposed to be the direct descendants of those pyramid builders. Nothing on this earth, even today, is more technological than the pyramids.

Having order is also a prerequisite to having technology. Technological societies have order on all levels. The basic core of this order is that they have laws for everything. They demand that everyone in their society and everyone that comes into contact with them live by these laws. The purpose of laws is not just to establish what is right and what is wrong, but more importantly to establish uniform behavior. This behavior ranges from business dealings to personal interactions. Why do you think that technological societies have the best buildings (skyscrapers), the best housing and standards of living. The reasons are because they have order which is maintained by their laws which in this case are zoning codes and ordinances which require that buildings be built to a certain standard.

These zoning laws as well as any other laws be they criminal, civil or administrative are compulsory. To insure that laws are followed, technological societies have stiff penalties, and in some cases death is required. The people in these technological societies don't mind so much following the laws because they understand that the laws make it better for everyone and are for the collective good which supersedes the rights of the individual. But again, the evolution from individual thinking and importance to collective thinking and effort makes it easier for these individuals to obey the laws than primitive people. Yes, I am saying that Blacks are primitive. Young Black males have no concept of this order and how it is the reason behind all of the criminal laws and statutes. It is so difficult for these young Black males to obey the laws because many times when they break some law, all they see is that on the surface it is not affecting any one but them. They can't understand why some things they are doing are even against the law because any harm done is only affecting them. As individualistic thinkers, they can't see that the laws are written to protect society, not just a particular person. Law are written to make the members of society operate in harmony and as safely as possible. So the fact that you run a stop sign at three o'clock in the morning because you are the only one on the road is still breaking the law since this action is potentially harmful to other members of society (another motorist that you may not see coming).

The second level of this order is record keeping. Technological races record everything. They put it in writing. They have amassed large libraries that contain everything that they have ever done. Technological races keep statistics. These statistics help them to gauge whether or not their society is improving or declining. In America, you can learn about anything by simply going to the library. This library can be public, private, university based or governmental, but it will contain the sum total of all of the history and knowledge possessed by the White race. Non-technological races do very little, if any, recording. They attempt to pass information and history to others verbally. Each time the information or history goes from one person to another, some of it gets lost or distorted.. Over time, both the history and knowledge are lost all together.

The third level of order found in technological races is standardization. You see this in the sizes of things like weights and measures, the sizes of door frames, lot sizes, street widths, keyboards, interchangeableness of parts and tools, power supply from electrical outlets, etc. Go anywhere in a technological society and the standards, the quality, the laws, the products, the buildings, all will be basically the same. They do not differ from village to village or tribe to tribe as in primitive cultures.

Another universal constant that is found in races that possess technology is that the people of the race are well educated. When you look at races that have no technology, they are going to be illiterate and uneducated. In order to have technology you have to have the people to design it, build it and distribute it. If it breaks, you have to have the people who have the ability to repair it. These technicians are going to have at least a college degree and in most cases a Masters and Ph.D. If you took the collective intelligence of a highly technological race (Whites) and compared it to a race that has no technology (Blacks), you would find that the amount of collective intelligence possessed by the technological race is approximately nine orders of magnitude (one billion) times that of the non-technological race. Image the collective intelligence of the non-technological race filling a Styrofoam coffee cup (small), while that of the technological race fills the Atlantic Ocean. To have education you also had to have had the discipline to study day in and day out. Technological races have the discipline to do what needs to be done and non-technological races don't.

There is another important universal constant possessed by races that have superior technology. It is a strong will. You can't have technology unless you have the will to work together, expend the resources and accept nothing short of the best possible outcome. Once you have the technology, you have to have the will to use it; even if its use is going to harm some people initially.

As stated earlier, no race or group of people have ever been conquered who possessed technology and strength of will. As a group of people, you won't win at something, be it war or business, unless you have the will to win. Let's use two examples here. In the first example, if a company or individual knows that a new product or invention will improve the condition of mankind, but that there will probably be a small number of deaths or potentially harmful side effects associated with the product or invention, then this company or individual must have a strong will to go ahead with the product or invention. This scenario has happened countless times in industrialized countries.   In the second example, let's say that you are at war and you are ready to end this war. You have developed a new weapon. You know that you will most likely win the war, that it is only a matter of time, say six months. If you deployed this weapon you could end the war tomorrow. You would save the lives of your soldiers and civilians alike. You would be able to see that the weapon in fact works with the effectiveness that you predict. And lastly, you can demonstrate to your enemies that you are technologically superior. The only problem is that you know millions of people, innocent civilians, will die if you deploy the weapon. What do you do. You guessed it, technological races deploy the bomb. This is exactly what happened when the U.S. was at war with Japan. They had the strength of will to drop two nuclear bombs, the first on Hiroshima and the second on Nagasaki to show the Japanese that they could duplicate the process.

There is yet another universal constant that is possessed by technological races that must be discussed. That is the concept of substitutability. This means that in highly evolved races, you have large numbers of highly specialized people in all areas that can replace the people that are no longer viable in that area. This replacement of people can happen and the society is not set back in any way. For example, in White society, if 1000 of their political leaders died, say the President, congressmen, governors, etc., it would not matter because they have enough skilled people so that the society would continue to operate. The same is true in other areas. If hundreds of their prominent doctors, scientists, lawyers, professors or architects died, they would still be able to operate, discover and build more technology. This is not true of primitive cultures and races (say Blacks for example). If you kill off ten of the top Black political leaders, chaos would ensue (more than Blacks already have anyway).

Now, once again, what does all of this have to do with the Black race and how does it add to the extinction of the Black male?

It could be that the reason that the Black male is becoming extinct is because he is inferior. Not inferior genetically, but inferior socially. By socially I mean human to human interaction. Genetically, Black males are superior both physically and mentally. The physical part is proven everyday in sports, but the mental part is my own opinion based on the intellectual ingenuity that is shown by Black males. If you have a problem that needs to be solved and a Black man works on it diligently, he can usually solve it when no one else can.

It has already been stated that technology is a manifestation of your social evolution. And that Black men were 500 years behind on the evolutionary scale.

Black men don't produce a single product. We don't make anything that we can call our own. We make no cars, phones, plastics, lasers, computers, or clothing. In other words, we don't make a damn thing. Because to make anything of substance, you have to work together.

Black men don't and won't work together. As stated earlier, working together requires evolving from thinking and acting as an individual to thinking and acting collectively. This means putting and valuing the group (race) more than yourself. You can see this thinking as an individual prevalent in every aspect of Black life and Black interactions. When a person or race of people put more emphasis (importance) on the individual (me, myself and I), this person or race will do anything to maintain that importance.

Look at the behavior of Blacks and understand how this is borne out everyday. Just try to enter into the street when the traffic is very heavy and see if a Black person will let you in. The answer is no. A Black person will even go so far as to block you out. This makes that person feel important and in control. Have you ever noticed when a Black person is behind you on the highway they will tailgate you unmercifully? No matter how fast you go, they will speed up and stay on your bumper. Even if you change lanes, many times they will change lanes with your and remain on your bumper. However, the moment this same Black person gets in front of you, they will immediately slow down. They will creep along, profiling and styling and blocking your progress. If you try and get around them, they will speed up. They want you to know that they are more important than you are.

This focus on self importance also helps to explain why Black people will not speak to one another. If they speak, they feel that it lessens them. By not speaking, they feel that I am more important than you are. How many times have you seen two Black men walk by each other and each one has their head in the air trying to show the other one that they are more important. Never mind that the one might just be that person that the other needed to complete a project or get a referral from. In order to work as a group, you have to meet and to know people. You can't do either if you don't speak to people because that is the way that any relationship starts.

Have you ever tried to schedule an appointment with a Black man only to have him tell you how busy he is and that he does not know when he will have a free moment, yet you can get an appointment with the White President of a large lending institution who has the responsibility of managing thousands of employees and millions of dollars. If you doubt this for a minute, try and speak with your own pastor. It is unlikely that you can get five minutes of his time even though he is paid to be full-time and yet he is rarely at the Church except on Sundays and Wednesdays. Even if he is there, he is too busy to talk to you.

Another aspect of this individualistic thinking is that I am so important that I will do anything to make sure that you know I am. For instance Black people will cut down or try to destroy a person sometimes just because they are popular or better looking. In other words, anything or anybody that detracts from a Black person's self importance will be fought against.

Black men are so caught up in this I am important and I must be an individual rather than part of the group that they can't do anything in which they will not be seen or known about. Drive to any mall and watch how many Black men will park their cars in the fire lane so they can be seen, even though the parking lot may be empty.

It was mentioned earlier that highly technological races were based on competition which lead to high standards and are based on order. Primitive races are based on emotion which leads to always asking for sympathy and making excuses.

Black men are very emotional. It manifests itself in everything that they do. When Black men interact, they get so caught up in jealousy and hatred or love. If you try and do business with a Black man, there is always going to be an element of if you don't do it exactly as I want it to be done, then you don't like me. If you try and discuss business, the moment you disagree, Black men will get angry. They wear their emotions on their sleeves. These emotions always get in the way of things getting done.

When Black men have a meeting, the first thing that happens is singing and shouting, neither of which accomplishes the task at hand.

This emotional way of doing anything has led to Black people only being able to transfer information by singing and feeling good. Our leaders, people that try and shift the direction in which we are headed, are either preachers or entertainers, rather than scientists or from some other meticulous step by step profession.

This emotionalism has lead to an expectation that everyone and everything is equal and competing to win is unfair (except in sports). There are so many Black men running around in America feeling that life is unfair or that they are owed something. They want to be liked and respected. They are so hurt. All they have to do is start competing, but they will make excuses, racism being the most often used. How many times have you heard Black men say, "Whites have changed the rules and increased the standards because they want to make it harder on us because they are trying to limit how many of us are in a particular profession." You rarely hear Black men say, "If they can do it, then I can do it. I don't care how hard it is."

The thing that is hurting Black men the most in this technological society is their inability to work at tasks that require sustained mental effort. The more meticulous a task, the less likely a Black male is going to be able to do it. Able meaning having the know how and willing to put in the effort. This is one of the main reasons why Black men can't produce anything of substance because in order to do so requires sustained, meticulous, mental effort. Anytime Black men complain about the level of standards or a change in standards, it is always the mental (knowledge) standards they are complaining about, never the physical.

What about conformity? We discussed in the section about history that Black men in America were descendants from a mixture of various tribes and countries. Perhaps that accounts for the extreme level of non-conformity among Black men that you see in America.   This non-conformity is seen in the differences in how Black men dress (suit and tie, dashiki, pants falling off butt, athletic attire, no shirt), how they wear their hair (Jheri curl, bald, big Afro, dreadlocks, dyed, waves, close smooth cut, designs in scalp), to education level.

Blacks really need to take a hard look at the things that they do and try to understand their behavior. One more thing that primitive cultures do, specifically Blacks, is to arrange and use things for show rather than function. Even when a Black purchases a Benz, he still will put flashy wheels on it even though they take away from the function of the car. Even the way Blacks dress is more related to show than function. Young Black males wear their pants hanging off of their butts, shirts out and shoes untied, all to be seen and make a statement, but there is no function. Most of the behavior that Blacks display is to be seen, rather than to do something constructive.

In the end, Black men display the hallmarks of primitive behavior. They display the elements of individualism which are look at what I got (i.e. what car I drive), look at what I'm wearing and how I'm wearing it (expensive tennis shoes and casual clothing hanging off their butts and two sizes too big) and look how fine or cute I am. This is opposed to evolved superior cultures whose hallmarks are look at what we were able to build and accomplish so that life is better for all of us.

As usual there are going to be a large of number of Blacks that will argue that they have evolved. But I am here to tell them that they are mistaken. Blacks think that if you have the stuff that evolved races have and live with them, then you have evolved (arrived). Most Blacks think that if you drive a Mercedes (or BMW or Lexus), you wear expensive clothing and live in an exclusive White neighborhood, then you are just as evolved as White people. Even the least uneducated Black person believes this. Observe the behavior of any Black person who comes into a large sum of money (at least to them). The first thing that they will purchase is a Benz. How many times have you been driving down the freeway and looked next to you to see a brother with his hat on backwards, mouth full of gold teeth, but driving a Mercedes. Even if a Black person can't afford a new one, they will buy a 10 year old Mercedes and hold their head up high (act stuck up) while they pass you. They even act like a snob and won't speak to you while the old Mercedes is in the repair shop. How many Black people do you see walking around on a daily basis wearing expensive shoes and suits and acting like they are better than you? And don't let a Black purchase (rent) a house in an exclusive White neighborhood. They think that their importantance goes way, way up. Even if a Black works in an area where there are mostly Whites, they think that they have evolved more than you.

The dumbest, laziest, dirtiest brother, who doesn't even have a pot to piss in, will walk around with a cellular telephone in his hand, with no shirt on, acting like he is somebody (i.e., he is better than you, more evolved because he has a cell phone and you don't.).

The reality is that these Blacks have not evolved. You can teach a monkey to drive a Mercedes. You can dress him in an Armani suit, give him a cell phone to hold in his hand, give him an address in a White neighborhood and let him work in a White firm. But this monkey has not evolved. The reason that he has not evolved is because he has no clue of how the technology that he is using works, how to build it, or how to repair it. You can have this monkey associate with Whites for four hundred years (sound familiar), using all the latest technology available and the basic make up of this monkey will not change.

Sure, inside he may feel that he is better than the other monkeys still out there in the jungle, but he is still a monkey and will always be treated like a monkey by Whites and other races. Because when you see him coming, guess what you see coming, not a monkey that lives, acts and tries desperately to be White, no, you see a monkey. Does this too sound familiar?

If you doubt any of the above discussion about Blacks possibly being inferior and being 500 years behind on the social evolutionary scale, consider the following hypothetical.

Suppose you woke up in the morning and all Black people (except you) have disappeared. There are no Blacks anywhere, just you. The buses are not running, the phones in businesses are not being answered, the food in restaurants are not being cooked, there are no security guards to be seen, the jails are empty, no one is standing on the corner. What would happen? The first thing that would happen is that Whites would ask the question, "Why are none of the menial, service jobs being done?" They would have a meeting and decide on two courses of action. One course of action that they would take is to have their scientists to study the phenomenon. Their scientists would be instructed to find out what happened to the Black people. Where did they go? Why did they disappear? Was it a virus that made Blacks disappear? Did aliens take them away? Was it the Rapture and God has returned to claim his people?

The other course of action that Whites would take is to form groups in order to teach the Hispanics to fill the role of Blacks. These groups would work on improving their English and raising their level of technical job skills so that the Hispanics could perform all of the tasks that Blacks used to do. Whites would continue to be serviced. In fact, they might be better off because the Hispanics would work harder, for less pay and Whites would not have to deal with all of the discrimination issues and racism. In the end, Whites would not miss Blacks and would adapt.

Conversely, suppose you woke up in the morning and all White people have disappeared. The only race left in America are Black people. (For the sake of argument, let's say there are no Asians, nor Hispanics). Overnight, Black people have inherited everything in America. All the cars, houses, businesses, the airplanes, the nuclear weapons, hospitals, shopping malls, space shuttles, land, phone systems, money, and everything that America has to offer is left to Blacks. What would happen? I submit that not only would Blacks be incapable of running this country, there would be total chaos and the country would be destroyed (due to vandalism and fire) within three months.

The reasons for this are as follows. Blacks have never worked together as a cohesive people in harmony (for the good of each other). It is unlikely that Blacks would be able to operate the airline system, the health care system with hospitals and ambulances providing medical care. What about fire and police protection? Would the mail be delivered? There certainly would be no more new technology created. So whatever is available now, is all that you would ever have and if it broke, there would be no one to fix it. Blacks are not the kind of people who would put in the long tedious hours and expensive resources to explore outer space or the bottom of the ocean. There would be no more new aircraft developed or nuclear fusion plants. How about sporting events? Would there be a World Series or NBA Championship considering the technical expertise needed to broadcast the event around the world. Would we even have television with the daily programming that we have become accustomed?

The reason there would be no more technology is also due to the fact that Blacks have concentrated on being entertainers and athletes rather than scientists and technicians. There simply would not be enough people with the know how to get the space shuttle off the ground, or to operate the vast array of laboratories. Then what about operating the manufacturing plants. Blacks have never even designed and built one skyscraper on their own. We don't have enough architects to design or enough qualified journeymen to do new construction. We don't have the collective intelligence.

The odds are that we wouldn't even have to worry about making any more scientific or industrial strides because we could not even manage the status quo. Blacks would destroy this country. You would have Blacks asking anyone who tried to maintain some semblance of order, "Who put you in charge? I only obeyed the laws when I did because the man (White man) was in charge. Now he is gone, so I am just going to take what I want. It is just as much mine as it is yours." You would have on a mass scale the same kind of behavior that you see when there is a blackout in a major city. There would be looting and complete disorder. Even thinking that the country could last three months might be optimistic.

PART V. 23 STEPS FOR THE BLACK MALE TO SURVIVE IN THE 21ST CENTURY

Up to this point, we have identified all of the problems that are leading to the extinction of the Black male in America. It is obvious that the problems are many and at the very least complex.

If you have read this book up to this point, hopefully you have gone through the same stages that Elizabeth Kubler Ross felt that terminally ill patients go through. First, there is denial and in this case, many Blacks who read this book will at first simply try and deny that Black males have half of the problems that are outlined in this book. They simply will not face up to the truth or try and act as though these problems are not real or not as serious as this book makes them out to be. The second stage is anger. There will be more than a few Blacks who will get angry (most likely with the author) and act as though me or someone else is a terrible person for pointing out the problems. They will be mad and not even know why they are mad. These people will want to lash out at someone, anyone. They may even go into a rage. The third step is bargaining. In this stage, the person will finger point time after time to justify these problems and will try to bargain with everyone he or she talks with in order to get them to agree that other people have the same problems and thus the problems of the Black male are no better or worse than other races. They will give countless comparisons as though this justifies the behavior of the Black male. The fourth stage is depression. If you have read this book in the order that it was written up to now, then you can't help but be depressed. Its possible that you may feel that there is no way to solve these problems of the Black male or you may feel that it is so unfair. You feel helpless and wish that you had not read this book. You would rather have been ignorant of what the reality of the Black male in this country really is in the 2000's. But now you do know and it is too late. The fifth and final stage is acceptance.[54] Now you know the truth and you realize that the first step to solving any problem is accepting the fact that you have it. Now your resolve is returning and you are feeling a glimmer of determination that someway, somehow you are going to deal with these problems of the Black male.

After you have accepted that these problems exist, then lets move to the next step of problem solving which is to review the things that have not worked in the past. Only a fool does the same things over and over and expects a different result.

Now what are some of the things that won't work in solving the problems of the Black male? For one thing, no one else is going to solve his problems except him. You can't look to or expect Whites to solve the problems of the Black male because it is not in the best interest of Whites to do so. This means that anything associated with the Civil Rights Movement, marches, and so forth are futile. Affirmative action suits and discrimination suits to get Whites to hire more of us is not going to solve our problems. They have already been tried and failed, miserably. Any strategy that is based on assimilation into the White culture or is done to impress or get White approval will also fail. Blacks must begin to understand that just because the White media covers an event, that in and of itself does not mean that the event is successful. Blacks have to get away from the media. No one can come up with the kind of hard nosed, meaningful solutions to this or any kind of problem with the cameras present. Not to mention that there are some things that you don't want to be recorded.

Other things that simply will not work are billboards and commercials such as "Stop the Violence". Having well known entertainers do public service announcements for Nike, Major League Baseball and the NBA urging young Black kids to learn to read are not going to work either.

Every year around the country, Blacks have numerous Christian retreats that are meant to empower Black men, these too are useless. What happens is that there is a lot of praying, singing and shouting and a whole lot of ethereal information given that would be applicable to any meeting, but nothing tangible and practical. The Blacks that attend go back home feeling good for a minute, but couldn't tell you if their life depended on it, what the message was and how to apply it.

Other things that are just as useless are Black Expos, Black networking gatherings and any of the numerous Black tie parties. Again, none of these things provide any practical information. These are just social gatherings, designed to be seen and pretend you are somebody.

Blacks cannot solve their problems through entertainment. Any time a large gathering of Blacks come together, there is usually some awards ceremony and if there is any attempt to get a message out it is sung, or danced, but not spoken, nor written.

Enough already. What is the next step? Well we have identified the problems and their causes; we have admitted that we have a problem; we have looked at what will not work in the 2000's; now we must do some considerations and probing.

Black males in America have a monumental task in front of them. We are going to have to change the core values, beliefs and modus operandi that we have learned and practiced for the last four hundred years and do things differently for the next twenty years. We are going to have to develop a strength of will and purpose that we have never had. Once we've done these two things, we are then going to have to make some decisions.

The first decision will have to be, will we try and save all Black men, both young and old? Will we concentrate on the youth mostly or will we put just as much effort on the homeless, the incarcerated and the uneducated? In other words, will we save those that are salvageable and let the rest go because it would be too time and resource consuming to do so?

Another consideration is that Blacks for the first time in history are going to have to become aggressive rather than benevolent. This kind of benevolence has led to Blacks being easy targets to conquer and enslave. Blacks are going to have to learn to have a good offense (best educated, best technology for weapons and goods, best up to date information) and use that as the best defense.

Blacks are going to have to decide to build a stand alone culture with its own infrastructure, capable of manufacturing and distribution rather than continue trying to assimilate with Whites and being dependant. Co-existence is the key, not integration. The reason for this is that Blacks and Whites as of this writing are fundamentally different people. Whites have had a thousand years in which to build upon a foundation to constantly improve in all areas. They have worked together to accomplish this. Not only that, for whatever reason, Whites are driven to conquer, explore and to build, Blacks are not there yet or were once there and lost it. Blacks are going to have to develop a whole new psyche and identity that has nothing to do with Whites.

Blacks are going to have to figure out how to evolve socially and culturally in twenty years where other races have had a thousand years. What makes a race evolve that fast. It is either by education, by some major environmental disaster caused by the weather or disease, war, or divine intervention or it is by greed. Whatever the method or reason, Blacks have to begin the process of evolution now.

One of the things that Blacks must do right now is to devalue entertainment and sports and value education. The smartest person in a skilled or technical profession must be valued higher than an athlete or entertainer. Remember, primitive people value entertainment and spend most of their time partying and trying to look good while evolved people value technical expertise and spend most of their time studying, building and improving.

Blacks are going to have to find a common bond, something that not only binds them together, but promotes loyalty, pride and most of all a collective goal. Again this is going to be difficult because right now there is nothing except skin color that is universal to Black people. Blacks don't have a religious bond. Currently, we have all kinds of religious affiliations such as Islam, Baptist, Pentecostal, Methodist, Presbyterian, Catholic, Jehovah Witness, Church of God and Christ, Seventh Day Adventist or some other religion that is predominately White. None of these religions were originally our own, but Blacks were indoctrinated into them by missionaries in Africa or when we got to America. Some Blacks are even constantly changing religious faiths. Nor do Blacks have a unified political ideology. Some of us are Democrats, some Republicans, some Socialists or some of us are politically inert. It has already been pointed out that Blacks have no common heritage upon which to unite. And what little heritage that we did have has been diluted with non-Black racial impurities.

The next thing in all of these stages is that Blacks have to develop a measuring stick. We have to know if we are on the right tract and if we are making headway or not.

There are ten indicators that Blacks must keep track of and I mean we must keep track of them, not look to Whites to do it for us. These ten indicators are (1) Increased percentage (relative to number of Blacks) and number of post graduate degrees in computer science, engineering (including mechanical, electrical, astrophysical, chemical and nuclear), architecture, and medicine; (2) Decreased number of Black men convicted of felonies and incarcerated; (3) Increase in number of Black businesses that provide necessities (food, clothing, mechanical repair, medical and legal services, banking, construction, transportation services, lodging, both hotel and motel, auto sales and repair); (4) Increase in percentage and number of marriages (obviously a divorce means one less marriage); (5) Decrease in number of teenage pregnancies; (6) Increase in number of Black households with an annual income above $100,000; (7) Increase in home and land ownership; (8) Decrease in number of Black athletes and entertainers; (9) Increase in number of Black owned and operated radio and television stations including cable; and (10) Increase in annual Black planning and strategic policy sessions.

Now how are Blacks going to accomplish all of this? We are going to have to develop a plan of action so that we are all working off the same sheet of music so to speak. In the above paragraph, we have the ten indicators that we can look at to see if we are making progress. We need a time line, a specific time frame in which to accomplish the things that we need to do. This time line should be twenty years. No ifs, ands, or buts. The first five years should be spent on accomplishing the twenty-three items listed in this section. These items are very basic in nature and have to be accomplished before anything else will work. Then the next fifteen years should be spent on accomplishing the goals and tasks outlined in *"The Strategic Planning Guide for Blacks in the World"*, which will be released in the year 2003.

For Blacks to do what needs to be done, they are going to have to initially focus on the basics. There are no magic or quick fix formulas. It is going to take hard work and sustained effort. This work and effort is going to encompass both mental and physical inputs. All available resources and time in the Black community are going to have to be channeled into this effort. The difference between us and other races is that we lack the ability to work. Simply put, other races outwork us and therefore have better quality of lives because of their ability to work hard.

The thing to remember is that Blacks don't have a resource problem, it is a mental and faith problem. Once we believe in ourselves and our abilities, then nothing will be impossible for us.

Trust and Follow the Teachings of Christ

The intent of this book is not to promote any particular religious doctrine over another. These doctrines are man-made anyway. What is being promoted is that the first thing that Black men must do is to believe in and follow (practice) the Word of God. It does not matter if this Word of God is recorded in the Bible (King James Version, old and new edition, the New International Version, the Life Application Bible, Todays English Version, The Living Bible, New Revised

Standard Version, Amplified Bible, Phillip's Translation, the Good News Bible, The Way Living Bible); the Qur'an; the Torah; the Holy Books; Bigadbahvita; or The Book of the Dead (the Book of Coming Forth by Day and Night).

Still let's review religion for a moment. There are really only two types of religion. There is human religion and divine religion. The human religion is all different types of denominations, each trying to spread its own word. Divine religion is non denominational, with Christ being the connecting point with man. Now what is the divine? The divine can be viewed (an analogy) as electricity. God the father is the electric source. The Holy Spirit is the electric power that flows from the source. Christ is the electric light powered by the power.

All of the above three (God, the Holy Spirit, and Christ) are collectively the Divine Essence. The Father (God) and the Holy Spirit work through Jesus Christ who provides the light to the inner man. Man's spirit thenn expresses the manifestation of God outwardly as peace, love, patience and understanding.

It is important to understand that likes attract and unlikes repel. Since God is light and Christ is the light of life, they attract and are one. Then sin and the Devil are darkness. Where there is God and lightness, there can be no darkness.

We must have light to grow both our spiritual bodies and our physical bodies. Why is light important to the physical body? Well, we eat soil (dirt) by way of proteins, vitamins and carbohydrates which we get from the ground and from animals which eventually return to the soil. No animal nor plant can survive without light. In terms of the Spiritual body, the only way for the spiritual body to grow is from the Word of God and the Holy Spirit. And both the Word of God and the Holy Spirit shine through Christ. Without the light of Christ, who is the light of life and the power of the Holy Spirit, the Spiritual body dies.

Let's shed just a little more light on this subject while we are at it. You see Black men, you must also understand the importance of Tunnel Separation. What this means is that we are living two lives. One is earthly and short and the other is eternal. Death happens to both the physical, i.e. soil and to the Spirit. The death of the physical body means that there is death of the soil (remember the old dust to dust). But death of the Spiritual body means that our inner spirit is reunited with the Spirit of God (if you are saved) or with the Devil (if you are not). Then when the Rapture comes, those who are saved, their Spirit and the old soil are reunited into a new body.

So now from our worldly standpoint, our starting point is what is the Word of God? We must know the answer to this question to find our way into the light of Jesus Christ. Well, the Word of God is like pure gold. You see, there are four types of gold. The Word of God is not (1) Glittering Gold, which is something that shines like gold, but is not really gold. This is the World Religions. These followers believe in a new age, I believe in what suits me religion. The Word of God is not (2) Coated Gold, which is where you have something (the message) gold plated. This is the Evangelical Religions where everything but God himself is worshiped. You know these religions as Buddhism, Hinduism, etc. The Word of God is not (3) Alloy Gold, which is where you have some gold plus some mineral like the Church which contains impurities caused because man split the Churches into all kinds of denominations, each preaching that their denomination's way of worshiping God is right and that other denominations' ways of worship are wrong   But the Word of God is (4) Pure Gold, which means that it is non-denominational. It is apocalyptic as in Philippians 1:27.[55] The Word of God and the inner spirit of all men touched by God is all the same.

So what does all of this mean? It means that there are two parts of man. There is his physical body with its five senses and there is his spiritual body, his eternal inner spirit. His inner spirit is surrounded by his emotions, his soul (your will) and his mind. Man needs the Word of God through Christ and the Holy Spirit to touch the inner spirit to ignite your emotions, your soul and your mind to direct your physical body so that through your physical body you can manifest the essence of God and the image of God will be restored within and without you manifested by your actions.

When you come into the light by way of Jesus Christ, you begin to know God and his word and begin to practice it, you begin to love God, which means that you love yourself, other Blacks and ultimately other races and peoples. You begin to understand that all people are different expressions (and there are more than man can comprehend) of the almighty.

Black men, by practicing the principles of God (seeing the light), you begin to end the chaos (the darkness) in your individual life and then the race itself. You then begin to get a sense of purpose and direction that will lead you to both your own personal as well as group destinies (as now the way is lit).

There are some things that you must understand about destiny. First, you, a Black man must have a sense of destiny. That sense of destiny begins when you understand that you were created by God to do God's work. Otherwise, you will think, as far too many Blacks do, that God only exists just to give you blessings (material stuff). You will waste half of your life praying to God and trying to live a righteous life, just to receive material blessings. God will always provide for the needs of those who trust and believe in him, but not every believer is going to be filthy rich. Second, you, a Black man are in a spiritual war. You can't stand still. The first thing that you must fight in this spiritual war is rebellion in your heart against God. Of all of the people in the world that have gotten away from God, the Black male tops the list. He therefore suffers as a result. Third, God expects the Black male to build a spiritual family. That family starts with your own wife and children. You must be responsible and prove your worth by taking care of and providing for your own family before God will give you your blessings. The more responsible, the more blessings he will give you. Again, when you look at the Black male, he is the least responsible when it comes to taking care of his family. The other races, (finger pointing I know), take care of their families. Just look at any prospering race and you will see that they are based on a strong family unit. Fourth, you the Black man must become a servant of God. You must give yourself away to others, especially in your own race. This is the only way that you can find out who you are. As you serve, not only will God bless you, but you won't be alone. People that are alone (lonely) are never good servants. People that have many friends and acquaintances are always good servants, doing more for people than people do for them. It is also the loneliness in people that make them do many of the negative things that they do. These things range from adultery and fornication, to vicious gossip, to theft, to hate, to suicide and just plain old unhappiness.

If the Black male does not get his own personal relationship straight with God, then nothing he attempts is going to be successful. He can blame other races all he wants for his pathetic existence, but the root cause of all of the Black males' problems are due to his own lack of faith and obedience.

Use the Church for Praise, Teaching Scriptures and Evangelism Only

In Part III of this book, there was a discussion of how the Black Churches have added to the extinction of the Black male by focusing on things that were not applicable in God's Church. The Church is not a business nor bar where you meet people. Nor is it a planning commission or construction company.

Still the Black Church is the key to stopping the extinction of the Black male. Without the Church playing the correct role, the Black male is doomed to destruction. First, the Church must be used as a place to praise God. You can only praise God by submitting to his will. The more Sundays in Church, the more you will praise him, the more you will submit to his will. And it follows that the more you submit to his will, the more you become obedient to his will.

Second, the Church must be a place that instills values in Black males by teaching the scriptures and what they mean in his daily life. What values are we talking about? The values are responsibility, honesty, love, trust, kindness, loyalty, hard work, high standards, excellence, winning attitude, preserverance, dedication, order and duty to God, family, race, community, and country.

Churches must begin to teach that the Bible is not some mystical document, rather it contains books, chapters and verses which serve as a practical guide with examples and analogies to keep you from making the same sinful mistakes and what to do when you make them. The Bible is just as applicable today, in 2000, as it was during the times before the birth of Christ. The reasons for this are because the motivations for committing sin, such as lust, anger, hate, jealousy, envy, greed, and revenge (just to name a few), have not changed. The emotional make up of man has not and will not change.

There is a simple formula to being a Christian (or whatever faith by which you acknowledge God), and receiving the blessings and forgiveness of God. That formula is you must believe in God with all of your might; praise him publicly, ask him to forgive you for your sins and repent; ask him to provide for all of your needs and a few of your desires; have faith that he will answer your prayers; work to fulfill your destiny (purpose) and for the things that you ask for with all of your strength; be obedient as he has instructed you to be; and if your intentions and requests are righteous and are within the scope of God's will, then your needs and desires will be fulfilled. This fulfillment will be more in terms of peace of mind rather than riches, although material wealth will be a part of it.

When it comes to instilling values and teaching the word of God to Black men, the Pastors of Black Churches must also play a significant role. Churches must strive to pay Pastors enough money so that they can be full time ministers. Full time minister means that the Pastor spends full time ministering to the needs of the members and in this case, especially, Black male members.   Churches must make the demand that the moment a Pastor gets too busy to speak with his members, or spends most of his time preaching at other Churches, or runs for political office, then he can no longer pastor that particular Church. Pastors must create a climate of nurturing and accountability to the members. He must spend time, especially on an individual or small group basis, teaching and training Black men in the ways of God. When the Pastor tells you that he can't spend at least twenty hours per week, not counting Sundays, at the Church, then it is time to get another Pastor. When the Pastor tells you that he is too busy to conference one on one with the members during assigned times during that twenty hours, then it is time to get a new Pastor. Otherwise, the Pastor is telling you that he is too important to talk with the members one on one or it is too boring to do so. Pick a community were there is a lot of crime and you will see that the members, especially male members don't know nor associate with the Pastor.

Black Churches must return to the business of saving souls and being places for cultivating spiritual growth rather than being in the business of temple building, i.e., building larger and larger structures. There was a time when the best place to learn to sing and to speak and develop poise and confidence before a large crowd was in the Church because the children and young adults were allowed to participate in the service. Churches must return to this practice.

What about tithing? Churches must begin to use the monies from tithing to do two things. First, to meet the spiritual needs of the community. This includes supporting the structure, the Pastor and fulfilling the requirements of God to feed the hungry, clothe the naked, visit the sick, visit the prisoners, be hospitable to strangers, and give water to the thirsty.[56] Second, to improve the community and give back to the people. See discussion on page 194.

What about time and talents? Black Churches must allow their members to devote the bulk of their time and talents to work in their own community. The Bible did not say that you had to give 10% of yourself just to the structure. In fact, Blacks must start spending less time at Church and more time doing the business of God in the community. The problem that Blacks have right now is that they spend far too much time at Church (the building) and very little time improving their community. Evangelism also comes into play here. You have a responsibility to go out into the community to spread the Word of God and to encourage others to follow him. Blacks have taken the Church like they do clothing and cars and taken it too far. They now think that success is going to Church four times a week (Sunday, Monday night, Wednesday night and Thursday night). That praying, singing and shouting puts them closer to God. The reality is that God only requires man to go to Church one time per week (remember the Sabbath Day and to keep it holy)   After attending Church on

Sunday in which you give God his praise, pay your tithes, fellowship with other believers, hear God's Word, then you go home and spend time with family and friends, not doing any work, but relaxing. Come Monday morning and through Saturday night, you do all of your work, letting the Word of God guide you in your dealings. Note: Wednesday night bible study is okay. The more Blacks are in Church (other than on Sundays) the less work they are getting accomplished. Even Jesus spent very little time inside the temple (some structure), but was out in the world working for the people (feeding people, raising people from the dead, and giving his life for our sins).   The bottom line is that going to Church increases your faith, but that faith without work is dead.[57]

A very strong argument can be made that Blacks would be better off if they got rid of Black Churches altogether. This would force Blacks to look at the dismal state they are in instead of going to a building, singing and shouting and feeling good. The atmosphere in most Black Churches is exactly the same as that at a rock concert. In fact, other than the minister talking about God, if you woke up and did not know where you were, you could not tell the difference. It is just one big party (complete with women in short dresses wearing no stockings and people doing the same dance in the isles that they do in the clubs), with most Blacks going home and being just a little lazier than the week before because they think that things are just going to fall from the sky as a reward for going to Church.

In terms of receiving blessings, it is better to work as hard as you can and not pray, than it is to pray as hard as you can and not work. God only answers blessings while you are in the process of working to accomplish something. God wants winners, people who do and give it their all. He does not want people who whine and complain and think that he is just there to crisis manage their lives. There is a small piece of God in each of us and it is called talents. By using your talents, you begin to receive your blessings as you complete the tasks God chose specifically for you. Remember, God works through you, not for you.

Forgive and Forget What Whites Did to You

During the period of roughly 1450 until 1988 (year Apartheid ended) Whites enslaved (the real name for colonization) Black males in one form or another throughout the world. They took Black people's land and the resources that went along with the land. Whites enforced and maintained this slavery by any method necessary. Very often, these methods of enforcement were very brutal and inhumane. Families were separated and destroyed. Slavery is one of the main reasons today why most Blacks will never know their lineage.

We have already discussed the reasons why Whites and other conquering races could do this and not feel any sense of remorse. These conquering, colonizing races actually justified enslaving Blacks (and others) on the basis of bringing these Blacks order and religion. In essence, Whites felt that they brought Blacks civilization.

It is time for Blacks to stop running around carrying the deep feelings of hurt. Start acknowledging that the important thing is not that you were enslaved, but it was the reasons that you were enslaved. Understand the reasons and start devising strategies so that it won't happen again. Now what were the reasons why Blacks were enslaved? You remember, it was because we did not have the technology and strength of will to prevent it from happening.

Black men must stop displaying the symptoms of an abused woman. That is always thinking that the reason that you were abused is because of something you did and that if you prove your worth to the abuser, things will be better. Like the abused women, Black men continue to try and be with the abuser (assimilate with Whites) who just continues to abuse her. Black men think (just like the abused woman) that things are getting better when the abuser (Whites) gives you something or temporarily does something nice (you know give you a job or promote you to an insignificant position), that things are getting better and the abuse will stop. But it never does. Once an abuser, always an abuser.

It is laughable that here it is in the early 2000's and there are still more than a few Black men who actually believe and are lobbying for the government

(Whites) to give them 40 acres and a mule. How stupid can Black men be? It would not make one shred of difference. In fact, the land would have no value without Whites in light of the current way that Blacks have of doing things. Within two years Whites would have gotten all of the land back and more Blacks would be in debt due to placing mortgages on the land to buy stuff.

It is equally idiotic for any Black man to think that Whites are ever going to set up a separate nation or state inside of the United States or somewhere else in the world. The closest that this has ever come into being was when the U.S. set up the colony (allegedly free land) of Liberia, in Africa in 1822. Here was supposed to be a place where freed slaves who wanted to return to Africa could go to. But like the analogy earlier in this book of what would happen if you woke up and all of the Whites were gone, Liberia turned out to be a disaster. No one is going to give you anything in the 2000's. Another thing to consider is most Whites who had anything to do with slavery are already dead. The Whites that are being screamed at now don't feel in anyway responsible for the plight of Blacks and look at Blacks as just being lazy. Whites have gotten tired of hearing Black men complain to them about discrimination and unjust treatment. In fact the term itself has become just a cliche'.

Any time you entertain idiotic thoughts such as Whites giving you land or money to clear their consciences, turn on the television set and watch an old cowboy and Indian picture. Ask yourself this question, "What makes me think that Whites are going to do more for Blacks than they did for the American Indians?"

It is time for Black men to concentrate on what we need to do rather than begging for forgiveness and respect from some other culture. By looking to Whites to do this for all of these years, it has made Black men emotionally dependant on what Whites call them (you know niggers, on welfare etc.) You can never win at life when you measure your self worth by how others view you.

Why is it so important for Black men to forgive and forget what Whites did to them? The reason is because God will never bless Black men unless they

forgives Whites. God never forgives those who don't forgive his (God's) people.
Actually failing to forgive someone cuts off your relationship with God.   If you
begin to follow the teachings of God, then you will begin to understand the
reason for forgiveness. For one thing, it clears your mind. It also gets rid of all
of the negative emotions of anger and pity. You basically feel better and spend
no time being mad at some person or race who may not even know that you are
mad, nor care. You can't build a meaningful relationship with someone that did
something to you if you have not forgiven them.

Not all Whites are bad, evil people. Just like all races, there are good,
bad and indifferent members of that group. There are many instances where
White professors, bankers, neighbors and the like have helped needy Blacks. The
number of Whites who have acted as mentors to Blacks are countless.

The simple fact is that if Whites around the world in the 1960's had not
decided on their own to end colonization (slavery), it would not have happened
because Blacks were in no position to force them to do so.

Ultimately, you are not responsible for what happened before you were
born, but you are responsible for what happens to you once you reach adulthood
because only you can control your destiny. It is time for Black men to move past
the fact that they were once enslaved. Quit crying like a bunch of women, get
over it and move on. Every race of people that Whites came into contact with
is worse off than before they came into contact with them. We have to get off
our butts and do what we need to do.

Stop Trying to Integrate With Whites

The biggest mistake that Blacks made in America was to try and integrate
(assimilate) with Whites in the mid-60's. Of course it is always easier to look
back and criticize what people did before you. And I admit that. The problem
is that here it is in the early 2000's and Blacks are still trying to integrate. Blacks
have been and continue to be the only race that has tried to integrate with Whites.
No other race has tried this idiotic endeavor.

The gains that Blacks had made up to 1960 were then lost. Blacks turned their backs on the things that they had built because they wanted to mingle and be around Whites. We let our businesses go out of business. We didn't build anything nor improve ourselves in anyway since 1960. We have not built any schools, hotels, exclusive restaurants, theaters or anything of substance since. If not for athletics and entertainment, there would not be any Black millionaires today. The prospering parts of town that we lived in then are slums or totally dilapidated now. We wanted to be around and be with Whites so bad that we were willing to give up our identity.

You can't mix apples and oranges which is exactly what you are doing when you attempt to assimilate Blacks and Whites. We are fundamentally different people. Whites (American Whites and their ancestors) have a thousand year foundation which they used to build upon and to improve themselves in every way. They are a people driven by greed, adventure, search for knowledge, and competition. As already pointed out, they have evolved socially to the point of being able to work together to build almost anything with the knowledge that they have acquired.

Black men must understand that we are different from Whites in more ways than skin color. We differ in our basic belief structures, in the way we do things and in the way we relate to each other as Black people. Assimilating into the White culture or race is not going to make any difference because we will always be Black and act accordingly. It will not make us Blacks smarter or harder workers. It will not even improve our quality of life in the long run. If you look at the condition of Blacks in America in the early 2000's versus the late 1960's, you will see that we were better off back then. We must discover our role and purpose in this world and I guarantee it is not the same purpose and role that Whites have.

There is another, more devastating side to all of this. Whites are never going to integrate with Blacks. You see, to actually have integration, the dominant race has to also want to integrate with the subordinate race. For the reasons given earlier, Whites don't want to integrate with Blacks and even if they did, they couldn't afford to do it. You remember, if you had integration in America, complete with widespread sexual mating, Whites would be wiped out in fifty years.

There will always be instances of racism and discrimination in this country because Whites (and all of the other races by the way) do not value Blacks. Blacks have no order and nothing to offer except athletics, entertainment and crime. The racial relationship between Blacks and Whites in America will never change. Can't Black males understand this and stop wasting time trying to make Whites change their attitude towards us?

Whites are going to continue to move away from Blacks once Blacks make up more than 10% of their neighborhoods. They move away because they believe that when Blacks move into their neighborhoods, it lowers their property values. They also don't want their kids mixing with Black kids because of the possibility of sexual mating and because Black kids change the values of White kids in a negative way. Whites also want to get away from the loud stereos, the dirty yards, the old cars being worked on in the driveway, Black males just hanging outside with no shirts on, the vicious dogs such as Rottweilers that Blacks always have running around without a leash and all the other things that having Blacks in your neighborhood brings.

Blacks have to understand that Whites look at America as theirs. It is their businesses that are located in their high-rises in their cities congested with their cars which are driven from their homes on their land. In other words, it is their stuff, all of it and contrary to what Blacks believe, Whites would have built it all anyway, with or without the presence or help of Blacks. Whites are not going to hire a Black to run or make a Black part owner of one of their businesses that was built over generations by White people.

So if integration is not the answer, then what is? The answer is co-existence. Blacks have to look at the way Japanese and other Asians exist in

America. Still the Japanese are the perfect model. Just like the Japanese, Blacks have to build their own infrastructure complete with the ability to produce (manufacture) profitable products. We have to begin to operate businesses that cause money to flow to Black people and not away from us. Like the Japanese, we have to be better than White people in all areas, particularly in the area of technology. You can't compete with Whites, nor the Japanese without having your own technology. Right now, the Japanese can build anything that American Whites can build. In many cases they can build it better. They can compete with Whites in all areas including computers, cars, and manufacturing. You never hear the Japanese complain about racism on the job because they don't work for Whites in large numbers. Japanese live in their own areas of town and work together for the betterment of each other. They solve their own crime problems. They demand the highest standards from each other, even higher than Whites demand of each other. The Japanese can survive in America without White intervention or help.

The bottom line to all of this is that as long as Blacks try to assimilate with Whites, the result is going to be the same as that of an individual taking poison. It is death to us.

And when you really look at Black men, we are not sincere about hating Whites for what they did to us anyway. In fact we are hypocritical at best. Can you imagine a Jew trying to integrate with a Nazi. Can you see this Jew trying so hard to fit in with the Nazis. Would a Jew go to work for a Nazi on a daily basis, live in a Nazi neighborhood and marry Nazis to prove how important they are. Would a Jew treat other Jews the way Nazis treated them? So every time you, a Black person, are trying to fit in with White people, think of this analogy.

Don't Waste Time Participating in Movements and Marches

Dr. King and all of the Civil Rights Leaders that worked with him did a wonderful thing that would not have happened had they not endured the pain and rigors of marching. They were able to draw national and international attention to the plight of Black people in America by organizing and participating in these marches.   These marches became a symbol for the struggle for freedom and equality under the law.   The willingness of the marchers to endure the beatings, the water hosing, the dog bitings and yet remain non-violent in the name of Jesus Christ, touched a nation.   Even spiritual Whites joined in to be a part of history in the making.

Those marches of the 60's were absolutely necessary as well as absolutely effective to stir the soul of a nation.   In the 2000's, marching for freedom and dignity are absolutely ineffective and absolutely unnecessary.   Unless you are marching in a high school or college parade, marching is, to put it mildly, dumb.

While it is true that an argument can be made that marches do work for temporary, emotionally charged incidents such as rallying support to demand justice for a police beating or killing of a Black youth.   And under these circumstances, this argument is correct.   But the moment the incident is out of the press, the memories of the march and why it took place also disappear.

Marches take a lot of time and effort to organize, not to mention the money needed for permits, porta-potties, insurance, advertising, etc.   In doing all of the planning and hoopla for the marches, people lose sight and begin to believe that you are successful simply because the march happened.   Marches make people feel good.   There is a lot of media attention given to them and they become the focus of that week.   People who were involved with planning of the march feel a sense of accomplishment.   They have something to brag about, even if it is only about the amount of people that participated.

But a bunch of people walking down the street with no specific message nor purpose other than a show of unity is nothing more than committing waste. You see the problem is that after the march, there is no follow-up because there were no specific goals to be accomplished.   Even if there were general goals (Black men unifying, being empowered or some other nebulous nonsense), there is no way to measure the effectiveness.

In the end, after the press has gone and the march is over, Blacks still face the same problems and are no closer to solving them than before the march because marching does not equal a plan of action.

One more time, the marches of the 60's were effective because they had a specific purpose to achieve a specific end, freedom and equality.   These marches were not a one time gala event (with the exception of the march on Washington).   Marches cannot achieve what needs to be done by Blacks themselves. Marches don't improve the individual and ultimately the race.

The same can be said about movements.   They too don't really accomplish anything other then giving people a sense of rebellion. Like marches, movements are nebulous and ineffective as it relates to solving the problems that Blacks have. Movements by their very nature are things that make people feel good and not face up to their individual responsibilities nor group responsibilities. Movements differ from Societies and Organizations in that Societies have a specific purpose (bylaws), specific membership requirements and dues. Societies and Organizations also have accountability. Movements have no real, objective membership requirements and thus anybody can claim that they belong and are acting in the name of the movement.

The Civil Rights Movement has already been discussed and all the reasons given why it is no longer applicable in the 2000's. We will not recount it here other than to say that any movement that is focusing on changing the behavior of Whites rather than concentrating on changing the behavior of Blacks, is worthless.

The reality of it all is that any Black male that is focusing on doing what is right and best for his family and community has neither the time nor the need to march.

Be Loyal to Black Race First, Everything Else Second

At the beginning of Part V of this book, there was a discussion about how Blacks would have to be able to find a common bond (page 136). This is not going to be easy. Blacks don't have the luxury of having a common ancestry or at least knowing about it like the British or Japanese know about theirs. We come from all over Africa, from many different countries and tribes. We don't have a common religious bond that unites us in our beliefs and value systems such as the Jews and Mormons. Blacks don't have a common ideology such as the Communists or Marxists.

There are some other potential bonds that may have worked had we not been the kind of people that we are. For example, what about educational level? This won't work because the more educated some Blacks become, the more ashamed they are of being Black. They try so hard to fit in and be White. They try to sound like them so that you won't know whether you are talking to a Black or White on the telephone. They try and dress like Whites and have the exact same mannerisms as Whites. In other words, these same Blacks try to completely disassociate with other Blacks. What about income level? Again, the behavior displayed by Blacks when they make some real money is the same as the behavior displayed when they get a degree. When Blacks get some money, the first thing that they do is find a house in an all White neighborhood. They want their kids to go to an all White school and they try and have only White friends and associates. These Blacks with money will quickly tell you that the poor Blacks are only in the position that they are because they are lazy. They will also tell you that Whites are not so bad and that some of their best friends are White. They will tell you that they worked hard and they had so much to offer their White employer that they had to hire them and if the poor uneducated Black worked as hard as they did, they would get hired too. Yet these Blacks never acknowledge the fact that they are the only Black in the entire company even though there were numerous other qualified Blacks. These Blacks will never spend time nor money assisting other Blacks in achieving any kind of success.

With no common bond, how are we going to work as a collective body to change our quality of life and reach our destiny as a people? The answer is that we, Black people are going to have to do something that no other race or group of people on earth have ever done. We are going to have to take the negative and turn it into the positive. As stated earlier, everyone including Blacks themselves lump all Blacks together. We are going to have to actually make this work for us. Blacks are going to have to unite and work together based solely on skin color at first. At first here means during that initial twenty years of the time line that was proposed. After that time period, our individual ethnicities may not matter.

When Blacks are loyal to each other, half the battle is won. This loyalty will keep us working for the betterment of each other and not give the best that we have to offer in terms of talent and money to a race that does not need it.

If Blacks unite based on skin color and are really sincere and proud to be Black, look at the immediate results. We go from being under 30 million in America to being well over 900 million when you add in Africa, the Caribbean and South America. We go from being a minority to second place, behind the Chinese only and running neck and neck with India.

Even if Blacks are not 100% loyal to other Blacks, at least we can be more loyal to each other than to some other race of people. Even if a Black is wrong about something, at least be neutral when you are in public.

It is important to understand that loyalty is the first step to conformity. Blacks must get their priorities straight. The priorities in your life are God first, then family, then community (Black community), then the Black race, then country. If you watch other races or groups, you will see that this is exactly the priority that they have.

Maintain Strict Order in All Areas of Life

Other than not working together, the thing that hurts Blacks the most and keeps them from being competitive is the lack of order. Why is having order so important? The reason is because without order, you have chaos. Right now, as a race we are more chaotic than any other race. Our faith, our families, our homes, our yards, our finances, our jobs, and our futures are all in chaos.

Where does order begin? Order begins with setting standards. You can't have order without high standards. The higher the standards, the higher the order necessary to achieve those standards. Why do you think that Whites and Japanese have so much order, it is because they have the highest standards on earth.

The next thing that you need to have order is cleanliness. Look at any person that is poor and down and out and the first thing that you will notice is that every thing that this person is responsible for is unclean which is another term for disorder. Things are not in the place and in the way they are supposed to be. Go into a poor neighborhood and look around. Start with the outside of their houses and the first thing you will notice is that the yards are filthy. The grass needs to be cut, there is trash and debris on the lawn, there are old cars and junk parts lying everywhere. There is oil all over the driveway. The outside of the house is in disrepair, meaning that it needs painting, the shutters and windows need replacing, and the roof needs fixing. Go inside the house and take a look around. The things that you will observe are that the inside is as dirty (in disorder) as the outside. You will see old clothing laying everywhere, dishes all over the place, the floor needs vacuuming, the beds are unmade, the bathrooms are dirty, people are lying around with beers in their hands, and loud music is playing.

One of the very hallmarks of poverty is poor record keeping and filing of paperwork. If a person is poor, you can bet that their personal paperwork (bills, receipts, contracts, purchase agreements, personal and business phone numbers, family documents such as birth certificates and marriage licenses) is a disaster. There is paper lying all over the place. Some things might be on the refrigerator, other papers might be in a dresser drawer, still others may be on a table, some might be on the floor in a corner, some in the closet and in other places in which this person can't find when they need them. The reverse is true if someone (you) are wealthy. These people know where all of their important paperwork is located. They can tell you not only where all of their bills and receipts are, but how much they owe, to whom and when their bills are due. They have a neat filing system complete with filing cabinets for the hard copies and a computer for the things that need to be constantly updated.

Another facet of order is discipline. All discipline means is the ability to work at tasks when they need to be done. It takes work to maintain order. This is why lazy people can never reach their destinies. Even if you know what your destiny is, you have got to work to accomplish it. Don't believe for a minute that most people don't know how to organize (put things in order). The simple fact is that they are too lazy (unwilling to put in the necessary work) to do so.

There are four major things in life that you as Black men need to work on and make sure that they are in order. The first is your spiritual life. This is your relationship with God. This involves going to Church on Sundays, tithing (money, time and talents), reading your Bible (studying the word of God), praying (getting guidance from God), evangelizing (spreading the word of God) to co-workers and friends and living your daily life and dealing with people the way God requires (practicing the word of God). The second thing to get in order is your mental life. This is your education. This is studying to get a degree or on the job training. This is to make sure that you have a usable skill or trade to make it in this world. The third thing is your physical life. This is getting the proper amount of exercise, sleep and eating the right foods. Your body is a temple and God expects you to treat it as such. You are responsible to keep it in tip top shape and free of illness and disease not just when you are in your twenties, but for as long as you live. Many Black men stop exercising when they turn thirty-five, not realizing that they are going to live to be seventy. So from about forty, their health is poor until death. The fourth area where we need to have complete order is our finances. Most Black people do not have peace of mind because they live in financial chaos. Their debts far exceed their income and still Blacks continue to rack up more debt. We need to pay off all of our bills and have monies saved before we run out and purchase items that feed our egos rather than things that secure our financial future.

Order is the way of the universe. Natural laws are based on order, from the orbits of the planets to the interaction of electrons. God created heaven and earth by bringing order out of chaos. God requires that we get our own lives in order before we can truly help someone else and ultimately receive our blessings.

Let's say you get your life in order. How does that really improve the quality and abundance in your life? Order for the sake of order is wasteful also. Order, once achieved, has to be used to accomplish goals. Goals give you purpose and allow you to see the light at the end of the tunnel. One of the reasons that so many Blacks can't complete their degrees and go on to become what they were meant to become is because they can't see themselves doing it. They can't see themselves doing it because they have no plan for accomplishing it. Setting goals is your plan, your road map. Getting a degree is just part of the process. Goals allow you to focus.

How do you go about setting goals? Accomplishing a goal is a twelve step process. (1) <u>Desire</u>. Your personal goal must be personal. It must be your own selfish desire. It must be in line with what motivates you. If you don't live your own adventure (your goals), then you are merely a part of someone else's; (2) <u>Belief</u>. You must believe beyond the shadow of a doubt that you can accomplish the goal. The goal should have a 50/50 chance for success. Goals should be challenging and cause you to stretch; (3) <u>Write the goal down</u>. This programs the subconscience. Write the goal in precise, vivid detail. Describe the goals exactly as you want to have them. You must have a clear representation of what you want; (4) <u>Determine how you will benefit from</u> <u>accomplishing the</u> <u>goal</u>. Write all the advantages and benefits of accomplishing the goal. The more reasons for accomplishing the goals, the faster you will accomplish them. The more you will believe in it; (5) <u>Analyze your position</u>. Analyze where you are right now with no respect to the goal and measure your current status; (6) <u>Set a</u> <u>deadline for accomplishing the goal</u>. Ask yourself, when is the latest date for accomplishing the goal? The goal must be measurable so that you know how you are doing; (7) <u>Identify the obstacles you will have to overcome to achieve the</u> <u>goal</u>. List everything that stands in your way. If there are no obstacles except you are too lazy to complete it, then this is not a goal, it is simply a task; (8) Identify the knowledge you will require in order to accomplish the goal. Figure out what knowledge and skills you will require to accomplish the goal; (9) Identify the people, groups and organizations whose cooperation you need to accomplish the goal. What can you do for them to get them to help you? And remember that you gain by serving others. You get out what you put in; (10) Make a plan for accomplishing the goal. Take the last three steps and make a plan of how you are going to accomplish the goal. It should be complete in every detail. List all of the activities that you have to do to complete the goal. Once you have the list of activities, then prioritize and list which ones you have to do first and second and so forth. Keep revising and updating until the goal is accomplished; (11) Get a clear visual picture of the goal already being accomplished. Every chance you get, visualize the goal as already being done. See yourself enjoying the benefits. Act as though you have already done it. Think about it all the time; (12) Back the plan with determination and persistence. Stick to it. Never give up. Your persistence in carrying out your plan is your faith in yourself. Self-discipline is persistence in action.[58]

Goals have to be specific and measurable, otherwise they are just wishes and wants. There are some things that are not goals. For example, "I want to be rich. I want to be famous. I want to make all the money that I can. I want to be popular. I want to be a star. I just want to graduate. I just want to be happy. I just want to get married. I just want a woman or I just want a man. I want a big house. I want a nice car." All of these things are not specific and are just wishes. Some examples of goals are, "I am going to be a physician, who has his own internal medicine practice located in Your Town, USA, seeing 10 patients a day. I am going to be an architect who designs and builds hotels for Blacks that can accommodate 300 guest in first class luxury." To be a goal, it must be specific and something that you want to do, not something that you think other people would look up to you for or that would make you popular.

Love, Respect, Date and Marry Black Women

While it has been said before, it will be repeated here. The Black race will never be free until Black men begin to respect Black women. The reason is because God made you responsible for her, to be her provider and protector. No man is ever truly responsible until he respects his woman. By respecting his woman, a man respects himself. God will treat you the Black man the same way you treat your woman.

In the case of the Black woman, no other woman on earth deserves more respect than she does. The Black woman has been the foundation of the Black race for the last two hundred years. Without her rock solid support of the men and the children, the Black race could not have survived. These women have endured the worst possible jobs under the worst possible conditions to put food on the table so the family could eat. When the spirit of her man was broken, she found the strength to continue on anyway. No woman has given so much to her man and gotten back so little in return.

All a Black woman wants is to be loved. If she is genuinely loved and cared for, there is nothing she will not do for her man. Somehow, Black men have learned or believe that loving and caring for their woman is a sign of weakness. They feel that if they are not dogging her out, then they are wimps and will be taken advantage of. Nothing could be further from the truth. Black women thrive off of love, not pain and when given love, they give it back ten fold.

Part of loving is providing. If you truly love your woman, you don't want her out in the world suffering and struggling to make ends meet. Why would you want her to wither and wrinkle prematurely from hard work. It is time for Black men to stop making the excuse that they don't provide for their women because they are materialistic. All women love nice things such as jewelry, clothing and a nice house in which to entertain. Provide these things and add in a little shopping and you truly will have the 'Jewel of the Nile'

Now what is love? Love is simply a manifestation of a Godly spiritual connection and is expressed by your feelings and actions toward that other person. It has already been pointed out that Black men were the least spiritual beings in the world which may account for the fact that they don't form a spiritual connection with their women. Another reason for the lack of love by Black men for their women may be again because they have not evolved. Remember, the primitive man thinks from an individual reference point rather than as a collective.   In order to have and build a relationship, you have to have the willingness to share and build something together. You can't be selfish which is what many Black men are. They do whatever they can to get all they can from a Black woman, including her money.

Contrary to what most Black men believe, there are countless numbers of available, beautiful, smart, loyal, loving Black women. How do you find these women? You find them by dating them. Too many eligible, successful Black men search for trophy White women to give their time and money to when they know a sister deserves it. You hear these idiots (Black men dating White women) always saying, "A sister does not understand me" or "A sister is too materialistic". Yet these same brothers will marry the worst looking White woman, work two jobs to support her and then pay alimony and child support the rest of their lives because they usually get divorced within two years.

What if you, a Black man, are smart enough to date a Black woman and you are fortunate enough to catch one? What then? You must have as your goal to marry her. It is time for Black men to understand that your ultimate goal is marriage, not just sex. Marriage brings stability and longevity to relationships and ultimately to the race. Finger point for a minute and look at other races. They get married. They do so right out of college. Sure, there may be women in other races walking around not married in their late thirties, but you can bet they are divorcees.

The Black man needs the Black woman more than anything else in this world. Black women can help provide the love and confidence and inspiration that you need to become successful and have peace of mind.

Black Women Must Work With Black Men to Solve Our Problems

Let's say you found a deserted, remote island and put some people on it and they had no way off of this island. What would the make up of these people have to be, say bare minimum, if you wanted these people to survive for the next couple of hundred years (we will assume that they have adequate food and shelter). The answer is that you would have to put men and women on the island. If you put just men or just women, they could not procreate and would die after one generation. The same holds true for a race. If the men and women are not together, the race will die out, albeit a slower death than the example of the island.

We have already talked about Black women being the mainstay for the Black race. We talked about how she endured every hardship imaginable, and yet she did what she had to do to provide for her family. This still holds true today.

We also talked about how Black women, in spite of all of their hard work and good intentions, were adding to the causes of the extinction of the Black male.

Be that as it may, Black men cannot solve their problems nor even survive without the help of the Black woman. The Black woman is going to ask the question, "What can I do? I have already broken my back doing the things that needed to be done while the brothers were either in the streets chasing women, in jail or in my bed while I was out working. I worked, paid the bills, gave birth and took care of the children, made sure there was food on the table and provided the shelter. What more can you, a Black man, possibly ask of me?"

This question is both a tough one and a fair one. The answer is both tough and fair. The first thing that the Black woman has to do is return to being a woman, complete with all the roles that go along with it. In order to understand what your role is, you have to look to the Word of God.

According to the word of God, men and women were created equal. In the beginning, God made both man and woman in his image. He blessed both of them and told them multiply and fill the earth and subdue it, you are the masters of the fish and birds and all the animals.[59]

Once God created both men and women, he then equipped them both for various tasks. These tasks all lead to the same goal of being masters over the earth and ultimately, honoring God. The point being that men and women are the same in essence but different in function. The functions that go along with being a man are not more important or less important than the functions that go along with being a woman.

The reason that Black women have caught so much hell over the years is because they have (for a variety of reasons, most of which are beyond their control) been attempting to do the functions of men. The point being made that no matter what you achieve in your career, no matter how much money you earn, no matter how big a house you buy, no matter how much you try to be both a mother and a father to your children, you simply are not fulfilling your role as a woman. Let's put a caveat in here at this juncture. We are not saying that women can't have a career, or that they can't make money. What we are saying is that a woman must carry out her God given functions first and foremost, and in addition, not in lieu of, then pursue all of the worldly things such as career and money making.

So smarty, what is the Black woman's role? Well, it actually has two parts. To find out what these two parts are, we must again look to the Word of God.

The first part of a woman's role is marriage. When God created man, he said, "It is not good for man to be alone; I will make a companion for him, a helper suited to his needs."[60] So the first thing that a woman must do in order to fulfill her role is to marry (find herself a man, a husband).

You hear Black women all day long complaining about how difficult it is for them to find a man. You hear them say that Black men are just dogs (dawgs). They say all Black men want to do is have sex. Once they have sex with you, they just want to move on to the next woman. They don't want to make any kind of commitment. Of course it never occurs to women that the respect and dignity or lack thereof that they get from men is in direct relationship to what they demand. Most Black women have lost respect for themselves and all they are seeing in the Black man is a response to that lack of dignity and respect. Sure, Black women complain that Black men are dogs, but it never occurs to them that they, the women act like Alpo.[61]   Black women have somehow been taught (by Black men probably) or believe that the way to attract a man is by wearing the shortest skirt possible and to reveal as much cleavage as possible. Some women's skirts are so short and their blouses so thin that you can see the cheeks of their behinds and the nipples of their breasts. Black women present themselves to Black men solely on a sexual level and the response that they get from Black men is purely sexual. If a man sees a woman who exudes sex, then all he wants is sex and once he gets it, he moves on since that was what the woman promoted and that is all she is going to get. It is time that women learn that men don't respect women in extremely short dresses. Men figure that if she dresses this way when he sees her, she dresses and does the same thing (has sex) with other men. A man is not about to put his trust in a woman who walks around all day with her butt and boobs out.

Another thing that women do is to think that when they set their sights on a man, that he is going to automatically fall for her and want to marry her. Nothing could be further from the truth. Every man that is physically attracted to you is not necessarily going to be spiritually attracted to you, nor is he going to want to take care of you, i.e., pay your bills, buy you a stereo and a car all in the first couple of weeks of knowing you.

So many Black women have such an inferiority complex, perpetuated by Black men having sex with them and moving on, that they measure their worth now by what and how much a Black man can do for them. They seek men based on possessions only. You hear them say, "Girl he has got to have a Jaguar, and alligator shoes and a gold card or I'm not giving him the time of day." The moment they met a man, they want him to take care of them, i.e., pay their bills, buy them a stereo and a car, all in the first couple of weeks and all in return for having sex with them. Sisters, you are not that fine. All you have done is to have men fool you that they have something only to discover after they have sex with you that they were playing the same game that you were. That brother that you met in a club only wears that one suit he has to the club and that car he drove was rented or borrowed or the clunker he took you home in is really the car he owns and he doesn't have a Jaguar that just happens to be in the shop.

It is time for Black women to stop seeking men based on what they have and what they do rather than how closely you as a woman match up with the companionship requirements and suitability of needs requirements. Believe it, when a man gets ready to marry, he is looking at a woman based on these two things and not how fine the woman is. It is almost laughable how many Black women there are who think that a man of wealth and means is going to want to marry her and take care of her simply because she is fine. The only time this happens is if the man is 80 and is seeking a trophy of 30. By this time in the 80 year old man's life, he has already had a real family including kids by his first wife.

The point again to all of this is that if you a woman are not suitable to your man's needs and can't provide the kind of companionship that he needs, you will not find yourself a man and if you do, you won't be married very long.

The second part of the Black woman's role is to be a good wife. Again, look to the Word of God and it will show you how. "When a women is a truly good wife, she is worth more than precious gems! Her husband can trust her, and she will richly satisfy his needs. She will not hinder him, but help him all her life. She finds wool and flax and busily spins it. She buys imported foods, brought by ship from distant ports. She gets up before dawn to prepare breakfast for her household, and plans the day's work for her servant girls. She goes out to inspect a field, and buys it; with her own hands she plants a vineyard. She is energetic, a hard worker, and watches for bargains. She works far into the night! She sews for the poor, and generously helps those in need. She has no fear of winter for her household, for she has made warm clothes for all of them. She also upholsters with the finest tapestry; her own clothing is beautifully made--a purple gown of pure linen. Her husband is well known, for he sits in the council chamber with the other civic leaders. She makes belted garments to sell to the merchants. She is a woman of strength and dignity, and has no fear of old age. When she speaks, her words are wise, and kindness is the rule for everything she says. She watches carefully all that goes on throughout her household, and is never lazy. Her children stand and bless her; so does her husband. He praises her with these words: 'There are many fine women in the world, but you are the best of them all!' Charm can be deceptive and beauty doesn't last, but a woman who fears and reverences God shall be greatly praised. Praise her for the many fine things she does. These good deeds shall bring her honor and recognition from people of importance."[62]

The bottom line to all of this is that if you the Black woman are not taking care of your household, which includes being a wife, mother, manager, coach, manufacturer and merchant, you are adding to the extinction of the Black male. A woman's worth does not come from her career nor her physical attractiveness, rather it comes from her character and the way she manages her household. The problem with so many Black women is that they spend so much time trying to build a career, that their families (their husbands and young Black male children) fall apart. Black women have somehow succumbed to the notion that being a wife and mother (being domesticated) is a sign of weakness and servitude. These women fail to understand that your role, job, duty or whatever, is to first and foremost run your household. It takes money to run a household. That money is supposed to come from your husband. The way that you make sure that your husband is bringing in the money and achieves a certain status in the community is by making demands on him. If you the wife don't make demands on your man, he will never be the man he was meant to be. Men respond to demands. Let's look at an example. Let's say the family needs a new car. You, the wife, should say, "Honey, this car is smoking and rattling, we need another one. All of the neighbors have a new car. Why don't we?" At first your husband will say, "Why are you nagging me? The car we have still runs. Why should we go into debt just because other people have done so?" But you keep after him a few more times and guess what? The man will begin to think about it. He will become embarrassed and will feel like he has not done what he is supposed to do as a man, in this case, keeping the family riding in a safe, clean, reliable, good looking car. He will think unto himself, "My wife gets on my nerves, but I guess we do need a new car." And sisters, he will go out and get one and surprise you. He will even try to act as though it was his idea.

In a sentence, your job as a Black women (the queen that you are) is to build kings. Behind (beside, in front of) every great man is a great woman.

Build, Maintain and Provide for Your Family

We live in a world that places a lot of importance on wealth, looks and having a good time. People spend two thirds of their lives trying to achieve one, two or three of these things. Anything else is viewed as mundane, old fashioned or simply being square. So many people are walking around, lonely and unhappy because they have chased these things and not found them. Many times people's outrageous debt stems from trying to satisfy these things even to the point of borrowing money to buy things that give the appearance of wealth and prosperity. People buy expensive cars, clothing and take trips and attend functions, all of which puts them in debt.

It is time for Black men to understand that your basic purpose in this life is to grow up and build your family. Your family starts with you. Whatever value system you have and live by will most likely be transmuted to your family. In order to have a loving, functional, God fearing family, you yourself must be that way. You have to make a decision that at this point in your life, you are going to get yourself in order. Remember those four things that need to be put in order were the spiritual, the mental, the physical and the financial. Concentrate on doing these things and work hard at them, then and only then should you consider taking the next step to building a family.

That next step is getting married. Getting married means more than just going down the isle or to the courthouse. Marriage was created and instituted by God. Marriage has three aspects: (1) the man leaves his father and mother (and all of his old girlfriends and male buddies) and, in a public act, promises himself to his wife; (2) the man and woman are joined together by taking responsibility for each other's welfare and loving their mate above all others; and (3) the two become one person or one flesh in the intimacy and commitment of sexual union which is reserved for marriage.[63]

To get married you have to find a woman to be your wife. What do you look for? Looking here does not mean visual, it means seeking substance and function. The thing that you don't want to do is to just look for physical (visual attraction). Men have made that mistake throughout the ages. Remember Sampson? Here was a man (maybe a brother) who saw a woman and fell in love with her based solely on her looks. He did not even know the woman (Delilah) or what she was about, yet he trusted and believed in her because of his burning lust for her.[64] Even when she deceived him the first three times, he could not see past her beauty and understand the deceit. So often, brothers look for the finest sister that they can find. They marry her without knowing what is in her heart and what skills she possesses, and later, they complain when all she wants to do is shop all day, put on make-up and look seductive and flirt with other men. Only after marriage and having to do the day to day things that life entails, do most men look beyond the packaging and often times discover that the contents are rotten inside.

You can't look for a good woman based on looks. You seek a woman to spend your life with based on companionship for you and a helper suitable to your needs.[65] You do this by deciding what kind of person you want to love before the passions of the flesh takes over. Determine if the person's character and faith in God are as desirable as the person's appearance. Sex is always going to be good, but is this woman's personality, temperament and commitment to solve problems also desirable? You must start exercising patience and give yourself time to get to know a woman (two years minimum) before you fall in love and put all your trust in someone just because she has big thighs, a big butt and big boobs. Don't forget the discussion about primitive people worrying about how something looks rather than how well it functions.

When should you get married? The when here is referring to how old should you be when you marry? While this answer varies depending upon who you talk to, the best answer seems to be that you should get married in your middle to late twenties. The reason for this is that the longer you wait to get married after the age of about 27, the more demanding you are about your choice. You also get set in your own ways to the point that you can't change. As you get older, the chance of having a child out of wedlock also increases. Then there are the bills that you begin to accumulate. You have to find a person who is willing to accept you and all of the additional baggage (bills, children, old flames, obesity) that you bring to the relationship. Of course this works both ways. The point to all of this is that the older you get, the harder it is for you to match up with someone. This difficulty of matching up is also increased by the fact that as you get older you seek companionship using logical criteria such as how much money someone makes, what possessions they have and what their social status is in life. This is opposed to when you are younger and your criteria are based on things that are far more long-lasting such as does the person love me and do I love them and do we want to we want to build a life around us and then spend the rest of that life together.

Once you find a good woman who is right for you, then you have to devote your life to this woman. Don't be fooled by society which would have you believe that the test of being a man is how many women you can sleep with, versus God's test which is how well do you treat your woman? Once you marry that woman, it is for life. If you are not ready to make that kind of commitment, don't marry a woman and then immediately have children with her, only to desert her and the children because you saw (see how sight of the flesh kills you) some other woman and she looked like she would be everything that your wife isn't.

The truth of the matter is that every relationship that you enter into is ultimately going to be the same because you are the same.

Okay, lets say that you have children. It is time for Black men to understand that you are totally responsible for raising your children. We already discussed that most of the young Black males in jail did not have their fathers in the home. Children, especially male children are a reflection of their father.

What is it that makes you want to be a father to your child (children)? The answer is bonding. If you, a Black male, don't bond with your child in the first two years of life, you are never going to. You have to be there to change the diapers, to hear them crying, to rock them to sleep, to feed them the bottle, to watch them crawl, and eventually begin to talk. You have to see your features in their little faces. Any man that forms this type of bond will never desert his child. When this bond is formed, you will want to be a father to the child. You can't imagine and would not want anyone else raising your child and you will not be able to sleep at night not knowing whether or not your child is safe and being provided for. And any man that has deserted his child, and never spent any time with him, or only sent child support payments, you can bet he did not bond with the child initially.

Being a father means more than putting food on the table, it means providing the nurturing (love), training and discipline necessary to instill the values that children need to become God fearing, productive, functional (able to raise and support a family of their own) adults. This discipline begins when a child is toddling. They have to be taught to obey the rules (not breaking the law and committing crimes) and learn to work at doing their personal chores (cleaning their rooms, cutting grass, doing the dishes) and their school work. Children have to be taken to Church every Sunday and made to participate in the service to get a solid spiritual foundation. They have to know God.

Speaking of discipline, how do you discipline a child? You discipline a child by going through a process. This process works like this. First, when you observe your child doing something that you deem is wrong, don't just yell at the child or hit him, rather, this first time that it happens, tell the child that what he did is wrong.   Tell him why it is wrong and that if he does this or similarly wrong behavior in the future, he will punished.   The next time he does the same behavior that is wrong, you spank the child, at least five strikes.   The next time the child does it, spank him only about twice.   After that, vocal reprimands should suffice.   When you spank your child, never strike them in the head, face, neck or shoulder area.   Always strike below the waist.   The reason for this is that if you hit a child, say in the head or the face, he will then be confused and afraid to accept your hugs and love taps when you reach for him because he will not know whether or not you are going to strike him or love him.   So when you strike a child, always strike below the waist so that he knows when you reach there, you are disciplining him.   Another thing, if you are going to spank your child, it is advisable to use a paddle or switch.   If you use your hand, again he will be confused as to whether that hand going to deliver love or pain.   Probably the most important thing about discipline is not whether you spank a child or not, but rather if you are consistent in your correction of wrongful behavior.   The worst thing that you can do as a parent when it comes to discipline is constantly threatening your child with discipline but never following up on the threats.   This makes your child lose respect for you.

Now there are those lazy parents who will argue that if you hit your child, you will go to jail or your child will be taken from you.   The response to them is that you are just telling a lie.   There is an obvious difference between discipline and child abuse.   If you don't know the difference, then you should seek counseling.   But if you spare the rod and spoil the child, you will visit them later in jail.   You may not spank your child, but the police will when they arrest them 16 years later.

Children, especially young Black males, must be taught order in their lives as children if they are going to have order as men.   Part of this order involves the way they dress.   As parents, we can't allow our children to dress sloppily and expect them to be organized and ordered in other areas of their lives.

The way you dress is a direct reflection on discipline and the ability to follow the rules. A child is not going to be an "A" student who is allowed to dress as a rapper with their pants falling off of their butt and their hair worn in some weird hairstyle. By doing this, children are trying to send you a message that they are rebelling against conformity, the rules and ultimately, against the teachings of God. Unfortunately, this rebellion against conformity and the rules also means not making good grades, nor earning a good living and nor raising a family.

It is equally important to understand that being a father is not just being a disciplinarian. It is also being your son's idol and companion. It is sharing the good times with your family and teaching your child the things that he needs to know. You are responsible for your child's memories. You have to buy the truck, tractor, or some other vehicle so that when they grow up, they will tell their children about how you used to ride them around in it. You have to teach them how to play baseball, how to fish, how to cut the lawn, how to wash the car, how to repair things. You have to take your children camping and let them experience nature and get an appreciation for the land. You have to teach your children respect for themselves, other people and for property. You have to teach them why it is important to respect other people's privacy. You have to explain what sex is and how it fits into love and marriage. You have to teach your son how to treat and respect women. You have to explain to your son what the meaning of life is, at least as best you understand it.

It is time to understand that God will hold you, the Black man responsible for how your children turned out. Making the argument that it is the system's fault (i.e., if I discipline my child, I might be put in jail), or that I didn't get along with their mother and I left (deserted them) or at least I wrote out the child support checks each month is not going to save you from God's punishment. There is only two things that God requires of you as a father and will judge you by: (1) Did you spend the time with your children and wife (not going to the clubs or spending it with the boys or another woman), as spending time (just being there) is more important than money and toys; and (2) As you spent the time, did you raise your children in such a way that they accomplished more in their lifetimes than you did in yours for this is the true test of parenthood.

Head of Household Must Move Family to Suburbia

It is understandable that in the 50's, 60's and 70's, there was a migration by Blacks from the rural South to Northern and Western States. This migration was usually from the farm or at least the country, to the big cities. It was believed that there were more opportunities and that there was less racism in the big cities to contend with than in the rural South.

The result to all of this was that Blacks as a race went from being primarily farmers and rural people to big city dwellers. What Blacks didn't know was that when you left the country, you left most of the values that you had that made you responsible people.

The disadvantages to now living in the cities were many. The first of which was that you no longer knew your neighbors. In the country, your neighbors were your relatives. You could leave your doors unlocked, your windows down and your belongings outside if you wanted. They would be safe. But in the big cities, nobody knew each other and they certainly were not related. The value system in the cities taught that if someone was stupid enough to leave a door or window unlocked, then they deserved to be robbed. When Blacks lived in the country, the children only came into contact with their relatives mostly. This was especially true before a child reached seven or eight years old. At that time, everybody disciplined you because they knew you and had a familial interest in you. If you did something wrong, you might get a whipping from the neighbor who was your aunt, your uncle, your grandmother, your grandfather, your cousin and then when you got home, your parents would lay into you. But in the big city, nobody had a stake in the children in the area where they lived. No one gave a damn. You were somebody else's child and it was their responsibility to chastise you. Living in the cities, children came into contact with strangers at an early age and on a daily basis. You met people (strangers) on the bus, the train, on the street, and even on your door step. When Black children lived in the country, they had chores to do. After they finished the chores and studying, they played outside on their own land with their own relatives. There was no trouble to get into and they certainly did not come into contact with dope dealers and police everyday. Living in the city was just the reverse. There was no place for a child to play that was safe and isolated from strangers. There was all kinds of trouble and people to help you get into it with. Children in the city were influenced by so many things other than their parents.

Black men, or if you are a woman and head of the household, must move your family to suburbia. You have to get your children and yourself out of the environment that has dope dealers, prostitutes, gangs, the police, crime, poverty and just plain inhumane conditions (too many people crowed into too small of an area) like the projects.

What do we mean by suburbia? We are talking about areas that don't have bus and train service. There are no sidewalks. There are no liquor stores, pawn shops nor video arcades within two miles. The minimum lot size is an acre or more. If you are merely moving away from the downtown to a community of cluster homes (a community of more than ten houses and the houses are on one-third of an acre or less each), you may as well stay downtown because you will encounter the same crowded, drug and crime infested conditions.

Once you get these kids into suburbia, they will get a different value system. You, the parent, become the primary influence in their lives. That is assuming you build and maintain a family as outlined in the above section. In suburbia, your kids will have no place to hangout. If they stand on the corner, they look like an idiot. The only way that they can get somewhere is if you take them. They will have chores to do such as cut the grass, paint railings, wash windows, etc. Most importantly, they will have time to think and to just be a kid.

Make Black Communities Safe, Clean and Desirable Places to Live In

We have already discussed that there are a lot of Blacks that value Whites more than being Black and will do anything to live next to and around Whites. Even when some Blacks don't value Whites more, they still want to live in a predominantly White neighborhood. The reason for this is simple, Whites take care of their neighborhoods. Even the worse, poor redneck keeps his yard clean. He may have a trailer and an older truck, but the trailer is clean and the truck is running.

Taking care of your neighborhood means nothing more than keeping it in order. Once again, maintaining this order requires work. It means that you have to put in the effort to maintain your lawn, trim your shrubbery, pick up trash and debris from your yard and do whatever general maintenance that is required to keep your property in pristine condition.

Blacks are going to have to demand of their neighbors that they keep their properties up. We have to demand that our children and our neighbor's children don't play their stereos louder than can be heard inside their houses only. We have to demand (even if it means calling the zoning office and making a complaint) that no one in our communities keeps old junk cars out in their driveways and not be allowed to do major repairs to cars on their property.

Blacks have to begin to respect their neighbors and other Black neighborhoods by not throwing trash out of their car windows when they drive by. We must begin to monitor crime. Black communities and crime seem to go together. We have to get tough on crime in our own communities. We know when something wrong is going on. When we see that house on the block with strange cars coming and going all day and night, we know there are drugs being sold.

We have to teach our young Black men that it is not alright to hang outside with no shirt on and play music all day in our neighborhoods. The same goes for bouncing basketballs all day.

Why do you think that Whites are so sensitive to Blacks moving into their neighborhoods? Why do you think that they complain that it drives the property value down? The answer is simple. It does drive the property values down. The truth of the matter is that when the number of Blacks exceed ten percent in a community, they past the tipping point of safety and quiet enjoyment. Even if the Blacks that live in a community themselves are trying to be good neighbors and keep their property up, the people that come to visit them don't give a damn and you hear them driving up a mile away because their car stereos are blasting. It seems as though the first few Blacks that move into a White neighborhood are afraid to do anything wrong, but the next wave of Blacks (and there always will be more moving in) don't give a damn and the neighborhood goes to hell.

How do you get your neighbors to do better? You do this by getting to know them. Visit them and have them visit you at least once a week. Too often, Blacks live in a community of other Blacks for years and years and don't even know the names of their neighbors. It is only when the neighbor either does something bad such as committing a heinous crime or becomes famous do you hear people saying that they had no idea that the person was this way or that way.

One of the main reasons why we have to concentrate on making our own communities safe and desirable places to live in is because, if our communities are good, we won't continue to follow Whites into the middle of nowhere. By doing so, we continue to dilute our political strength. We also can never concentrate on having something that we can control. We also live around people that can't stand us nor our children.

It is bad enough that Blacks already do not have a connection with the land. But all of this moving by Blacks to get away from Blacks and with Whites moving to get away from Blacks, it is little wonder we don't have any unity.

Take a Vacation Every Six Months

God created the heavens and earth, but even he himself had to rest just after six days. The pressures of work and life in general run you down. Once run down, you are not operating at peak efficiency. You become irritable and don't even know it. Everything and everybody gets on your (cotton picking) nerves. If you allow yourself to continue on this way long enough, you will have an emotional breakdown which manifests itself through mental or physical illness.

A vacation helps to relieve stress. It relaxes the mind. It is not only good for you the breadwinner, but is also good for the entire family. Vacations allow for uninterrupted family time. It allows families to get to know one another again. Husbands and wives can re-kindle some of the lost romance in their lives while in some tropical place on an exotic beach.

Aside from having fun, vacations expose you to new places and new people. Seeing these places in person helps to increase your knowledge base. It makes you more culturally aware. It works wonders for the kids. Many of our Black kids have never even been out of the city or state in which they were born.

Vacations allow you to think and to reflect on your life, not only on where you have been but where you are going. You can also get a different perspective than the one you have day in and day out, hustling and bustling to make a dollar.

Still you will hear so many Blacks complaining that they can't afford a vacation. But they are wrong. Instead of spending money on those expensive clothing items and shoes, take a couple of hundred dollars and just drive somewhere and book a room for a week. The beauty of this country is that it has so many wonderful places, many of which are within four to five hours of where you live. You don't have to go on a cruise to call it a vacation, just going to a national park may be the get away you need. Just do something, go somewhere.

When you come back you will feel refreshed and ready to take on the world. Never, never allow yourself and your family to become stale towards each other and the world by not taking a vacation at least every six months. Your life and your relationships will improve immensely.

Educate Self and Family, Especially in the Area of Technology

There are many things that Black males need to do. We have identified many of them up to this point. But to understand why we need to do the things we have to and how to go about doing them, we must increase our knowledge level, first as individuals and then collectively.

It was pointed out earlier that the collective mental output of Blacks was far below that of Whites and Japanese. It was estimated that it was on the order of nine magnitudes less. In other words, the collective intelligence of Black males is one-billionth that of Whites. The analogy used was if you took Black collective intelligence and it fit in a stryrofoam coffee cup (12 oz size), White collective intelligence would fill the Atlantic Ocean.

We have said it for years, "Education is the Key", and it is. But of course there are some Blacks who will argue that it is the White man's education that hurt us so much. That we are being taught that he is superior and we are inferior. Some Blacks say we need to get our own education. Still others will say that education is not just book learning (of course they are confusing formal education with knowledge gained by experience). Still others argue that you don't need an education, just drive and hard work.

No matter which of these arguments people are making, the thing to keep in mind is that you never hear a person who has gotten an education say that they wish they had not gotten one. The truth is that anytime you hear someone knocking getting an education and telling you that you don't need one, you can bet that he doesn't have a degree.

Blacks need formal education. You need to get a college degree at a bare minimum. We must educate ourselves. Until we do so, we will always be victims, that is mental victims.

Why is getting an education so important? Education improves your ability to put life and to do things in order. Getting an education is a process which in and of itself increases order. It requires study and discipline. While studying and completing the requirements of a course of study, you increase your problem solving ability. You learn to focus your mind and concentrate on a particular thing. You learn to organize your thought process. You also learn to communicate your ideas in a way that others can more easily understand and follow them. Educating yourself allows you to open your mind up to new ways of looking at the world, and to discover new methods and solutions to old problems.   Education also takes the mystery and magic out of things (phenomenon) which previously seemed awe inspiring to you.

There are also the practical benefits to getting an education.   An education teaches you a skill which leads to an increased ability to make money (assuming you apply yourself).   More importantly, in today's world, education prepares you to understand and build technology.   An education allows you to compete in a world that has gone stark raving competition wild.   He who is the smartest wins.

There are residual effects of having an education that ultimately can determine your quality of life.   For one thing, your level of education is directly related to your health, income level, and stress level (educated people tend to have more hope that their lives will get better if they keep working).   There is a relationship between educational level and crime.   Educated people do not commit petty crimes as a rule.   As stated earlier, go to any jail and you will discover that the brothers that are in there are not educated.   This does not mean that only dumb people are in jail, but it means that people who are educated tend to feel that they can earn whatever it is that they desire, from just putting food on the table to the finest that life has to offer.   Whereas, those without an education feel that the only way for them to get the things that they need and don't need is to steal it or take it from someone else's person.   They feel this way because they don't have a usable skill nor trade.

How do you know you have become educated?   The answer is not just when you receive your degree, but is when you can take what others have done and build upon it, to create something new. When you can take what you have learned and help not just yourself, but others.   When your horizons have broadened so much that you can envision shaping the universe because as a man thinketh, so is he.

What the mind can conceive, can be made reality.   Why do you think Whites are about ready to enter into an era of space travel? It is because their mental conscientiousness believes it is possible.

When does an education start? It starts the moment a child is born. The first three years of life are some of the most important. The reason is because it is during this time that children learn language and problem solving skills. If you don't teach your child proper grammar then, they will never acquire it. If you don't teach your child how to look at things logically, then they will never acquire it to the level that they would have. It is unfortunate that so many Black children are exposed to cursing and broken grammar during this period. You as a parent must take an active role in the education of your child including looking at their report cards, making sure that they study and going to the school to check on their progress regularly. Get to know the teachers and let them know that you want to be notified the moment your child does something that is detrimental to himself (herself).

Once you have all of this education, (knowledge and skill), what should you do with it? Well, the obvious thing is to try and earn a decent living so that you and your family can have peace of mind and enjoy what life has to offer. Once that is accomplished, the next thing is to begin to put your talents to work to help build the infrastructure that Blacks need. You have to take the knowledge that you learned in your particular area of expertise and combine it with the knowledge that other Blacks have from their areas of expertise so that you can build whatever project that is needed at that particular time. You also have to begin to help educate others. A chain is only as strong as its weakest link. One uneducated Black can destroy the efforts of 100 educated ones. To put this another way, when you achieve, you have to give something back to your community and your race. Giving something back does not mean that you have to move back to the ghetto. It means that you help at least one person do better by giving them inspiration, direction, information, financial assistance or a job. Help more than one person if you can.

Equally important, there are some things that you should not do once you get an education. For instance, don't dissociate yourself from other Blacks, especially those who might not be as educated as you. Don't do like too many Blacks do and that is make the mistake of thinking that just because you are as educated as your White counterparts, that they will accept and hire you with open arms. Don't spend half of your life thinking that once you become educated, that your racial troubles are over because Whites will look at you as being equal to them and treat you differently than other Blacks. Too many Blacks believe this and become bitter after discovering that this is not so. Just because you are qualified does not mean that Whites have to hire you to a vacant position.

Let's focus once again on technology for a moment. It has already been stated that technology is a manifestation of your social evolution. It was stated that Blacks had not evolved because they had not arrived at the point of being able to work together. Well, education speeds up this process. The more a group becomes educated, the faster it learns that it needs to work together to accomplish things of substance. The simple fact is that you can't have technology (produce it) unless your race or group has a certain educational level. That level of education right now is college level. If you look at what the overall educational level of Blacks is right now, you will find that is roughly at the sixth grade level. If Blacks remain at the current educational level, we will never have technology.

The rate of technological advances is going to escalate. It won't be too long before there will not be anything such as cash money because every transaction will be done by debit cards. Even people to people transactions will be possible by way of cellular phone technology. Right now your social security number or drivers license is the way you show proof of your identity. Very soon, there will be fingerprint recognition devices located everywhere identification is done by you placing your thumb up to a screen and it scanning the data base and giving or denying approval. It won't be too long before communication between two people may no longer require verbal speech. Chip technology will allow the implantation of a chip that will allow your thought processes to be transmuted from your brain directly to another brain with the aid of a booster pack worn by you. As Black people are styling and profiling, Whites are building a space station right now. The space shuttle is not going into space on a monthly basis just to do rat experiments. It is more than conceivable that once this space station or city this is being built is at a certain stage of completion, they will need workers to do the high risk (death a high probability) jobs and guess where they are going to find the work force? It will be the people that are not valued in this society, i.e., Black men who are incarcerated.

There is one more important point to discuss here and that is the controversy regarding leaving school early to play sports versus getting a college degree. On the surface, it seems to make more sense to accept a million dollar contract at the age of 20, rather than going to college for four years, then going to graduate or professional school and then only making $100,000 per year or less. There is nothing wrong with playing sports in and of itself. The problem is that if you are a dumb person, money and fame are not going to be a good substitute for it. Even if you make millions, you can't keep them because you are not smart enough to manage your money or not be wasteful. There is a relationship if you remember between educational level and incarceration, and many athletes still wind up in jail because of drug use or failure to follow the rules. At best, an athlete has ten years, give or take, to play a professional sport. Why not get your college degree, making sure it is in a field that you can ultimately contribute to the building of an infrastructure. Once you graduate, play sports for ten years, while still learning more about your degreed subject in the off season. At the end of the ten years you should have most of your earnings put aside earning enormous interest. Then you can start your own business in your particular field and have the know how to run it successfully. All the while, your family and friends will still have benefitted from your sports career and you won't be washed up and broke when it is over.

Up to now we have really been talking about Darwinism when it comes to education. It is survival of the smartest. Without an education, Black men don't have the ability to understand and produce technology, and as such, Black men will become extinct. They will have no value in a world that no longer needs human labor to do physical nor repetitive mental tasks.

But there are also divine consequences to being uneducated. First, if you don't get an education, you will never learn to fine tune the talents God gave you to a level sufficient to achieve your destiny. Second, those people, Blacks in particular, who don't have a certain mental capacity to understand technology will not be able to receive God. For when God returns to retrieve his saints, it will be in a technological fashion. Look to the visions in the book of Ezekiel. Those descriptions in Chapter One are nothing but a spaceship and the beings described within are what ignorant (uneducated) people would call aliens. The people that have not educated themselves to the point of technological competence are the ones who will lose their minds during this time of the Rapture because these events will be beyond their ability to mentally grasp them.

It is not too late for Blacks to gain and understand technology. The way to build new technology and to acquire existing technology is outlined in non other than *"The Strategic Planning Guide for Blacks in the World"* in Part Three.

Build Personal Financial Empire for Self and Next Generation

Let's clear up some misconceptions right up front. Money is not the root of all evil nor is the accumulation of a large sum of money in and of itself going to bring you happiness. Being poor and the victim does not mean that you are closer to God (more spiritual) than someone who has earned wealth. There is no honor in being poor. Anyone who thinks that God rewards you in heaven because you were poor on earth, does not really know God. The converse of these statements are also untrue. God is not going to send all of the rich, wealthy whites to hell either. In other words, it is not a sin to be wealthy. More importantly, wealth (the abundance of or the lack thereof) is not an indicator of how much you are blessed. Everybody poor is not being punished and everybody wealthy is not being blessed. Too many people, especially Black people confuse the principle of tithing whereby if you tithe, God will provide for your needs versus God is going to make you rich. The Word of God is telling you that when you tithe, God will make sure that it does not ruin you and that he will make this part up to you, even give you back more than you gave because you had the faith in him which you showed by tithing. If you merely tithe to receive wealth from God, you are simply investing and have already lost your blessings. You tithe because you believe in God, you love God and because he asked you to.

Now let's talk reality. In the world in which we live in, and it has not changed for eons, you have to have money. The amount of money you have is going to determine so many other factors in your life. If you don't have a means to earn money and no one is supporting you financially, you will starve. Most Blacks in the world feel like they are victims because they are poor and dependant. The lack of money controls your outlook on life which always seems to be one of gloom and doom.

The lack of money (being poor) causes you to make poor decisions. Most Blacks allow themselves to be charged the highest interest rate allowable under the law because they don't have the money to buy an item, but they still want it so they charge it.

How do you become wealthy (having more money than you need) instead of becoming poor (not having enough money to meet your needs.)? The answer is that you have to work at one (being wealthy) instead of the other (being poor). You see, you don't just become poor, you or someone responsible for you had to work at being poor. You or they had to do the things that cause you to be poor. And believe it or not, you had to work really hard at being poor until you reached poverty.

To become wealthy, you simply stop doing the things that make you poor and start and continue doing the things that make you wealthy. The first step to take in accumulating wealth is to ask yourself this question. Is the thing that I am getting or the action that I am taking going to make me money? If it is not, then I won't do it. The only exception to this is when you are helping (serving) someone in the form of giving one-tenth of your time and talents and giving back to the community and race as mentioned in the section on education. You have to manage your time. Everybody has the same number of hours in a day. But to become wealthy, you have to use your time better than everyone else. When they are taking long lunches, or having after work cocktails, or socializing with friends, you have to be working to achieve your financial goals. When you really start to account for your time and begin going down the path to riches, you will lose many of your friends, especially the ones who take two hour lunches and gossip about other people. Don't worry, these so called friends will find you when you become wealthy.

There are some obvious things that you can't do if you want to build wealth and that is to put your hard earned money into buying expensive cars. The worst investment in the world is a car. The moment you drive it off the lot, it loses one-fifth of its value. The corollary to this is buying (or worse yet, leasing) a new car every three or four years. Don't waste your money in buying expensive clothing and shoes until you actually become wealthy. This "Dress for success" attitude displayed by so many wanna-bees has lead to millions of Black people being in phenomenal credit card debt. Speaking of charging, never charge anything unless it is a necessary item such as a refrigerator or stove or, it is a high dollar item such as a car. If you can't buy something other than these three things, don't purchase it until you have the cash. Never buy anything just to impress your friends and neighbors. Don't buy or lease anything just for show or convenience. Right now there are millions of Blacks walking around with a cellular telephone (and a phone bill for hundreds of dollars per month) and can't pay their light bill or put food on the table. Stop eating out all the time. It costs $5.00 per person at the local greasy spoon and goes up substantially when you go to a decent restaurant. In fact, quit going out three or four nights a week to a club. It costs you money when you do.

There are some obvious things that you have to do in order to be wealthy. But before you can do these obvious things, you have to do the second step to becoming wealthy and that is you have to understand two principles: (1) The practical definition of wealth. True wealth is having enough money to live on for ten years without having to work. This means that in our society, since it takes roughly $100,000 per year to live debt-free (pay tithes, pay utilities, buy clothes, buy groceries, take a vacation, pay school bills, etc.), then you need one million dollars before you can say that you are wealthy; (2) You can have anything or any amount of money in our society if you are willing to earn (work) for it, with the only limitations being the amount of time you are willing to put into it and the talents you possess. You will never accumulate money without working for it. You have to work at least 12 hours a day, five days a week minimum if you are even thinking about financial freedom. If you ever talk to someone who is wealthy, they will always tell you that they worked at least this much. If you meet and talk to someone who is poor, you will always find out that they are basically lazy.

The obvious things that you want to do are really simple when you hear them. For instance, only purchase things that go up in value. We are not talking about the disposables such as necessities (utilities, food). Buy tangible assets such as land, buildings, your house, etc. Buy things for their function, not appearance. In order to be wealthy you have to learn to save part of your earnings. It is easier than you think. When you earn some money, pay the first ten percent to God, then pay the next ten percent to you in the form of savings. Put the next ten percent into some kind of pool with other Blacks so that we can build our infrastructure. Pay the next ten percent to your family to splurge and have fun with. Then pay everything and everybody else. So the standard of saving is ten percent of your earnings. Take those savings and put them into something that earns compounding interest. Compounding means that the next interest payment due on your savings or investment is calculated on the balance as of that date which includes the principle plus any prior interest paid as opposed to simple interest that only pays on the principle balance each time. Good investments include mutual funds, the stock market or any place that a good investment advisor recommends. Only purchase a new car every seven years because the savings in interest and payment are enormous after the car is paid off.

Never lease because you never accumulate equity. Leasing is just a fancy name for renting.   It is designed for people who don't have the money but who have good credit and want to appear wealthy by driving an expensive car.

There are those Blacks out there who as usual will argue that you can't save. You just have too many bills to pay. But if Blacks would just save the monies that they use to play the lottery every week, they would be amazed at how much money they would have. Some Blacks spend hundreds of dollars per month on the lottery. You will never be rich from playing the lottery. The odds of winning the million dollar jackpot are one in 46 million or higher. The only fools who waste their money in the lottery are poor people (Blacks mostly) and people who have a gambling problem. You can't get something for nothing.

Why should you a Black man, work to become wealthy? The answer is that your family deserves it. You have an obligation to provide for your family in such a way that they don't have to worry about where their next meal is coming from. They should be able to enjoy the things (within reason) that God has placed on this earth, for ultimately the earth is the Lord's and the fullness thereof. Not only does this obligation run to your immediate family, but it also runs to your descendants. Most true wealth is generational. The previous generation is responsible to those that follow. Just as the following generation must be left knowledge upon which to build and not have to reinvent the wheel each time, the same holds true for wealth. The problem with Blacks is that each generation has to start from scratch. The reason for this is that Blacks want to have it all now. They don't give a damn about the future. They will spend every dollar they earn to pay for that Mercedes and won't put a penny away for their grandchild so that he does not have to borrow a student loan to go to college or get a loan from the bank to buy a house or beg in vain to get a small business loan. It is time for Blacks to understand that it is not how you live your life and what you have, but rather it is what legacy you leave that is important. The ultimate goal of any parent is to put their child in a position that they can do more and become more than you were because they had a better start than you.

Don't Work for Anyone But Yourself

In the above section, one of the principles to being wealthy was that you could have anything and any amount of money in this society that you wanted provided that you were willing to earn it. The only limitations were how much you are willing to work and how talented you are. This willingness to work is dependent upon both your motivation and the opportunity be in a position (place) to actually work toward your goal.

Most Black men are not working in the place they want to be, nor the field in which they were trained. Most Black men are working in jobs that are three to four levels below their education, training and abilities. The reality is that at least 98% of all Blacks are working in a job that they don't want to be in or they consider it beneath them. We have Ph. D.'s working in jobs that high schoolers could do. You have women working in delivery jobs that require heavy lifting, never getting to use that business degree. This may explain why Blacks are so bitter all the time and seem angry at other Blacks who have made it. Most Black men are working just to get a pay check rather than for self-actualization (meaning they enjoy what they doing while reaping the financial rewards).

The main reason why the average Black comes into contact with Whites and has to act so subservient is because he needs a pay check. What most Blacks don't understand is that Whites are never going to let you, a Black person, achieve the financial and skill level that you are capable of in their companies. It does not matter how smart, how educated, how talented you are, they are not going to promote you in the position that has any real power or pays any real money. Again, it is their companies, owned and built by their grandfathers (remember the importance of leaving a legacy).

Blacks and hispanics are the only two races on earth that are totally dependant on Whites in America. The reason that they are dependant is because they are the only two races that have to depend upon Whites for a job. Every other race employs itself.

It is time for Black men to work for themselves. We must move from being employees to being employers. If you are going to be truly wealthy, you have to be able to control your time, when and where you devote your energies and how you do things. In other words, if you see an opportunity, you have to be able to act on it immediately. You have to have decision making authority.

There will be more than a few Blacks who will say that not everyone is capable of setting up and running their own business. This is true. So if you are either incapable or too lazy, or too scared to set up your own business, you should, at the very least, work for another Black. Again, we and the Hispanics are the only races that work for Whites. As long as we do, we will always be crying about they won't hire me or that they fired me or I need affirmative action to make sure that I have a job. In other words, you will always be the victim.

Some Blacks are afraid to venture out on their own because they feel that they won't have the security that they do with a job. Well, you are wrong. In today's world, there is no such thing as job security. Companies have no loyalty to their work forces anymore. When they need to show a profit, they downsize i.e., they get rid of some of the workers and save on payroll. Many companies are going to temporary help so that they don't have to pay benefits nor do they have to worry about discrimination suits because you are not really their employee, rather you work for the temporary agency. Even if things are going okay for you today, there is always the take over bid waiting in the wings to strike you when you are the most in debt. No matter what the buying company says, every time a company is acquired, there is a loss of jobs. In today's work environment only one thing is certain, that being that there is no such thing as job security.

It is understandable that some of us may be in fields in which there are no Black companies and are not likely to be in the near future. An example would be a nuclear weapons builder. Still, if you have to take a job, don't look upon it as a career, rather look upon it as a source of capital. Work the job until you are in a position to go out on your own.

The bottom line to all of this is that Blacks will never be free in America (or the rest of the world for that matter), until they employ themselves. Right now, most Blacks can't even voice their real opinions about things for fear that their White employer will not like it and will fire them.

Trust and Work With Other Black Men (Network)

As mentioned earlier, the only unifying thing that Black men have in common is skin color. Black men are going to have to look past everything else, from religious differences, cultural differences and places of origin and work together as one mind and one body. We must begin this practice right now.

The rest of the world treats us, Black men, all the same anyway. The world makes no distinction between us based on religion, national origin, or ideology. Black is Black. Let's use it to our advantage. As already pointed out, there are roughly 900 million of us. This makes us the third largest group on the planet outnumbered only by the Chinese and Indians (people from India).

Remember, that to have any thing of substance, you must work together. The time has come for Black men to work together, with and for Blacks. Up until now, we have given our loyalties to everybody except us. Well, it is our turn.

The first step in trusting and working together is getting to know each other. The way to do this is to personally meet and greet every Black man you meet. Stop pretending that you don't know your brother when you are working for and around Whites. Walk over to your brother and introduce yourself. Find out if there is something that you can do for him or that he can do for you to make both of your lives better. It is time for us to be more honest with one another and stop fronting (pretending that you have more and know more than you actually do). One of the best places to network for Blacks, but is totally untapped, is your own family. Blacks have family reunions all over the country. Yet most Black males don't have a clue what their brothers, their brother-in-laws, their cousins, their uncles or male friends of their women relatives do. Blacks must start getting along as families. If you can't trust your family members, how can you trust strangers who have no insight or common origin with you like your family members do. Blood is thicker than water, but you have to stick your finger in the two of them to find out. You should know what everybody in your immediate family does and how it can help you.

It is time for Black men to quit being afraid that some other brother who looks better than you or who has more money than you is going to steal your woman. Not every man wants your woman and if they do, get on your knees and thank God for blessing you with such a desirable woman and to make you man enough so that she doesn't run off with every other man she comes into contact with. Black men must get past the barrier of not being able to support ideas that come from other Black men. You can't be the leader all the time nor can you be the originator of every idea because no one knows everything. You must learn to support other Black men, especially financially by way of donations when they are working on a project that will benefit the race. Every time a Black man succeeds, the entire race succeeds.

The most successful man is the man who knows and can get along with the most number of people. You can't do anything without the help of other people. What you have to do as a Black man is to network, know as many Black men as you can in as many fields of endeavor as you can. Get to know other Blacks in banking, in law, in medicine, in accounting, in construction, in entertainment, in carpentry, and so forth. Anytime that you need something to be done, you should be able to pick up the phone and call one of your buddies and get some advice on the subject.

Black men, from janitors to doctors, from dishwashers to ministers, have to begin to pool their resources (skills and materials) and capital (money) and work together if we are ever going to build our own infrastructure which we need so badly.

Right now, in the 2000's, Black men are no real threat to anyone because they don't work together. We can't compete on any level. In fact, we are the laughing stock of the whole world. We talk of revolting against the system, when we don't even have a unified objective nor do we know which other Black men would work with us.

Let's talk about networking for a moment. Networking by definition is the act of planning secretly by a group to gain some advantage over some other group. It is having the ability to have people you know do things for you and nobody else knows about it. Blacks must learn this art of working together as a secret network. The time has come for Black men to stop advertising on the radio and television that they are coming together to do something. This is not networking, this is ego tripping.

The advantage to networking is that it allows you to do things that you would not be able to accomplish by ordinary channels. Why do you think that most of the major planning done by Whites is on the golf course or at a secret retreat? The reason is because they don't want you (Blacks) to know about it because if you did, you would try to prevent the things from happening. At the very least, you would devise strategies to counteract them.

It is understandable that many Blacks feel that they have been taught to mistrust each other. This may be true. But now you must learn to trust each other, it is that simple. The alternative is death. Surely, rather than die, you can do something different. If nothing else has motivated you up to this point to trust other Black men, at least the threat of extinction should. And another thing, has putting your trust in other races, especially Whites, helped you? The answer is no.

Concentrate on Building Black Service Businesses

This discussion on this section is taken out of Part Two of *"The Strategic Planning Guide for Blacks in the World"*. That particular section deals with showing Blacks how to build their own infrastructure.

The first step to Blacks surviving on their own, that is truly being free, is to have the ability to provide the necessities of life for themselves by themselves. Right now, everything that we need on a day to day basis is provided by some other race. People of other races come into our communities, people who do not live there and don't even like us, yet get rich day after day, year after year, selling stuff to us. We are the only race that allows that to happen to us. Why is that?

To understand this, we must face some ugly truths. If a Black person puts up a business in an Asian neighborhood, it will not survive. The reason for this is that the Asians will not set foot in a Black business. Even though most of their businesses thrive because of Black patrons, they will not purchase a nickel's worth of merchandise from a Black person. It does not matter if your prices are half the going market rate. They simply will not let you make money off of them. If a Black person sets up a business in an all White neighborhood, it will not survive. The reason for this is because Whites will at first stop patronizing your business. If you are able to keep your doors open, they take the next step which is to vandalize your business. They will write racial slurs on the walls, break out the windows and so forth. Finally, they simply will burn the place to the ground. Either way, they will not allow a thriving Black business to be located in their neighborhoods. But Blacks are the reverse. They will allow, even be proud, that every other race is in their neighborhood, siphoning off black money and putting none into the neighborhood. Most of these places owned and operated by other races won't even hire Blacks. It is ridiculous that Asians and Arabs make so much money from us and they like Blacks even less than Whites do.

Why must we own our own service businesses in our neighborhoods? The reasons are many. The first reason is that it stops the dependency of Blacks on other races on a day to day basis. Secondly, it keeps most of the Black dollars in our own community, increasing our overall wealth. It also gives us the ability to provide jobs to each other. So we don't have to work and earn our livelihood from other people. Thirdly, it allows us to take back control of our own communities because other races are only in our communities because they are getting rich. If we stop supporting them and go to our own businesses, we will get these other people out of our communities.

How do we get our own service businesses? How do we get Black owned liquor stores, convenience stores, gas stations, grocery stores, hair product shops, dry cleaners, etc. in the Black community? It is easier than you might think. The hard part is having the strength of will. You can do this by a four step process.

Part one of this process works like this. Right now, Black people are in a unique position. We have a ready source of capital that we can tap anytime that we want to. That source of capital is Church collections. Every Sunday, around this nation, the congregations of large Black Churches take up in excess of $10,000 each. This money is from the tithes. We have to start using these tithes more productively. One half of the monies should be used to maintain the current building and to do the things that are in the book of Matthews such as feeding the hungry, visiting the sick, the prisoners, being hospitable to strangers and so forth. The other half of the tithes should go to the central credit union.

Part two of this process is the establishment of central credit unions. Each grouping of ten Black Churches located geographically close together should form a credit union. Every Monday morning, they should deposit their one half of their tithes into the central credit union. Just imagine for a moment how much money we are talking about. It is $5000 times ten which equals $50,000.

Part three of this process is the hard part. In this part, the central credit union silently targets specific businesses that are of necessity and are in their neighborhoods. They should target only the best ones, those that are clean and well kept and profitable. For example, suppose the target is a dry cleaners. The credit union would send out the directive to the ten churches that Blacks in the community will not patronize this dry cleaners for four months. The owner of that dry cleaners, usually Indian or Asian or Arab, would see his business go from thriving to zero. He would not know why. He would contact his buddy down the street and ask him what is going on. But his buddy would not know and would tell him that he is actually seeing an increase in business. And he would be right because the Blacks are coming to him because he is the next closest dry cleaners to them. After about four months, the selectively targeted dry cleaners would have to close. He would have no choice. He would not have any and I mean any business. He would have already tried half price sales and the like. At this point, a representative from the central credit union would approach the owner of the dry cleaners and offer him fair market value. The owner would have no choice but to sell.

The hard part of this is that Blacks are not used to keeping things quiet nor supporting the efforts of each other. Would they keep their mouths shut? Or would they tell the owner what is going on based on the fact that he has smiled at them and called them by name for years?

Part four of this is also somewhat difficult. Once the owner of a business in our community was forced to sell and we actually took the cash out of the central credit union and paid for it, how would we run the place? The way to do this is to screen qualified Black applicants (preferably those living in the community). The central credit union would tell the selected applicant that you get to run the place with no money down for five years. During the five years, you have to give 20% of your gross earnings back to the central credit union. At the end of the five years, the place is yours, free and clear. The Koreans and some of the other Asian groups already do this by way of what they call "Associations". The beauty of this system is that you don't need to get approval from financial institutions. You simply do what is best for your race and your community.

The hard part of this is that Blacks have a tendency to haggle over everything and to be emotional when it comes to business. It would be difficult to keep favoritism and incompetence down to a minimum. But this could be done.

This four step process could be repeated time and time again, all around the country. It can be done. Once accomplished in significant numbers, Part

Three of *"The Strategic Planning Guide for Blacks in the World"* could begin to be implemented.

Acquire as Much Land and Buildings as Possible

Other investments may come and go, but the one that will never lose value over time is land. There is a relationship between the amount of land a person owns and the wealth that person has.

Land is a diminishing resource. The reason for this is because the population is increasing every year and there are more and more people buying property which is not increasing. This means that you have a limited supply and increasing demand which always means an increase in price.

There are other reasons why Blacks need to acquire and own as much land and buildings as possible. You can't control your own community unless you own it. Blacks complain constantly about Whites always putting something in their Black neighborhoods that adversely affects the community. These complaints are about gas stations, truck stops, cheap hotels and motels which bring crime, video arcades, liquor stores, adult movie houses, the building of cheap, overcrowded subdivisions, and so much more. You hear Blacks complain that Whites are, by design, trying to undermine the orderly development of our communities. But the reality is that the community belongs to the land owners, not the apartment dwellers nor the people renting houses. When people buy land for investment purposes, they expect to make a profit. The last thing on their minds is how their development affects Black neighborhoods.

Another aspect of land ownership has to do with the right to vote concerning the zoning of land. In most instances, you don't have any standing (which means say so) to vote on what is going to be approved in a neighborhood unless you are a land owner. Of course you can show up at the public hearing and talk all kinds of trash, but ultimately, the land owners get the final say.

Land is also the best legacy you can leave for future generations. It is shameful that in the 2000's Blacks own less land than they did in the 1890's.

It is easy to see why this is so. Earlier in the section on moving your family to suburbia we said that many Blacks moved from the farm or rural setting to the cities. When they did this, they left behind land that was given to them by their grandfathers and grandmothers or mothers and fathers. These Blacks who moved from the South, now live in one of the five Burroughs of New York, Los Angeles, Chicago, Oakland, Washington D.C. and every other city in which slums were bred. These Blacks have the nerve to walk around talking about how much they love the big city and how cultured they are compared to their country bumpkin relatives they left behind. These city dwelling Blacks live in high-rise apartments that have a floor space of less than 800 square feet in most cases. Most are too poor to enjoy the cultural attractions that are in the cities in which they live. For example, there are Blacks who live in Brooklyn, New York who have never been to downtown Manhattan. Over time, these city Blacks have lost touch with the land that they left behind. Most of the land down South is grown up in trees and weeds because no one has kept it up.

Since the Blacks that left to go to the cities have no feel for the land, they then sell their land to developers. When you think about it, you want to cry. Here you have a Black living in a crime ridden slum catching hell and yet back in the South they have a hundred acres. When they sell the land, they use the monies to buy expensive cars, clothing and jewelry. So something that took someone 50 years of sweating and dying for; something that has been in the family for four generations, is sold to buy items that will last about five years and are worthless at the end of that time.

The result is that there has been a negative progression. The great grandparent got the land either by sharecropping to own, was given it by the slave master or bought it. This person worked the land, fed his family from it and improved the land. The next generation lived on the land and worked it. He too may have fed his family from it. He no longer improved it, but at least he maintained it. The third generation lived on the land, but did not work it. They worked in factories such as textile mills to earn a living. But they still kept the land, i.e. did not sell any of it off. The fourth generation not only did not live on the land, but they began to sell it off. At the start of the fifth generation, the land is gone.

Blacks have to reverse this trend. They can do this by buying five acres of land instead of a Lexus. Instead of spending $500,000 on a house in a predominately White subdivision on one acre of land, buy a house on 10 acres of land that costs $250,000. Your duty as a young Black male is to add to the family's holdings in land. Buy more land than your mother or father did.

Once you as a Black male have bought your personal land, then begin buying up as many buildings in the downtown areas as possible. Start with buildings that are run down and in the worst parts of town. The closer to downtown the better. The reason that you want to do this is because sooner or later that part of town will undergo regentrification (a fancy name for Whites returning). That building that you bought will then be worth ten times what you paid for it. Every town in America goes through the same cycle. That cycle is White flight to the suburbs, Blacks create slums in the areas Whites moved out of, Whites get tired of driving for two hours one way each day and eventually decide to move back to the downtown.

Participate in Political Process in America on Local Level Only

There is no question that Blacks must participate in the politics of this country. The problem right now is that too many Blacks waste time running for Congress, for Governorships, and State Legislators. The number of Blacks that win these political offices is so small, that they can't make any kind of meaningful difference as it relates to improving the condition of Blacks. What these Blacks fail to see is that while these offices may boost your ego, they are not at the level that affects your day to day life. Think about this for a second. If you become governor of a state, you are not the representative of the people because most of your constituency is White. The only reason that you were elected in the first place is because Whites made the decision that they would rather have you as an ineffective figurehead rather than another White who did not share the views of majority Whites. Once in this position of representing majority Whites, you have little choice but to do what is in the vested interest of Whites anyway since it was most likely their money that helped get you elected.

Your daily life is affected at the city and county level. It is at this level where zoning occurs, property taxes are accessed, signage is approved, the locations for toxic waste dump sites are approved, permits for service stations, all the school funding bond measures voted on and so forth.

Blacks must control their communities if they are ever going to enjoy the quality of life that is possible in this country. If you control the city and county politics, you control the nation.

If Blacks controlled their local politics, then they could decide what is built in their communities. They could control what the minimum lot size would be and zone for single family housing instead of multi-family dwellings. Speaking of lot sizes, you should never have a lot size less than one acre. If you do, there is going to be rampant crime in your neighborhood. If you kept up with and controlled the local politics, there would never be any surprises as it relates to your community. You would not have to picket out in front of something being built in your neighborhood only after it is in the near completion stage. By this time, all of the permits have been granted and there is nothing legally you can do about it.

The one thing that Blacks can do now to immediately affect their neighborhoods is go to the polls and vote. We are not talking about voting in Presidential elections. These are meaningless to Blacks. It does not matter who is President, you will not see any difference in your day to day living because ultimately the Presidency is controlled by large corporations and all of the decisions that he makes are to benefit his campaign contributors. When we say vote, we mean in any local election or referendum. Go to the polls when it is time to decide on sales tax increases and county commissioners. Vote on how city and county funds are to be spent. Don't be so stupid and crowd the polls when it is time to vote for someone that has no effect on you and yet be completely absent from the polls when something that is going to completely change your neighborhood is on the ballot.

It is time for Blacks to be active locally. We live in a country that lives and dies by majority vote. Yet Blacks don't take advantage of it. You can vote in this country to do almost anything. Speaking of voting, we must teach our Black men that if they are convicted of a felony, they lose the right to vote.

Demand the Absolute Best From Self and Other Blacks

Blacks must raise their overall standards. This applies to every area of life. Right now, our standards are so low that we as Blacks don't want to deal with things that are Black owned or that are predominantly Black because we believe that they will be substandard and we are right.

When it comes time to deal with something that is life and death, say you the Black person needs an operation or you need a million dollar house constructed, you will go to a White person because you know that you will get the best job done possible.

What is the best standard? The answer is simple. We must do everything that we do better than American Whites, the Japanese, the Germans, the British, the Russians, the Jews, the French, the Koreans, the Chinese and the Hispanics. We, as Black people, must adopt and demonstrate the philosophy that being Black means being the best, no exceptions.

How do you begin to achieve those kind of standards? You start with yourself. You begin to do everything that you do to the best of your ability. You become your own monitor and be accountable to yourself. How do you know when you are doing the best that you can? Again the answer is simple. You work on anything that you are doing until you can't lift another finger, you can't keep your eyes open anymore, you can't take another breath, you can't add to the job or product in any way. You have to do more than you are asked to do or are getting paid for. You begin to revel in the knowledge that no one could have done the job better than you did. If you think that something should be done, then do it.

Once your own personal standards are the best, then you begin to demand the absolute best from other Blacks. Don't let them provide you with poor services and products. Tell them immediately when they are not doing their best. Don't be afraid to get into an argument. Tell them that you gave them the courtesy of using them and they are required to give you their best service. The service that they give you, a Black person should be better than that they give to another race. As more and more Blacks require the best service from other Blacks, the faster the other Blacks providing the services will fall in line.

The benefits to Blacks will be unlimited. First, other Blacks won't mind dealing with other Blacks and spending their money on Black goods and services because they know that they are getting the best that money can buy. This will keep our dollars in our communities. Other races will begin to use our products and services too because they are also getting the best that money can buy. They will begin to rely on Blacks for other reasons than just sports performances. Other races won't be running from us, but will run to us. There won't be any such thing as White flight from the cities because they won't be afraid of being around Blacks only to get robbed and assaulted. They will hang around us to learn our expertise for a change.

What standards should Blacks strive for? As a Black man your minimum standards are to make the best grades, especially in English. There is no reason to try and justify Ebonics because any good student knows that Ebonics is not on the MCAT, the LSAT, the GMAT, the Bar Exam, the CPA exam, or in architectural plans. If a baby can learn language by the age of two, then a teenager can learn correct English. Black men must be the most trustworthy. We won't commit crimes, we especially won't rob nor steal. We will make the best husbands and fathers. We will make the most amount of money. We will perform the best on any job. We simply will be the best.

Black Men Must Reunite With the People of the Continent of Africa

It has already been stated that if you see a Black person coming towards you, it is not possible to tell where that Black person is from until they speak to you (and most Blacks as you know don't speak). It is only then that you will be able to determine if this person is from America, a country in Africa, the Caribbean, Central America, South America or some other country.

As Blacks we have to begin to understand that not only do we look the same, but we have the same heritage. Yes, we are born in different countries, 53 of them in Africa, in North, South and Central America and the Caribbean Countries, but we share the same origins. Our ancestors are exactly the same.

Just as important, all Black people around the world, especially American and African were treated the same by other people of the world, especially Whites. We were all colonized (enslaved) somewhere around the 15th century and freed for the most part around 1960.

The parallel between what happened to Blacks in Africa and the negative consequences that followed, the crime, the lack of self-esteem, the poverty, the disease, all came about as a result of western contact. The same thing is true for the Blacks in America. The funny thing is that American Blacks think that they were freed (granted Civil Rights) in America in the early 1960's just because of the marches and protests going on in America. But the reality is that this granting to Blacks basic human rights was going on all around the World. It is time for Africans to admit that their history is identical to the Blacks in America because most African countries were granted independence in 1960, some even later than that (Ethiopia in 1974).

This slavery or colonization may also help to explain the individualistic thinking displayed by both American and African Blacks. Both were forced into conditions where you had to survive as an individual. You were separated from your immediate family, sometimes from your immediate familiar surroundings and overseen by brutal masters. You had to develop an instinct for self survival. It would have been hard for you to develop a sense of collective purpose when you were placed among other Blacks who were complete strangers to you and Whites who killed anyone who encouraged group resistance.   It became increasingly difficult to trust any other Black because that Black in most cases was the master's eyes and ears among the slaves. You just didn't know. The sad thing now is that the very behavior that allowed Blacks to survive under conditions of slavery, is completely detrimental to them under almost free conditions.   You can never work together as a group to build anything of substance if the members of that group don't trust and believe in each other.

American Blacks must feel the same responsibility that other races feel toward their homeland. We have to take back the technical skills (the few that we have) to our native continent. Notice, I did not say our native country. Most Blacks have no clue as to which country in Africa they came from. We have already discussed the reasons as to why this is so. We are unable to trace our true lineage because of all of the intermixing and families being broken up during slavery. Many times, people took on the surnames of the masters. The bottom line is that there is no way to weed through this kind of web to find your ancestors in Africa by normal methods of tracing family trees.

But all hope is not lost. There is a way that you can find the people in Africa that are the most like you. This will not guarantee that they are your true ancestors, but it will be the closest to finding your ancestors than any other method. That method is by DNA testing. Using genetic markers, you find the people in Africa that most closely match you. The way you do that is by cataloging all of the people of Africa, that means every tribe. You put the data in a large computer data base. You then take a sample of your own DNA and see who it matches up with. This can be done, it is just that we have to do it. There is another way that is not quite as accurate as DNA testing, but will still work. This method is by blood marker matching. There are markers in the blood, other than blood type and Rh factors, that are unique to each group or race of people. Again, you follow the same cataloging methods and then test yourself.

Once you find out where your people are located, then you immediately go to that country in Africa and get acquainted. Learn their customs. Ask them why they dress the way that they do and so forth.   Learn as much as you can about the political structure of the country, study the country's history, especially history that preceded the 1400's (pre-colonization).   Equally important, ask about their religion prior to colonization. After this, exchange information, tell them everything you can about America. Merge the information to create something better and new.

Even if you can't afford to go to Africa, begin to get acquainted with the people from African counties who you meet here in America. Every time you meet a Black person who has a different accent than you (we all have accents relative to one another), introduce yourself. Ask them where they are from. Get them to tell you something about their history, their culture, their geography and their commerce.   Sure, they may be reluctant at first, but they will eventually open up to you.

The next step is to implement Part IV of *"The Strategic Planning Guide for Blacks in the World"*. This part of the book shows Blacks how to utilize the natural resources of Africa to build an empire for all Blacks around the world. It is important to understand that Africa contains most of the world's copper, manganese and other precious metals needed to build computer parts, diamonds, and oil. For instance, Nigeria is the 7th largest oil producing country in the world, but the oil is being extracted by foreign countries while the people of Nigeria live in poverty. The same is true of South Africa, which has the richest repository of diamonds on earth, yet foreigners get rich while the natives starve. It is very easy to reverse this trend as you will discover when you read the strategic planning guide. The important thing for you to see is that all races are recapturing their lands. Look at China with Hong Kong, the Philippines, etc.

The truth of the matter is that Africa is our link to our past and our link to our future. We have to learn who we really were and what our true nature is. The heart of civilization was and still is Africa. We have to stop being ashamed of our heritage which is more than the colonial period of Africa. Earlier, we questioned whether or not Blacks built the pyramids. The answer to this question is only going to be found by Blacks. This is not the only question that has to be answered. What about who was Jesus? We know that he was Aramaic. He spoke Aramaic. Were Aramaic people Black? Was he Black? Let us also be reminded that Africa is more than the Africa that Westerners have carved up today. Ancient Africa included all of what is now termed, the Middle East. There was a time when Blacks inhabited all of that region.

When we know Africa, Blacks will know the truth. The truth is not what is in the history books of others, nor is it found simply by wearing African attire and dreadlocks in our hair. We must go to Africa to seek the truth.

Black Men Must Strive to Participate in the Black World Order (BWO)

This part of the this book is taken from Part I of *"The Strategic Planning Guide for Blacks in the World"*. The Black World Order (BWO) is not a movement nor is it a march. It is not a fraternity for entertainment or for showing off your possessions. In fact, it is only open to a very select few.

The BWO is a society created for the purpose of changing the status of Black people in the World. It's membership is limited to 1000 members. The criteria for membership can be found in detail in the strategic planning guide. A few examples of those criteria are listed here. To belong to the BWO a person must have completed a doctoral program in Medicine (M.D.), Law (J.D.), in the Applied Sciences, Education or Municipal Planning (Ph.D.), and Accounting (CPA). The person must have cash (not assets or paper net worth) on deposit of $1,000,000. The person must be at least 40 years old (no exceptions). The prospective member must pay the annual membership dues of $50,000. Membership is reviewed every two years. Members must take a sworn oath never to reveal membership in the BWO. Likewise, the candidates that are selected for membership in the BWO must take an oath of death, meaning that they will die before they will reveal any information to a non-member about what is being done by the BWO. The candidate for membership in the BWO cannot have been an elected governmental official on any level during the last seven years prior to application for membership.   Approval for membership requires approval by 100% of the existing members. There are ten other requirements listed in the strategic planning guide.

The basic premise of the BWO is that it is time for Black people to move from being on the bottom to the top.   The bottom means being a slave, both physically, mentally, spiritually and economically for the rest of the world.   It means ending the practice of whining and moaning and all other pathetic practices of victimization.   The BWO will teach Blacks how to go from being beggars to takers.

Another premise of the BWO is to end assimilation and begin co-existence. The BWO does not believe in separate but equal, rather it believes in separate but better.   As such, it goes without saying that the BWO does not support affirmative action, welfare nor any other form of entitlements.   The BWO will help Blacks become the best in manufacturing, electronics and computer production, space exploration, oil production, and the other items listed in the strategic planning guide. The ultimate commerce goal of the BWO is that Africa, unified as a single area, will become the number one export continent in the world.

No other information can be given regarding the BWO at this point other than if you would like more information on this society you may pay the information fee of $5,000 and send in a set of your fingerprints along with passport photograph for purposes of identification and background check as the BWO has very strict criteria as to whom it provides information to. Make check payable to Xavier C. Dicks, who is one of the retained attorneys for the BWO. The mailing address is P.O. Box 361166, Decatur, Georgia 30036.

One thing is certain, the BWO will provide the leadership necessary to assure the survival of Black men in America and the world.

PART VI. WHITE SOCIETY EITHER HELPS OR ELSE

Most of the discussion in this book has been about Blacks, their problems and what needs to be done to solve them. The reality is that while Blacks do indeed have a lot of problems, they are not the only inhabitants in America. As pointed out earlier, a country is like the human body. When one part of it is sick, all of the other parts are affected. If the infected, sick part is not attended to and is allowed to exist in the diseased state long enough, eventually the whole body gets sick and dies.

If any Whites in this country think that what is happening to Blacks is not affecting them and will eventually lead to their destruction, then consider this. If Blacks don't follow the steps outlined in this book they will become extinct, but the country will be destroyed in the process. The more civilized and technological this country becomes, the less number of Black males will be able to operate productively in America. What you will have is the "Bull in the china shop syndrome". Everything that is built that is beautiful and orderly will be vandalized and stolen or you won't be able to enjoy it because of the fear of being a victim of crime.

Whites must overcome their fear of Black males. This is a sexual fear for the most part anyway. Not all Black men want White women. Black men are not going to replace you. It should be obvious by now that hurting the Black males does not make you more of a man. It does not prove anything except that you can take advantage of some group that over the generations did not have the opportunities that you had.

It is time for Whites to understand that the highest expression of civilization is not who has the most money, or who has the most toys, or who is smartest or who has the most technology. The true test for the highest form of civility is the ability to empathize. It is to have the ability to help those less fortunate than you, with the only reason for doing it being that you know it is the right thing to do. When Jesus Christ walked this earth, he was the most powerful, smartest, wealthiest, human alive. Yet, he did not use his abilities to hurt, rather he sacrificed himself for the good of mankind.

Sure, there are Whites who believe that Blacks are lazy. They believe that Blacks want something for nothing. They believe that Blacks make excuses and babies and nothing more. They believe that they are in no way responsible for the plight of Blacks. They wish that Blacks would just go away. But these Whites are wrong. The destinies of Whites and Blacks in America are tied together more than anywhere else on the planet. The reason for this is because only in America were Blacks brought from their homeland to a strange land to be slaves. In all of the other places on earth, Blacks were enslaved in their own lands by colonizing (invading) Whites. American Blacks did not have the luxuries that Blacks had in other countries of Africa (or the people of India). When these people were granted independence, they had a place, their native land, to fall back on. Even though the countries had been raped and pillaged, they were still home. The majority of Whites that were there up until 1960 left with the exception of the few that remained to continue to exploit these countries for their natural resources (oil, diamonds and precious metals). But the Blacks in America were simply given minimal human rights, which most of the time were not enforceable. American Blacks then are in a land that is not their homeland (except by birth), populated by a White majority of 20 to 1, most of whom hate Blacks. These two races in America, Blacks and Whites are absolutely intertwined. This is different from the American Indians who were rounded up, killed or placed on space restricted reservations. These Indians were never really mixed in significant numbers in White society.

If the Black Male is Destroyed, So Will America

Most Whites believe that the way to curb the destructive behavior of Blacks, as they head toward extinction, is to increase the criminal penalties when they break the law. They think that by putting more and more of these young Black males in jail, that at least they will be out of sight and at least not committing crimes while they are behind bars. Of course there are some subtle factors that also come into play that help Whites to justify this incarceration of the Black male. These factors are things such as if they are in jail, they are not a sexual threat to White females. Putting Black men in jail helps to destroy the Black family and ultimately the Black race. The more Black men that are in jail, the fewer Black males there are to compete for jobs, or to vote to make changes in favor of Blacks. The other subtle factor has already been discussed. That is the Black male is the perfect consumer in that while he is in jail and being made totally unproductive in this society, Whites make billions.

Again, this kind of thinking is going to destroy America. While stiffer criminal penalties may work in some countries that have a different racial make up, they will not work on the young Black male. Not now, not ever. The fear of incarceration is not a deterrent to criminal behavior for Black males. This will only work for the college graduates. It can already be seen that most of the Black men in jail (95 plus percent) are not college graduates.

There is a pattern developing here. The stiffer the criminal penalty, the more violent the young Black male is becoming. He expects to go to jail, so he figures, why not kill the witness, otherwise he is going to do jail time.

The result of this cycle is that it won't be too long before no one in America is going to feel safe. Why have all of this wealth if you can't enjoy it? People are going to be afraid to walk around in the daytime. There is just going to be more death and destruction since the stiffer criminal penalties are desensitizing Blacks males to fear of incarceration.

What about the Black female? Every time a Black male is placed in jail that has children, the mother suffers and eventually so does society. There is no one to help her raise the young Black male child with the proper values or to even keep the mother's values up to par. The result is that more and more law breakers are made as the young male child matures. This child may have to enter a life of crime just to help support the mother who is going to be living in less than ideal housing conditions anyway. The odds are that with her first mate in jail, the mother will eventually mate with someone else who does not care for her and will eventually impregnate her with another child which she cannot take care of financially nor emotionally. This cycle is picking up speed in America.

Saving the Black Male Increases Overall Wealth

The violent behavior that is exhibited by the Black male is eventually going to become a drain on American society. Sure the criminal justice system is making money now, but that will not be for too much longer. As more and more young Black males are put in jail, there is going to be a critical point reached where Blacks families can't finance the criminal justice system any longer (bonds, lawyer fees, fines, accepting collect calls etc.). As the older Black male population (above 50) dies off, there is not going to be any financial base to pull from. The younger Black males will not be able to support their families because they did not learn how to make money while in jail. The Black female will need public assistance. The undisciplined Black male child will be a criminal in the making. This reality, while it will not break America financially, will lead to enormous costs in manpower and money.

It does not have to be this way. With just a little encouragement, Black males could be guided back to the schoolhouse rather than the Courthouse. Imagine the possibilities for achievements in this country if the brain power of young, energetic, enthusiastic Black males was added to the think pool. Instead of this country wasting energy and time building and sustaining jails, we would begin to solve some of our most compelling questions because those monies that used to go into the criminal justice system could now be channeled into scientific research. It might be young Black males who would find a cure for the common cold, a cure for all types of cancer, discover what makes a person age, or a host of technological innovations that would raise the capabilities of the human race. We might enjoy space travel sooner. We might discover the way through the time and dimension barriers. It might very well be Black men who will be able to communicate the most effectively with Aliens when they really do decide to make significant contacts with mankind.

It is a sad commentary on a society that in the 2000's continues to place its youth in jails instead of working sincerely on the alternatives. The first thing to do is to change the criminal penalty structure. Offer drug treatment for drug offenders rather than jail time. Get rid of all of the party to a crime statutes which merely require physical presence even though you had no knowledge that a crime was taking place. Reinvest in neighborhood recreation centers complete with computers.

Whites should make a decision to help control the behavior of poor hopeless young Black males. Otherwise, their behavior is going to be out of control. Whites in business and industry must re-institute the mentor programs so that underprivileged Black youth can be exposed to the way things are done and then build upon what they learned. This would begin to spark this country to move in the direction of true diversity which is what it needs instead of maintaining a system of haves and have nots based on race.

PUBLIC SERVICE ANNOUNCEMENT NO. 4

If you need the best hair care services in the Atlanta, Georgia area, use:

Styles

By

Rosetta

Salon One 23

Rio Mall

595 Piedmont Ave. NE

Suite D-102

Atlanta, GA. 30308

(404) 325-4900

Owner: Rosetta Sanders

PART VII. THE XAVIER DICKS SURVIVAL FITNESS TEST

This is a test that was devised to allow anyone to have the ability to look at a Black male, be he young or old, and make a determination as to whether or not he is likely to survive in the 21st century. It is important to note that even if a Black male meets all of the criteria in this test, he still may not survive. It is just that the more criteria he does meet the better his chances are for survival.

Another reason that this test is so important is because if you find a Black male that is suspect, you at least have a set of criteria to use to guide him in the proper direction.

This test is broken down into two parts. One part deals with Black males that are over the age of 25 and the other part deals with Black males who are under the age of 25. The important thing to remember is that whichever part applies to the Black male you are measuring, he must meet at least all of the criteria. For each criteria that he does not meet, his chances for survival decrease by 10%. If he fails to meet more than four of these criteria, then the odds say that he will not survive. Don't let Black males make excuses to you about meeting these criteria such as I know someone who is very successful and he does not meet these criteria or that my father or uncle did not meet them. The fact is that this test applies in the early 2000's, not back in the 70's or 80's.

If He is an Adult (Over 25 years old)

(1) <u>Is he Spiritual (follower and practitioner of the teachings of God)</u>? If this particular Black male that you are looking at does not believe in God and the teachings of God, then he is more likely to not have the necessary values and

morals to do the basic things in life to provide for his loved ones and be the kind of man that he is supposed to be. He is more likely to be without purpose and live a life of chaos. He will not be the nurturing father and role model that he needs to be. If he is spiritual, then he is more likely to be a man of destiny and a pillar of strength and dependability. He is more likely to be an example for other Black men and he will be willing to act as teacher and counselor to others. He also will know that life is more than just getting women and having some money to buy booze and some material things. He will understand that life is about spiritual growth, which leads to an increase in knowledge regarding the meaning of life, which ultimately leads to an increase in faith, which leads to the ability to do more in life for the benefit of self and others.

(2) <u>Is he Married</u>? The purpose of any man is to grow up in the spirit of God, get married, have children, provide for his family and work to improve the community for the betterment of all. If an adult Black male is not married, especially if he is over 27, the odds are that he is not being a man. He has an increased possibility of having children out of wedlock who will suffer for the rest of their days because they won't have the love and nurturing of two parents. In most cases they won't have their father. The women that he comes into contact with will suffer because this unmarried, sexually active male will aid them in committing fornication or adultery. Black men who are not married have no purpose, direction or stability because they are not building a future for themselves or no one else other than they may have some financial prosperity. But they have nobody to share it with and must live in a constant state of fear that someone is trying to steal it from them by sexual trickery. Or they use their financial success to lure women into quick sexual relationships. If a Black male adult is not married, he is a detriment to the Black race and himself because he is not strengthening the basic unit of existence which is the family unit.

(3) <u>Does He Own His Own Business</u>? The importance of this has already been underscored. It the Black male that you are looking at is working for someone else, particularly for a White firm, it will only be a matter of time

before he is laid off or fired. The longer that a Black male adult works for someone else, the more vulnerable both he and his family becomes. The odds are that he will acquire more debt resulting from material stuff purchases. Once fired or laid off, he will have no immediate way of replacing his income either in the form of another job or his own business because it takes time to build a successful business. A Black man working for someone else can't get rich. All he can do is accumulate capital in order to start his own business. If a Black man does have his own business then he is more likely to control his own destiny. He is surely more likely to become wealthy. The reason for this is that if this Black man comes up with an idea that is a money maker, he gets the money, not just a salary. This Black man can control his time and plan his activities around his family. He is also in a position to help build the infrastructure that Blacks need so desperately. He can provide jobs to other Blacks who have not reached his level of entrepreneurship.

(4) <u>Is He a College Graduate</u>? You can't over emphasize the old cliche´, "Education is the key". The reason is that it is a true statement. The minimum education that a Black male adult must have is a college degree. You simply can't understand, create, build and use the technology that Blacks need to stay competitive (win) in today's world.   Education is about having both the knowledge to acquire necessary skills and the vision to make yourself stretch to achieve more than what was possible up to now. There simply is no place for an uneducated Black male in this world of the next century because a technological society will not value the Black male athlete nor entertainer financially as they do today. Once again, in order to build that infrastructure we need, we must have the skills to do so and getting an education helps to acquire those skills.

(5) <u>Is He Computer Literate</u>? There are very few tasks that are done in today's world that don't require the intervention and use of a computer at some stage of the process. It's going to be more so in the future. Any Black male that does not own and know how to use a computer will become extinct faster than the rest of us. In the future computers will be required to do all banking, make

reservations, pay your bills, communicate (talk to other people beyond the sound of your voice) and basically to get anything done. Computers will be the only way to access information because books will be obsolete and most of the information you need will be on the Internet.

(6) <u>Does He Earn $100,000 per year (net)</u>? A Black male adult must earn at least this much in order to survive. This amount is required to be able to pay his tithes, to buy groceries and clothing, pay utilities, pay for schooling including college tuition for two kids, purchase two autos and pay for their maintenance, pay a mortgage and furnish and upkeep his house, improve his business, take a yearly vacation and save a part of his earnings for a rainy day. If the Black adult male you are looking at is not making this much money per year, then both he and his family are suffering and eventually his debts will strangle his spirit and his relationship with his family.

(7) <u>Is He a Homeowner</u>? Owning a home is the first step to financial freedom. This is because of all of the necessities that you need, a roof over your head tops the list. You have to pay for this above all else. If you own your place, you are building up equity. And as stated earlier, you can't control your community unless you own it and home ownership is the first step. If a Black adult male owns his home, it says a lot about his maturity, commitment to the future, his financial sophistication and his ability to provide for his family. Of course as a homeowner, you are building up equity (wealth) and you are able to deduct your mortgage interest payment off of your taxes, which is also adding to your wealth.

(8) <u>Does He Donate 10% of His Time to His Own Community</u>? When you are looking at a particular adult Black male, you must also look to see if he cares about others besides himself and his family. As Black males, we don't live in a vacuum and the things that need to be done in our communities as a whole must be done by us. For example, who is going to make sure that our neighborhoods are free of trash and debris? Who is going to make sure that dope dealers stay out of our communities? Who is going to make sure that our kids

have a recreation center in which to play? Who is going to make sure that our neighborhoods are safe for our elderly members? Who is going to be responsible for community development, both residential and commercial? The answer is that Black male that you are looking at to see if he is going to survive. If he intends to survive, his community must survive, otherwise, he may be the victim of a drive by shooting or he may see his community inherit a garbage dump. In other words, if a man does not care about his community, he does not care about his family who lives in that community. And if he does not care about his family, he does not care about himself.

(9) Is He Drug-Free? Again, if you had to pick one thing that has added to the extinction of the Black male in the 2000's, it has to be drugs. How many Black males that you knew from childhood, who you played with and went to school with, are now in jail because of drugs or something related to drugs? Drugs, particularly crack cocaine, have led to Black men doing things that they otherwise would not do. Drugs cause Black men to steal and to rob in order to support the drug habit. If a Black does not have a personal drug habit, then drugs cause him to believe that he can make the quick money necessary to have the expensive car and clothing that the athletes and entertainers have. If a Black man is ever involved with drugs, he is finished. He will never recover (unless he lives a Godly life). Sure he will have periods where he is able to not take them. But sooner or later he will return to his old habits either because of his own actions or the actions of others around him. In the end, he will become extinct.

(10) Did He or Does He Have Contact With the Criminal Justice System? There are some people that will say that the better question is did he commit a crime or ever been convicted of a crime? Arguably that is a good question, but just by having contact with the system is enough to cause extinction of that Black male. This includes working for the system (policeman, detective, prosecutor, defense lawyer, judge) as well as committing a crime within the system. The reason for this is because either you at some point will be a victim (policeman who got shot, or judge murdered or disgraced for inappropriate acts) or you will

add to the incarceration of untold numbers of other Black males. Ultimately, you may even have to be responsible for the incarceration of one of your own family members. This only adds to the self-destruction of other Black males and since we are all connected, you are destroying yourself. Of course when you commit a crime, you have a record and therefore are no longer entitled to the full privileges of the ordinary, crime-free citizen. This affects the business licenses you can get and the political offices you can hold. You need both of these to be an active participant in your community.

If the Black Male is Between the Ages of 12 and 25

(1) Does He or Did He Have His Father in the Home? Who is going to teach him values and show him examples both living and verbal of what it means to be a man? If you see a young Black male who does not have his father in the home, the odds are that this young Black male will not make it. As already pointed out, the mother cannot provide the discipline nor manly examples that the male child needs. Society can't do it because it is not involved on a hourly and daily basis. A boyfriend or stepfather can't do it because they don't have the love for the child necessary to cause them to do the things that the male child needs. Every time that they look at the boy, they are reminded that some other man was intimate with the woman that they are now involved with and they wonder if the woman can ever love her son without continuing to think about and love his father. Without a father to give the child a sense of purpose, hope and love, the male child is not going to make it. In the 2000's, there are few if any uncles or grandfathers to fill the bill and act as surrogate fathers.

(2) Is He Spiritual? The same reasons for the adult Black male apply here. It is the spiritual value system that a young adult Black male has that will determine to a large extent whether or not he gets into trouble. His values are the only thing that stands between him and his friends when the decision has to be made if he is going to participate in a crime or not. It is this same value system that will affect how he treats his teenage girlfriends and may even keep his head

on straight when he is sexually aroused so that he thinks about the consequences of sex before he acts.   It also determines if he will use drugs or not.

(3) <u>Does He Have a Normal Hairstyle and Wear Normal Clothing</u>? Teenagers and young adults have been rebelling against the accepted dress codes and styles since the beginning of time.   It is their way of showing that they are nonconformists. By not conforming to the rest of society, they feel that they can maintain their own individuality and their own sense of youth.   Following the rules is boring, a sign of getting old and just not being cool (or whatever the phase happens to be at the time).   The fact is that if you see a Black male that wears his hair in weird styles (this is somewhat subjective), and his clothes in such a way that it is perceived as negative, you also see a Black male that is not an "A" student, nor crime-free.   There are exceptions, but not really.   The more a person wears weird stuff, the less likely his is going to be responsible because it takes discipline to be responsible and these types of individuals are not disciplined.   These types of individuals also tend to be poor as adults if they continue this practice past the age of 22.

(4) <u>Is He Enrolled Full Time in High School or College</u>? You know the phrase about education.   If a teenager or young adult is not in school, then he is a loser.   Not only does he lose, but we as other Black males lose because it is one less brother that will be available to assist with the building of an infrastructure. This Black male will not be able to provide for himself nor his family when he grows up.   The odds are that he will enter into a life of crime because the less educated a person is the more crimes they tend to commit in order to get some money to make it in this world.

(5) <u>Does He Maintain a G.P.A. of 3.5 or Better While in School</u>? The fact of the matter is that anything less than a 3.5 G.P.A. in high school or college is just a waste of your time and your parent's money.   The standards of high school and college have increased.   Young Black males can't count on minority set asides and quotas and anything even remotely resembling affirmative action to get you admitted into college or a job.   Colleges and employers should not do

this anyway because it makes Blacks lazy. Another reason why G.P.A. is so important is because it is a reflection of what you learned and how well you learned it. It also shows how much discipline you have since it takes discipline to study and make good grades in the first place.

(6) Is He Majoring in a Usable Skill or Trade? It is not enough that the young Black male is in high school or college and maintaining a good G.P.A. The real question is will he be able to use what he learned in school to run a business or work for someone temporarily while saving enough money to open a business. In other words, will what he learned allow him to make enough money to provide support to his family and the community? If he is in a field that society no longer values nor needs, he may as well not even go to school because he will be no better off than someone who did not attend college. Usable trade or skill here also must be looked at in the context of building a Black infrastructure.   If the Black male is not in something that can aid in this infrastructure building, then it too is useless.

(7) Has He Gotten a Girl Pregnant While He Was a Teenager? Nothing will kill your dreams faster as a young Black male than getting a girl pregnant. If you do, then you have to make choices that other teenagers don't have to make. You (and the girl) have to decide if you will keep the baby or have an abortion. You have to decide if you will get married or not. And you have to decide if you will drop out of school and work or not. If you see a Black male that is a teenage father, he is already heading to extinction. He most likely will never be the father that he could have been nor the person he could have been. He has a child that he can't take care of and if he does, he can't get an education and will eventually not be able to take care of himself since he has no usable skill nor trade.

(8) Does He Use Drugs or Alcohol? If he uses drugs or alcohol as a teenager, he is most likely to use them as an adult. If he uses drugs long enough, it will eventually interfere with his school work. Over time, he will mostly likely have to either take money from his family (food off the table) or rob and steal

to get the money to support his drug habit.   In the alternative, he will think that selling drugs is not so bad since he himself used them.   If he uses drugs long enough, he will eventually come into contact with the criminal justice system and possibly serve time.   Then he will have a felony criminal record and his life will be effectively over.

(9) <u>Does He Work at Least Part-time</u>?   When you are looking at a young Black male to determine if he will survive or not, look to see if he works.   This will tell you several things.   It lets you know if he is responsible.   It tells you whether or not he is industrious.   He understands that you have to work for a living.   He starts to learn the work ethic early and it will be easier for him to work hard as an adult.   If a young Black male is willing to work, the odds are that he is less likely to steal or get involved in criminal activity.

(10) <u>Has he Ever Been Arrested or Convicted of a Crime</u>? When you are a teenager, there really is no real difference between being arrested or being convicted of a crime.   The result of both is that you have a stigma attached to you that you can't get rid of.   The earlier a person comes into contact with the criminal justice system, the more likely he is going to be a criminal as an adult. When you see a young adult that has been arrested or convicted of a crime, he is effectively already extinct.

PUBLIC SERVICE ANOUNCEMENT NO. 5

If you need a realtor, please use the best office in the Southeast:

PART VIII. PROBABLE FUTURE FOR BLACK MALES IN AMERICA

This is the final part of this book. Up to this point, the discussions have centered around the status of Black men, what caused them to get to where they are now, how to fix it and how to measure the effectiveness of the fix. This final part of the book will now deal with what the probable future is for Black men in America.

It has been said that you have to be very careful about which words you choose to describe something because words have the power to make what is said become true. The future is what you make it and it is never set until it becomes the present.

Still, life is about planning, with predictions being a part of planning because you are projecting the future and planning to have a strategy in place to deal with it. One can never predict with 100% certainty, but you can come very close if you are diligent enough and ask the right questions.

The questions that have to be asked now are as follows: Is it too late to turn things around? Even if you could turn things around, is it possible to catch up with the rest of the world? After all, the rest of the world, meaning other races, have had 1000 years to evolve to where they are. They had a foundation upon which to build upon and centuries to do it. Blacks have 20 years to do what they did in 1000. Even if the blueprint given in this book is the right one, do Blacks have the will power to implement the things that need to be done?

Life, evolution, existence is ruled by no other principle than survival of the fittest. Those who evolve the fastest are by definition the fittest. Will Blacks see that the catastrophe known as extinction is upon them and take the appropriate steps to save themselves before their last breath?

The predictions of what will happen to the Black male are given below. Perhaps by reading them you will be inspired to take action, any action that will add to the possibility of our survival.

Extinction Most Likely Will Occur

Blacks will continue to blame external (outside) forces as the cause of their problems. While these external forces must be factored in, they are not the main reasons for our extinction. It is us. We must now look inside of ourselves. We must face and deal with all of the ugly truths that stare us down.

But Blacks won't do it. They will continue to blame Whites for all of their troubles, rather than admit and deal with the fact that we are the biggest part of our problems.

Blacks will continue to do the same old things that don't work such as marches and movements. They will continue to focus all of their attention towards changing the feelings that Whites have for us. This is not possible and has been demonstrated time and time again. Only a fool does the same things (in this case, takes the same actions) over and over again and expects different results. And in this sense, Blacks are fools. Blacks have told Whites since 1865 that they were not treating us fairly and it has not made any difference. Dislike and discrimination will never go away in this country nor any country inhabited by Whites in large numbers because they only value other Whites.

Yet, Blacks will continue to try to assimilate with Whites. Most Blacks will not even consider the possibility of working together as hard as they can to build their own infrastructure. They will feel that why should they have to build a complete infrastructure when Whites already have one. Most Blacks will feel that it is their God given right to be treated as equals by Whites resulting in equal jobs, equal pay, equal opportunities and equal value. They will operate from the premise that all they have to do is continue to demonstrate and they will get the same fair share of America as Whites.

Blacks will continue to not work together. The reasons are because they will not make the effort to find a basis of conformity upon which to unite and rally around. Rally here means trust and value each other. Education will not be the conforming basis because Black males are becoming less and less educated as they worry about pursuing a sports and entertainment career to make the quick big bucks. Right now and even more so in the next five years, the education level among Black males will vary much more than it has in the past. The majority of Black males will not have more than a high school (if that) degree.

Blacks will continue to be divided based on religious differences. They are too focused on their own particular religious beliefs rather than the spiritual nature of those beliefs. They will not look at the fact that all of the religions that Blacks so zealously practice are religions that were brought to them by the White missionaries in Africa or the slave masters here in America. But for the grace of (God, Allah, Jehovah etc.) the religion you practice might be completely different had your ancestors lived in a different place in Africa or on a different plantation in America in which case you would be Christian rather than Islamic or Methodist rather than Pentecostal, Presbyterian rather than Catholic, Jehovah Witness rather than Jewish and on and on. Blacks most likely will not be able to get past their religious differences and focus on the tide that binds us which is skin color. No, they will continue to turn their backs on their brothers when they need their help only because they have a different religious belief. So we all suffer and eventually, we will become extinct.

Only 10% of Black Males Will Survive and That is Enough

The beauty of what is happening now in America is that Whites are showing Blacks that the party is over. Whatever illness that Whites had that made them treat Blacks in this country with any respect and dignity in the sixties and early seventies, has been cured. Whites have reverted back to their status quo. That means that they are as they always have been, conquerors and self-serving, for Whites only. This is the best thing that could have happened to Blacks because it will force Blacks (those that will) to get off of their butts and become men. Those that do will survive and those that don't will not survive.

Just how many Black men will survive and which ones will survive? To answer that question you have to understand the groupings that Black men are in. In the next twenty years, the group you are in will determine if you survive. Each group will make up a certain percentage of the Black male population.

There will be four groups of Black men in the next twenty years. The first group is called the Paradise Lost Group. This will be the largest group of Black men in this country. This group will account for 40% of the Black males in the next twenty years. This group is in a technological, financial paradise filled with opportunities known as the USA, but they will never experience the bliss that it has to offer because they are not prepared educationally, emotionally, nor spiritually. This group contains all of the Blacks that commit crimes and become incarcerated, the homeless, the unemployed, the Blacks that are on welfare, the uneducated Black males who dropped out of high school and college, and the Black males without a father in the home.

The second group of Black males is called the Church Assimilators. This is the second largest group comprising 30% of the Black males. This is the group that will spend most of its time either in Church services or participating in marches and movements to improve their chances for assimilation into the White culture. This is the group that wants to be absorbed by Whites. They are not concerned with their own history, their culture or heritage. They could care less about building their own infrastructure and being independent. They will argue that there is no reason for them to waste time building an infrastructure since Whites already have one and since they live in America, they are entitled to use it. As Whites continue to cut back on minority set asides and affirmative action and just quit hiring Black professionals at all, this group will continue to march and demonstrate. They will still try to change the psyche of Whites. This group of Blacks will spend the rest of their lives trying to accumulate a Mercedes Benz, a house in a predominately White neighborhood and a job in a White firm. These are the Blacks that front as well. They will continue to go around pretending that they have these things when they in fact are living a life of credit slavery. This is the group that goes to Church four times a week, praying, singing and shouting and expecting God to reward them with riches. They will spend so much time in Church, that their homes and their families will deteriorate right before their eyes and still they will be in Church. The children of this group will make up the highest percentage of group one (Paradise Lost group). The reason for this is that the Church Assimilators will be so busy trying to accumulate stuff and singing and shouting, that they won't have time for their children and this group won't know why their children became part of group one.

The third group is called the Performers. This group will comprise 20% of the Black males. This group contains all of the athletes, the recording artists, the actors, the comedians, the radio and television personalities as well as the wanna-bees who spend their lives trying to achieve stardom. This is the group that performs for the entertainment of Whites. These Blacks don't care how silly they have to act, how long and how fast they have to run, or how many balls they have to hit, shoot or catch as long as they can get paid. They will not worry about an education or anything that helps to improve the race. In fact they could care less about the plight of other Blacks. It is about being a performer to a group of people that can't stand you, yet will laugh at what you do and pay you while they are laughing. These Performers are the greatest detriment to the race because they are broadcast into our homes on a daily basis, perpetuating the message that as long as you are funny, vulgar and dumb, you can make money and live happily in America. This group will also become extinct because they are gambling that the sports and entertainment cash cows will continue to give milk, but they are mistaken. The gravy train of sports and entertainment has ten more years at best and then these Performers are going to find that they have no use in society and thus are extinct. Because these Performers are uneducated, and have no financial sophistication, they will themselves become a part of the Paradise Lost group in a very short time after the gravy train crashes. The children of this group will also become part of the Paradise Lost group because these parents don't have the time nor the education level to teach them how to survive in the twenty first century.

The fourth and last group is called the BWO Followers. These are the Blacks that will follow the directives of the BWO and will do the things that need to be done to ensure their survival. This group will comprise 10% of the Black males. While this a very small number at first, it will grow as the other groups become extinct and realize that this is the only way if they want to save their children and themselves from total extinction.

The BWO group will understand the harsh realities that exist in this country and how to utilize the spiritual talents that Blacks possess to become the high priests once again.

The BWO group will work to build the infrastructure that Blacks need so badly in this country. They will be smart enough to understand that this is not being separate but equal or anything else designed to be a mental barrier to Blacks. Rather, they understand that the very foundations of this country are built on the doctrine of self-determination and the pursuit of your happiness. The BWO group will be able to get past the religious barriers that has paralyzed Blacks in this country for too long. The BWO will be unified by the only possible basis of conformity for Blacks in America which is skin color. These Blacks will achieve things that were thought to be impossible for Blacks up to now only because Whites said so. The BWO group will once again begin to unite the Black people of the world. The BWO group is the future for Blacks in this country and the world.

All Hope is Not Lost, God Has His Plan

No one knows what the creator has in store for us. Many Blacks believe that he created us to suffer on earth so that we would experience eternal happiness in heaven.   Others believe that we are re-living the history of the children of Israel and will one day be delivered.   This second guessing goes on and on.   The only thing that is for sure is that no one knows why the creator does what he does nor why he does it.

Again as mere mortals who believe in God and his goodness, we have to look to the analogies and history that has happened before.   For Black people, the best analogy is in the book of Habakkuk.   In this book of the Bible, Habakkuk had doubt and questioned God.   God explained his ways to Habakkuk and he understood and worshiped God even more.   I think it is wise to include what transpired herein.

From the Living Bible it reads as such beginning in Chapter 1, verse 2: *O Lord, how long must I call for help before you will listen?   I shout to you in vain; there is no answer.   "Help! Murder!" I cry, but no one comes to save.   Must I forever see this sin and sadness all around me?*

Wherever I look there is oppression and bribery and men who love to argue and to fight.   The law is not enforced and there is no justice given in the courts, for the wicked far outnumber the righteous, and bribes and trickery prevail.

The Lord replied: "Look, and be amazed! You will be astounded at what I am about to do! For I am going to do something in your own lifetime that you will have to see to believe.   I am raising a new force on the world scene, the Chaldeans, a cruel and violent nation who will march across the world and conquer it.   They are notorious for their cruelty.   They do as they like, and no one can interfere.   Their horses are swifter than leopards.   They are a fierce people, more fierce than wolves at dusk.   Their cavalry move proudly forward from a distant land; like eagles they come swooping down to pounce upon their prey.   All opposition melts away before the terror of their presence.   They collect captives like sand.   They scoff at kings and princes, and scorn their forts.   They simply heap up dirt against their walls and capture them! They sweep past like wind and are gone, but their guilt is deep, for they claim their power is from their gods."

O Lord my God, my Holy One, you who are eternal--is your plan in all of this to wipe us out? Surely not! O God our Rock, you have decreed the rise of these Chaldeans to chasten and correct us for our awful sins. We are wicked, but they are far more! Will you, who cannot allow sin in any form, stand idly by while they swallow us up? Should you be silent while the wicked destroy those who are better than they?

Are we but fish, to be caught and killed? Are we but creeping things that have no leader to defend from their foes? Must we be strung up on their hooks and dragged out in their nets, while they rejoice? Then they will worship their nets and burn incense before them! "These are the gods who make us rich," they'll say.

Will you let them get away with this forever? Will they succeed forever in their heartless wars?

I will climb my watchtower now, and wait and see what answer God will give to my complaint.

And the Lord said to me, "Write my answer on a billboard, large and clear, so that anyone can read it at a glance and rush to tell the others. But these things I plan won't happen right away. Slowly, steadily, surely, the time approaches when the vision will be fulfilled. If it seems slow, do not despair, for these things will surely come to pass. Just be patient! They will not be overdue a single day!

"Note this: Wicked men trust themselves alone [as these Chaldeans do], and fail; but the righteous man trusts in me, and lives! What's more, these arrogant Chaldeans are betrayed by all their wine, for it is treacherous. In their greed they have collected many nations, but like death and hell, they are never satisfied. The time is coming when all their captives will taunt them, saying: 'You robbers! At last justice has caught up with you! Now you will get your just deserts for your oppression and extortion!'

"Suddenly your debtors will rise up in anger and turn on you and take

all you have, while you stand trembling and helpless. You have ruined many nations; now they will ruin you! You murderers! You have filled the countryside with lawlessness and all the cities too.

"Woe to you for getting rich by evil means, attempting to live beyond the reach of danger. By the murders you commit, you have shamed your name and forfeited your lives. The very stones in the walls of your homes cry out against you, and the beams in the ceilings echo what they say.

"Woe to you who build cities with money gained from murdering and robbery! Has not the Lord decreed that godless nations' gains will turn to ashes in their hands? They work so hard, but all in vain!

("The time will come when all the earth is filled, as the waters fill the sea, with an awareness of the glory of the Lord.)

"Woe to you for making your neighboring lands reel and stagger like drunkards beneath your blows, and then gloating over their nakedness and shame. Soon your own glory will be replaced by shame. Drink down God's judgment on yourselves. Stagger and fall! You cut down the forests of Lebanon-- now you will be cut down! You terrified the wild animals you caught in your traps--now terror will strike you because of all your murdering and violence in cities everywhere.

"What profit was there in worshiping all your man-made idols? What a foolish lie that they could help! What fools you were to trust what you yourselves had made. Woe to those who command their lifeless wooden idols to arise and save them, who call out to the speechless stone to tell them what to do. Can images speak for God? They are overlaid with gold and silver, but there is no breath at all inside!

"But the Lord is in his holy Temple; let all the earth be silent before him."

This is the prayer of triumph that Habakkuk sang before the Lord: O Lord, now I have heard your report, and I worship you in awe for the fearful things you are going to do. In this time of our deep need, begin to again to help us, as you did in years gone by. Show us your power to save us. In your wrath, remember mercy.

I see God moving across the deserts from Mount Sinai. His brilliant splendor, fills the earth and sky; his glory fills the heavens, and the earth is full of his praise! What a wonderful God he is! From his hands flash rays of brilliant light. He rejoices in his awesome power. Pestilence marches before him; plague follows close behind. He stops; he stands still for a moment, gazing at the earth. Then he shakes the nations, scattering the everlasting mountains and leveling the hills. His power is just the same as always! I see the people of Cushan and of Midian in mortal fear.

Was it in anger, Lord, you smote the rivers and parted the sea? Were you displeased with them? No, you were sending your chariots of salvation! All saw your power! Then springs burst forth upon the earth at your command! The mountains watched and trembled. Onward swept the raging water. The mighty deep cried out, announcing its surrender to the Lord. The lofty sun and moon began to fade, obscured by brilliance from your arrows and the flashing of your glittering spear.

You marched across the land in awesome anger, and trampled down the nations in your wrath. You went out to save your chosen people. You crushed the head of the wicked and laid bare his bones from head to toe. You destroyed with their own weapons those who came out like a whirlwind, thinking Israel would be an easy prey.

Your horsemen marched across the sea; the mighty waters piled high. I tremble when I hear all this, my lips quiver with fear. My legs give way beneath me and I shake in terror. I will quietly wait for the day of trouble to come upon the people who invade us.

Even though the fig trees are all destroyed, and there is neither blossom left nor fruit, and though the olive crops all fail, and the fields lie barren; even if the flocks die in the fields and the cattle barns are empty, yet I will rejoice in the Lord; I will be happy in the God of my salvation. The Lord God is my

Strength, and he will give me the speed of a deer and bring me safely over the mountains.[66]

The point to all of this is that God has his plan for Black people. We have to continue to believe in him and to serve him by being obedient and humble. We have to be ourselves even though we are tempted to try to be like those who are around us, living in wealth and prosperity at any expense.

This book was written to give hope and to let you know that all is not lost. Somehow, someway, Black men will survive in America. Some day, we will once again live as God intends. It will be in our lifetimes, i.e., within the next twenty years. God have mercy and bless us all.

PUBLIC SERVICE ANNOUNCEMENT NO. 6

Black men must set the example for young Black males by making sure that they are well groomed and the Barber Shop that provides the best hair care is:

NICK'S BARBER SHOP

The Best In Hair Care For Men"
Your Return Is Our Concern!"

Vance Harper

Owner

4830-B Redan Rd.

Stone Mountain, Ga. 30088

Phone: (404) 508-9525

ENDNOTES

1. American Heritage Dictionary, 4th Ed. (Boston: Houghton Mifflin Company, 1995, p. 120).

2. Wilford, John Noble, *Riddle of the Dinosuar* (New York: Alfred A. Knoff, 1988, p. 212).

3. Ibid.

4. Ibid., p. 213.

5. Ibid., p. 215.

6. Blacks Law Dictionary, Fifth Ed. (St. Paul, Minn.: West Publishing Co., 1979, p.1113).

7. *Statistical Abstract of the United States, 1997,* prepared by the U.S. Dept. of Commerce, Economics and Statistics Administration, Bureau of the Census.

8. Smith, Jessie and Horton, Larrell, *Statistical Record of Black America,* 4th Ed. (Detroit: Gale Publishing, 1997).

9. Ibid.

10. Pappas, G.; Queen, S.; Hadden, W. and Fisher, G., "The Increasing Disparity in Mortality between Socioeconomic Groups in the U.S., 1960 and 1986" (*New England Journal of Medicine,* July 1993, pp. 103-15).

11. Smith, op.cit.

12. Sequell, Michael, "The Pinnacle of Creation (penis size)" (*Esquire,* September 1997, p. 136).

13. Average age of incarceration of Black males is best estimate from statistical data from annual Crime Reports and Statistical Abstracts.

14. *Uniform Crime Reports for the United States, 1996,* prepared by the United States Department of Justice and the FBI.

15. My own calculations based on total black males divided by athletes, corporate presidents, etc.

16. My own conclusions based on Health Department data from various states and hospitals.

17. Faust, Drew, *Ideology of Slavery* (Baton Rouge, Louisiana: Louisiana State University Press, 1981).

18. Chappell, Keven, "How Black Inventors Changed America" (*Ebony,* February 1997, p. 40).

19. Schafer, Edward and The Editors of TIME-LIFE Books, *Great Ages of Man: Ancient China* (New York: TIME-LIFE Books, 1967, p.85).

20. Leipold, Andrew D., "Jury Nullification: A perversion of justice?" (*USA Today*, September 1997, p. 30).

21. Schleif, Robert, *Genetics and Molecular Biology* (Reading, Massachusetts:. Addison-Westley Publishing Company, 1986).

22. Kornbluh, Peter, "Crack, the Contras, and the CIA: The Storm over 'Dark. Alliance" (*Columbia Journalism Review*, January 1997, p.33).

23. Smith, Julia Floyd, *Slavery and Rice Culture in Low Country Georgia 1750-1860* (Knoxville, Tenn.: University of Tenn. Press, 1985, p. 94).

24. Whetstone, Muriel L., "Why Professional Women Should Consider Blue-Collar Men" (*Ebony,* March 1996, p. 25).

25. Leland, John and Nadine, Joseph, "Hooked on Ebonics" (*Newsweek*, January 13, 1997, p. 78).

26. Ibid.

27. Ibid.

28. Ibid.

29. "Black Leaders Cancel Planned Texaco Boycott" (*Jet*, January 13, 1997, p. 8).

30. *Crooklyn,* Universal Studios, produced by Spike Lee, 1994; *Harlem Nights,* Paramount Pictures, produced & directed by Eddie Murphy, 1990.

31. *Corrections Corporation of America*, traded on the New York Stock Exchange and specializes in building and managing correctional facilities.

32. Fischer, David, "And gouge someone: The boom in prison phone systems" (*U.S. News and World Report*, May 5, 1997, p. 52).

33. "Black Judge Cites Unfair Cocaine Sentencing Law" (*Jet*, March 4, 1997,. p. 4).

34. Hatsukami, Dorothy and Fischman, Marian, "Crack Cocaine and Cocaine Hydrochloride: Are the Differences Myth or Reality?" (*JAMA*, November 20, 1996, p.1580).

35. USCS Constitution, Amendment 4.

36. GA. CODE ANN. § 16-3-25 (1996).

37. Simons, John, "Improbable Dreams" (*U.S. News and World Report*, March 24, 1997, p. 47).

38. Ibid., p. 48.

39. Ibid., p. 52.

40. *Leviticus* 18:22, *Romans* 1:24-27, and if you need even more proof, see *1 Timothy* 1:10-11 (King James).

41. Shoumatoff, Alex, *African Madness* (New York: Alfred A. Knopf, 1988, p. 135).

42. Ibid., p. 136.

43. Henry, William A., "The Appalling Saga of Patient Zero" (*Time*, Oct. 19, 1987, p. 40).

44. Shoumatoff, op. cit., p. 161.

45. Ibid., p. 135.

46. Bellenir, Karen and Dresser, Peter, *Aids Sourcebook* (Detroit, Michigan: Frederick G. Ruffner, 1995, p.53).

47. Jones, James H., *Bad Blood - The Tuskegee Syphillis Experiment* (New York: Free Press, 1993).

48. Edwards, I.E.S., *The Pyramids of Egypt* (Harmondsworth, Middleser, England: Penquin Books Ltd., 1985).

49. *Revelations* 1: 14 (King James).

50. Shoumatoff, op. cit., p. 154.

51. Ransdell, Eric, The Telltale Signs of the Next Genocide (*U.S. News and. World Report*, November 13, 1995, p. 64).

52. *Genesis* 11: 1-9 (Life Application).

53. Comer, Douglas, *The Internet Book: Everything you need to know about computer networking and how the Internet works* (New Jersey: Prentice Hall, 1993).

54. Kubler-Ross, Elizabeth, *On Death and Dying* (New York: Collier Books, 1993).

55. *Philippians* 1:27 (King James).

56. *Matthew* 25:42 (King James).

57. *James* 2:14-17 (New International)

58. Tracy, Brian, The Psychology of Selling (Sound Recording) (Niles, Ill.: Nightingale Conant, 1985).

59. *Genesis* 1:27-28 (King James).

60. Ibid., *Genesis* 2:18

61. Alpo is a registered trademark of Friskies Petcare Company.

62. *Proverbs* 31:10-31 (Life Application).

63. Ibid., *Genesis* 2:24.

64. Ibid., *Judges* 16:4.

65. Ibid., *Genesis* 2:18.

66. Ibid., *The Book of Habakkuk.*

PUBLIC SERVICE ANNOUNCEMENT NO. 7

If you need Telephone Systems installed and or maintained, I recommend that you use:

AVD

AMERICAN VOICE AND DATA, INC.

Herbert H. Hamlett, Sr.
President

1280 W. Peachtree St. • Suite 310 • Atlanta, GA. 30309
(404) 897-5880 • FAX (404) 897-1376

SYSTEMS INTEGRATORS: Specialists in Telephone Systems,
WAN/LAN, Structured Cabling, Residential Wiring,
Teleconferencing/Video Systems, Paging/Sound Systems.

Moving? We can move and maintain your telephone system.
Nationwide service to businesses large and small.

To order additional copies of this book directly from the publisher:

Send check or money order in the amount of $24.95 (per book) to

> Farry Bell Press
> P.O. Box 361166
> Decatur, Georgia 30036

Make check or money order payable to Farry Bell Press

Please make sure that you print your name and address.

A 20% discount is given on each order of 50 or more books.

To make arrangements for Speaking Engagements by the Author:

Mail your requests to
> Farry Bell Press
> P.O. Box 361166
> Decatur, Georgia 30036
> (404) 298-9098
> Fax: (404) 298-7969

My e-mail address is: XDicks @ Bellsouth.net

You may purchase copies of the book online at: www.farrybellpress.com

For up close and personal visit me at: www.xavierdicks.com